THE POLITICS *of* ETHNICITY
and NATIONAL IDENTITY

PETER LANG
New York • Washington, D.C./Baltimore • Bern
Frankfurt am Main • Berlin • Brussels • Vienna • Oxford

THE POLITICS *of* ETHNICITY
and NATIONAL IDENTITY

Edited by Santosh C. Saha

PETER LANG
New York • Washington, D.C./Baltimore • Bern
Frankfurt am Main • Berlin • Brussels • Vienna • Oxford

Library of Congress Cataloging-in-Publication Data
The politics of ethnicity and national identity / edited by Santosh C. Saha.
p. cm.
Includes bibliographical references and index.
1. Ethnicity. 2. Ethnicity—Developing countries. 3. Ethnic conflict.
4. Ethnic conflict—Developing countries. 5. Developing countries—
Social conditions. I. Saha, Santosh C.
GN495.6.P65 305.8—dc22 2006101477
ISBN 978-0-8204-7888-3

Bibliographic information published by **Die Deutsche Bibliothek.**
Die Deutsche Bibliothek lists this publication in the "Deutsche
Nationalbibliografie"; detailed bibliographic data is available
on the Internet at http://dnb.ddb.de/.

Cover design by Joshua Hanson

© 2007 Peter Lang Publishing, Inc., New York
29 Broadway, 18th floor, New York, NY 10006
www.peterlang.com

Printed in the United States of America

For:

Dr. Kartick Chandra Saha,
of Calcutta, India,
with whom I spent the formative years of early life

Contents

Introduction

Santosh C. Saha

Hypotheses and assumptions of ethnic identification in disturbing civil conflict may have two broad generalized conclusions. First, materialistic interpreters of various persuasions, including simple economism, postulate that the masses as well as elites are guided by people's benefits in land, positions, and jobs, demonstrating modernity's perennial "discontents." Second, sociological and psychoanalytical theories of ethnic conflict, using at times clinical tools, observe that origins of conflict have emotional causes, at times bordering on primordial ancient habits in social contact. The basic stance in both of these existing assumptions leads us to believe that there is hardly any positive moral consideration in human calculations in identity construction. In reality, the ethnic identification issue remains complex simply because ethnicity concerns the experience of exclusion that may be real, or imagined.

The current book, *The Politics of Ethnicity and National Unity*, argues that the vexed ethnicity issue is the combination of two prime forces—emotional and material. A basic conclusion of these collected essays offered by scholars from different countries claims that ethnicity's impact on national identity formation and state-building may be positive in the sense that the ethnic elements, for instance in Rwanda, Burundi, Nigeria, Liberia, Post-Soviet Ukraine, and other places, may not be as destructive as presumed by the existing literature. Linking identity to relational settings, these essays, with a coherent theme in positive ethnicity, maintain that beyond ethnicity's "political tribalism" there are helping aspects in ethnic attachments that act for reconstitution of state structure. Ethnicity, mostly based on language, has no real meaning unless understood in the interactions with other processes in human relationships and viewed in a social context. It is not a cultural basis of a "folk" populist theme but an analysis in several political and non-political factors that help in the process of state-building. Indeed, the essays here, resting on a cumulative consensus, and with historical and sociological tools, argue that interethnic cooperation is largely based on man's moral consideration. Examining several conflict sites, including the U.S., the book refutes mono-causal theories and political polarities to add that morality, though at times ignored, has a role to play in state-building around the contemporary troubled world experiencing severe social unrest and even politically motivated genocide.

Most designs in social policies, government activities, and independent agencies promote interethnic cooperation, depending on circumstances. No doubt, ethnically diverse societies are prone to political instability, but there are unrecognized undercurrent activities helping institutional performance. The empirical evidence in this book suggests that in several countries, including Rwanda, Liberia, Sierra Leone, and Sudan, the work of diverse communities as well as governmental activity have had considerable success in many areas such as religion, economics, and politics. David E. Kiwuwa, in his essay on post-ethnic-conflict reconstruction in selected countries in Asia and Africa, offers a theoretical explanation, arguing that the renegotiation of areas of citizenship for national identity aids to bridge the gap between various identity groups, which, in turn, helps subordinate ethnic, racial, and cultural prejudices to the assimilating logic of common civil culture that is not hostile to national identity. He argues that the post-conflict reconstruction discourse should be crucial to redefine national identity, not necessarily through a primordial notion of ethnicity or a monolithic conception of culture and identity. For instance, he adds, the two-decade-old southern rebellion in war-ravaged Sudan was not so much seeking political power, but primarily the restating of the individual and southern group identities as part of the Sudanese national identity. Within post-genocide Rwanda, there developed a "new national identity" promoting a centralizing Rwandan identity, submerging sub-group loyalties. His conclusion is that the current government in that East African country moved to banish ethnic identification in Arab-dominated Sudan. Methodologically, Kiwuwa depends on psychological and sociological aspects in human calculation, because, as he suggests, collective myths have not evolved and thus a new sense of territorial unity has been fostered. He highlights, with some justification, the political "general will," rather than cherished imagined traditions in some countries in Asia and Africa.

In chapter three, Michael Grossman takes up the identity issue from a different angle to argue that the Ukrainians have used external relations to formulate a pragmatic solution to the national identity formation issue. Observing the peculiar nature of the newly imagined and innovative identity in that East European country, he affirms that Ukrainian society is divided between a strong nationalistic population in the western part of the country and a more Eurasian/Russian-focused population in the eastern part, with a mixed identity conception in the central regions. Using adequate published literature and appropriately based on statistical data, Grossman finds a linkage between domestic issues and foreign relations in emerging nationhood. His findings suggest that the majority of Ukrainians do not consider themselves as Europeans. Interestingly, he adds, the political leaders in the country chose a national identity that corresponds to a minority view, exclusive to only one part of Ukraine, instead of reconciling the different identities to adopt an identity that would balance the different views about special ethnic values. In a materialistic interpretation, he uses the political data to submit that the elites have been guided by economic interests rather than usual inherited socio-political cultures. He observes that the central governing politicians in Ukraine prefer to forge a unified nationality out of various ethnic groups for better beneficial connections between Ukraine and the West, largely because Russia, with its weak economy, is unlikely to help the new country financially. This novel path to national identification—espousal of a pro-Western political identity—may help the process of national identity that certainly tries to avoid social conflict as well as political instability within emerging nationhood. This pragmatic means implies an absence of a popular social consensus on the unified national identity of the country, which had long economic and political connections with Russia. Here a kind of moral justification is offered to forge unity in the midst of narrow ethnic differences.

In the subsequent chapter on American race-based divisive ethnicity, Paul J. Magnarella summarizes the activities of the militant group, the Black Panther's, to explain the sudden and tragic fall of the Panther's. His essay notes Panthers' political confrontation with ethnicity and race. With a historical perspective, the essay examines the work of the key leaders and their shifting ideologies about race and ideologies that incorporated elements of vaguely defined "black nationalism" and "revolutionary nationalism." His chief argument is that the primacy of "revolutionary" inter-communalism allowed various ethnic groups to cooperate in a spirit of mutual aid to form a general American identity. What is interesting in his presentation is that the militant Panthers, in their brief spell of political ascendancy, did not stand for reverse racism. The Panthers argued that they could eliminate both unrestrained class-based capitalism and racism to build a national American identity. Like many others writing on the Black Panthers, the author argues that the fall of the Panthers should be examined in the light of internal conflict rather than negative ethnic pride. In this case, public morality shaped the course of action. After all, the Panthers tried to resolve the existing ethnic anomalies in American society. Their frontal attack was against often unjustified and excessive police brutalities that created more social problems. Their message was clear. "Do unto others as you would have them do unto you." The Panthers asked the general public to put themselves in someone else's shoes. Frans De Waal (2006), the great ethnologist and biologist, connects humanity's desire for fairness and its morality with primate behavior, offering a view of society that contrasts sharply with the untrue interpretations some authors have of Darwinian evolution. Survival instinct does not come with ancient primordial habits. We often ignore the nicer side of human behavior. Even the much-maligned Panthers did not desire confrontation, unless social injustice prevailed in a polarized society.

In chapter five, Rita Kiki Edozie, returns to the traditional theme of ethnic violations, but with a difference in political analysis. As Edozie examines the centralizing trends in Nigeria, she traces some hope in reintroduction of democracy in a country that has seen repeated military dictatorships. She claims, with reference to factual information, that centrist politics have gained some respectability by way of national reconstruction. Here in line with a variety of "delegative democracy" in other developing countries, Nigeria is making progress in democratic procedure. Her recommendation is that Africa's centrist democrats need to adjust their political strategies to incorporate a democratized and globalized social order, redesigned by Africa's vitalized civil society and not by ethnicity. This middle path, Edozie seems to suggest, does negate ethnicity's negative role in the political discourse. The RDP/Obasanjo regime has introduced a kind of moderate multiparty democracy cutting across ethnic separateness and regional special interests. Edozie's message is that the active civil society in Nigeria stands as the custodian of moral imperatives for cohesiveness and political fair play. It is not certain whether Nigeria's experiment will produce a prolonged and sustained political system. Nevertheless, her analysis depicts Nigeria on a correct track of political progress, despite problems related to ethnic and religious demands. One aspect in her analysis deserves our attention. Nigeria's political problems are connected with regionalism, not always with ethnicity.

Clayton D. Peoples, in chapter five, has scrutinized a broader subject in discrimination against ethnic minorities in various parts of the world. Following others' interpretations, he finds that there are relationships between group identity and discrimination; at the same time, he observes, with the help of existing data, that there is a positive side as well in ethnic interaction. His argument is that there is no significant relationship between ethnic identity strength and interethnic conflict; groups with stronger ethnic identities are neither more nor less likely than groups with weak identities to engage in conflict. His secondary hypothesis is that social movements are organized to attain specific goals or changes in the existing political power structure.

In his essay on Liberian democratic development, Edward Lama Wonkeryor, a Liberian historian, argues how ethnicity contributed to problems in national identity. He maintains that recent elections and democratic development under the leadership of President Ellen Johnson Shirleaf provides some hope in ethnic harmony. The general public is being tuned to the new democratic government, which is following a pragmatic path toward political reconciliation and economic development to create a national identity that was vague since the arrival of the Americo-Liberians in the early 1820s.

Abdul Karim Bangura employs a combination of theories to analyze on a case-by-case basis some special features of "politicized ethnicities" in Liberia, Rwanda and Sierra Leone. While agreeing with the book's core line of argument that suggests that civil conflicts have not always been ethnically motivated, he opens a new avenue in discourse. His submission is that in Liberia the ethnic domination of the Americo-Liberians, who were former slaves or descendants of slaves in the US, contributed to a separate social identity. It was the genesis of conflicts in Liberia, and this genesis provided a background against which lowly placed Samuel K. Doe rose to power after a military coup, killing most of the leaders in the ruling Americo-Liberian groups. Like Christopher Clapham (1996), Bangura suggests, with justification, that when government purposely limits political participation to small elite groups, the exploited ethnic groups are bound to react violently when the state fabric appears, as in the case of Liberia, to be "soft" because of the lack of any clear political and institutional structures. There existed a kind of black colonialism. In a materialistic interpretation, Bangura brings in Rwanda's tragic genocide to put forward the same argument that Hutus historically suffered at the hands of a complicated hierarchy that had little regard for social justice or political obligation of fair play. In Sierra Leone, Bangura adds, the Creoles, who constitute only 2% of the population, played a dominant role in professional and state jobs. Bangura's underlying thesis strengthens Saha's theory (below) that the need for good participatory governance is the key to avoiding recurring civil conflicts. Here again, the fundamental issue is not only the question of legitimacy but also moral responsibility of the holders of power. The social context is relevant in the sense that friction derives its strength from unjust economic conditions.

In the last chapter, Santosh C. Saha examines the political and social contexts in sub-Saharan state-building, and he differentiates between Antonio Gramsci's (1971) cultural consciousness which accepts or challenges cultural hegemony, and African long-cherished internal morality, based positive ethnicity, which stands for social autonomy as well as territorial harmony. Saha, of course, makes it clear that people are not programmed to abide by earlier traditions. He raises an empirical question: Who can take the initiative and reestablish social control of state in Africa. Admitting that cultural relativism encourages an uncritical acceptance of atrocities, Saha is in line with the sub-alternists, who gained eminence in Australia, the U.K., and India in the 1970s, and who argue that the derivative westernization model may not be helpful in analyzing African ethnic and civil conflicts. Saha affirms that the "African" economic model accepts some basic premises of progressive liberalism such as the state's role of directing citizens' organizations and associations that may cut across cleavage lines in conflict-ridden regions to build social trust. In African consciousness, for instance, an ethic of the environment, nature, and religion, demands that the moral standing of non-human entities of the cosmos is given equal value with the human species. Here indigenous cultural norms shape basic courses of action in state-building, although the contemporary elites ignore the relevance and legitimacy of the issues involving ethnic demands.

In a way, Saha negates the "veneer theory" that in the post-war era argued that humans were violent and as such amoral. He posits that people in general and ethnic groups in particular do not generate fighting instinct and aggressive drive unless professional predators come to guide us. As Paul R. Brass (2003), writing on India's ethnic violence states, the "production" of violence is manipulated by politicians as well as anti-social elements who can use even unfounded "rumors," that get currency under unhealthy political atmosphere.

The book opens up the old debate with varied methodologies and new angles. The existing literature is flooded with causes and circumstances of ethnic conflicts and genocides, providing hopeless situations in different parts of the world. Instead the present work invites readers' attention to moral issues and pragmatic solutions so far undertaken in different countries. Contributors in this book argue that instead of creating an ethnic distinction, actual social actors in the countries under scrutiny have examined the identity issue from pragmative angles. The book tries to avoid the trap of essentialism that relies on the ascriptive shared features in a group. After all, human cognition operates variously under various conditions. In short, the volume focuses on the construction and spread of the acceptable idea of national identity that refuses to accept the terms of negative ethnicity.

CHAPTER TWO

Post-Ethnic Conflict Reconstruction and the Question of National Identity in Asia and Africa

David E. Kiwuwa

Every post-conflict society is unique and there is no one-size-fits-all approach to its post-conflict reconstruction needs. However, when conflicts have been underlined by identity dissonance, post-conflict response ought to place issues of national identity as an integral part of the general reconstruction efforts. But since there has been minimal theoretical and normative development expended to this task, this essay seeks to address this shortcoming by treating national identity as a crucial theoretical construct to post-conflict reconstruction. Approaching this debate largely from a theoretical perspective, the paper seeks to analyse the theories of post-conflict reconstruction and that of national identity, how these fuse within post-conflict scenarios and how national identity can be made an integral component of a revamped post-conflict reconstruction theory and practice.

The central thrust of this essay is the argument that the theoretical and normative treatment of the critical question of national identity has often been considered and treated as marginal within post-conflict reconstruction discourses. Given persistent faltering of post-conflict reconstruction, this has raised questions of the ability and viability of current post-conflict reconstruction approaches to achieve and sustain over the long term durable peace, group co-existence and a viable state structure. Firstly, the essay starts by offering a brief empirical overview of the extent and nature of the problem in a number of selected countries. Secondly, it proceeds to analyse post-conflict reconstruction theory and its shortcomings. Thirdly, the essay offers an analysis of national identity, its contemporary relevance and finally how it can be brought to inform the broader debate within post-conflict reconstruction discourse. The use of empirical evidence through case studies will be used to bolster our theoretical analysis.

It is hardly novel to note that many states today are far from homogeneous and increasingly have had to grapple with the tensions inherent in their diversity or multiple identities within their borders.[1] These states are of interest to political scientists, conflict mediation strategists and post-conflict reconstructionists because they are more at risk of and often suffer from violent ethnic conflict, secession movements and pervasive socio-political instability. However, within multiple identity states, there has been a mixed bag of political fortunes in respect to political stability and social cohesion. Whereas in some states such diversity has fostered political stability through group bargaining and trade-offs, in others they have been a catalyst for incessant and bitter group conflicts and tensions. The conflicts in Lebanon, Sri Lanka, Congo (DRC), Rwanda, Sudan, Ethiopia, Burundi, Ivory Coast, former Yugoslavia and now the festering sectarian violence in Iraq have been explicitly characterised by the question of identity: ethnic, race or religion. These, a 1997 World Bank report "A framework for World Bank Involvement in Post-Conflict Reconstruction" classified as suffering from state erosion or failure due to ethnic, racial, regional conflicts. This however has not always been the case. For a long time, inter-state conflicts had dominated the political landscape, though with the end of the Cold War, there has been a gradual shift in the nature of conflicts towards intra-state conflicts. During the Cold War, ideological battles overshadowed and in most cases made redundant identity based conflicts, though in reality, these lurked in the background. With its end, instead of an emergence of a much-vouched 'new world order', local tensions and conflicts simmered into full-scale communal civil wars or what elsewhere has been referred to as the 'new wars'.[2] In fact, the Institute for Democracy and Electoral Assistance 1998 report noted that some 80 percent of the major conflicts taking place in the 1990s (predominantly in Africa) had a clear identity component. However, while it is incontrovertible that many contemporary conflicts are characterised by competing identities, it is also true that they sometimes obscure the 'real' root cause of conflicts, which could be structural inconsistencies or socio-political dysfunctions.[3] Following sustained local and international efforts to prevent escalation of identity-based conflicts, primarily through liberal approaches like constitutionalism and democratisation with inbuilt conflict prevention mechanisms and secondly through elaborate post-conflict reconstruction approaches, the question of subgroup loyalties' compatibility with national identity has become apparent following importunate communal conflicts.[4]

Perhaps to situate our analysis in context, it is relevant to offer a brief overview of the scale of the problem. From an empirical perspective, groups in

Ivory Coast have separated the country into two, creating a north (largely Muslim)-south (largely Christian) divide, while the pattern in Sudan follows a similar dimension. Along with perceived systematic discrimination of the people from the north in Ivory Coast and south in the Sudan, the two conflicts also highlight problematic issues of group security, national resource sharing, political representation and national identity broadly understood.[5] In former Zaire (now Democratic Republic of Congo), the recent civil war was partially sparked by a systematic purge of the *Banyamulenge* Tutsi by the Mobutu government as unwelcome 'non-Congolese' aliens. Despite over a century of unchallenged settlement within Congo's South-West Kivu province, domestic and regional political conflicts saw the *Banyamulenge* playing some role but also in the process reigniting the debate about national identity and their citizenship.

The Rwandan civil war was perhaps the ultimate manifestation of contested identity that culminated in genocide as an attempted solution to the question. This genocide seems to have been underscored by the survival strategy of the competing groups born out of perceived or real threat to group identity and security. Hence, the logic was you either get 'them' first or they get 'you'. Rwanda's neighbour to the south, Burundi, has too grappled with the question of the place of identity within politics for a greater part of its contemporary politics and its subsequent implication.[6] This socio-political dilemma stocked systematic group violence and an entrenched mutual distrust which ensured political instability and quasi permanent war footing. What is common to all the highlighted cases is that subgroup identities and loyalties have fundamentally challenged the nature and behaviour of the state. In seeking to prevent significant state fissure, some of these states have sought to seek and actively pursue an overriding 'collective identity' by homogenising their multiple identities. However, Hannum Hurst has cautioned that 'the search for "homogeneity" implicit in the pursuit of a national identity may...' be more likely to lead to repression and human rights violation than to promote the tolerance and plurality which many would claim to be essential values in the twentieth century.[7] Hurst's argument can be understood in two ways. On one hand, it may reflect the incessant political tensions, violent civil conflicts and socio-political fissures that engulfed and still plague some of the multiple identity states, and on the other, it may be highlighting the need for a cautious approach to the question of national identity, a debate that we shall return to in the later part of this essay. For now, the perennial 'national identity' crisis in multiple identity states, particularly emerging from civil conflicts seems to be indicative of some systemic weakness of existing approaches. In focusing on the theory of post-conflict reconstruction here-under, we seek to identify and analyse its weaknesses and therefore establish the rationale for a theoretical revamp.

Reassessing Post-Conflict Reconstruction Theory

It is assumed that when conflicts of whatever nature end either temporarily or permanently through military victory, formal peace agreement or a stalemate, a period of post-conflict is ushered in preceded by efforts to secure some form of short- or long-term political stability and social tranquillity. Most importantly, efforts to prevent a relapse into violence are actively pursued within a broad framework of what has come to be known as post-conflict reconstruction. A rather ambiguous and broad term, post-conflict reconstruction is understood differently by many scholars and practitioners. Mari Fitzduff has noted that 'reconstruction' implies that one reconstructs society to resemble what it was like before the conflict, hence failing to sometimes address the very problems that caused the conflict; while to others, it may imply righting a moral wrong done to the victims of violence.[8] In our discussion, we do not wish to be caught up in such definitional complexities. Rather, considered in a broader context, post-conflict reconstruction will be understood as a complex system that provides for simultaneous short-, medium- and long-term programmes to prevent disputes from escalating, avoid a relapse into violent conflict and to build and consolidate sustainable peace.[9] This has normally involved efforts to create and restore physical infrastructure and facilities, minimal social services and structural reforms and transformation in the political, socio-economic and security sectors. While post-conflict reconstruction proceeds in three stages, namely, emergence, transitional and development, the dynamics within each stage are not mutually exclusive as there is a tendency of overlap. Elsewhere, various scholars have considered a number of issues as critical to post-conflict reconstruction theory and practice: security, political reconstruction, justice, human rights, economic and social reconstruction and civil society.[10]

From a general literature overview, a comprehensive engagement with post-conflict reconstruction theory is relatively thin on the ground but also clearly wanting and inept in offering adequate analysis of political stability and social cohesion in contemporary post-conflict states. In the past, post-conflict reconstruction has been more concerned with infrastructural reconstruction and the resuscitation of development processes. Also, according to the World Bank, post-conflict reconstruction is particularly focused on the rebuilding of the socio-economic framework of society and the reconstruction of the enabling conditions for the functioning of a peacetime society to include the framework of governance and the rule of law. Within the emergence stage, the immediate concern is for states or groups to halt active hostility, while the transitional and development stages provide an opportunity for societies to recover from the systemic 'shock' of the conflict, take stock of the causes and move to systematically address them. Hence, within the latter two stages, it is possible to envisage an attempt at social transformation and creation of enabling conditions for sustainable peace. Nevertheless, it is evident that there has been disproportionate scholarly attention in favour of economic development while very little attention has been paid to more complex and ideational abstracts like national identity.[11] Though on closer analysis, it is possible to argue that issues of security, human rights, justice, social reconstruction and transformation are clearly relevant to national identity post-conflict, this interconnectedness is not explicitly developed within the theory. Hence, in this context, the general theory of post-conflict reconstruction and its practical implication appears relatively inadequate in responding to national identity crises. Having briefly analysed post-conflict reconstruction theory and its inadequacy in the face of national identity, it is only prudent that we also engage on a theoretical and functional level with the meaning and relevance of national identity post-conflict.

Problematising National Identity

For a while now the phenomenon of national identity has occupied a central place in social sciences, most evident within a number of contemporary seminal works by Anthony Smith among others.[12] Smith has argued that national identity has been a basis for the creation and maintenance of the modern state, a catalyst for social cohesion, but also hastens to add that it has been problematic; a root cause of protracted civil conflicts.[13] Additionally, there has been a healthy level of research in understanding the dynamics between identity and protracted communal conflicts. Peculiarly, within post-conflict reconstruction discourse as earlier argued, there has been a relatively weak explicit theorisation of national identity and consequently the efforts to establish a robust and comprehensive mechanism that would ensure enduring caveats on such conflicts occasionally falter.[14] In reflecting on such a problem, it is important to address ourselves to a number of questions; what is national identity and what is its relevance to individuals, groups or states? Most importantly, how would reconstruction practitioners address the complexity of national identity post-conflict, to bring about lasting political stability and peace? In addressing these questions, we shall hope to highlight the need to position national identity as a key issue within post-conflict reconstruction.

As a concept, national identity has been considered complex, fluid and multidimensional.[15] As a phenomenon and its contemporary political relevance, contrary to modernists' expectation of its waning, it has proved quite pervasive and highly adaptable. Broadly however, national identity can be understood in relatively two simple ways; first, where it represents a subgroup identity like an ethnic group in a multiple identity state (particularity) and second, where it refers to a collective identity in reference to a sum total of all existing subgroups (universality).[16] In this essay, the understanding of national identity will be primarily within the context of the latter though occasionally overlap is possible.

According to Smith, the concept of national identity involves some form of a political community, which in turn implies at least some common institutions and a single code of rights and duties for all members of the community, with a definite social space and a fairly bounded territory.[17] It is therefore a considered view that people who tend to share all or most of these attributes will form a national identity that in turn enhances the smooth function of a state and the maintenance of some form of unrestrained political allegiance. Kelman too has argued that:

> ... national identity is the group's definition of itself as a group, its conception of its enduring characteristics and basic values, its strength, and weaknesses, its hopes and fears, its reputation and conditions of existence, its institutions and traditions, its past history, current purposes and future prospects.[18]

Within states, individual or group identification carries a very intrinsic value, considered basic and foundational, to be nurtured, promoted and preserved. Elsewhere, national identity can be perceived as an end in itself and for many serving as an identifier, a source of distinctiveness and continuity and overall providing a sense of belonging and unity for the members.[19] On his part, Giordano saw it as a psychological foundation offering the individual a 'ground on which to stand' that 'no one can take away'.[20] Membership to a defined national identity accords groups and individuals particular and sometimes exclusive rights and benefit and are likewise expected to manifest this membership through a shared consciousness, shared dispositions or solidarity and sometimes collective action. It therefore seems to justify group claims to resources, control of power and most importantly demarcation or exclusive claim to territorial space. Likewise, Smith has argued that national identity tends to not only determine the composition of the regime's personnel, but also legitimate and often influence policy goals and administrative practices that regulate the everyday lives of citizens.[21] Within a post-conflict scenario, this carries with it very important implications.

Derived from the logic of ethnic entrepreneurs, national identity mobilisation can be considered functional and practical where groups tend to stake their claims based on their perceived distinctiveness from the 'other'. Increasingly, within societies that possess multiple identities, the mobilisation of distinct identities will always be attractive to political opportunists, elites and groups who seek to gain an advantage over the 'other' through seeking collective identification and subsequently, collective bargaining and action. Hechter has employed the rational choice theory in explaining such use of collective identity in pursuing collective goods.[22] Yancey et al have argued that the activation of collective identity may have something more to do with the exigencies of survival and the structure of opportunity than mere expression of distinctiveness and pursuit of state power *per se*.[23] Within many societies, the emphasis on national identity serves as a rallying notion for development and claim to cultural distinctiveness, norms and values, all of which are interwoven into a kind of narrative that binds such groups together with myths of origin, territorial claims and a shared history.

The attractiveness and political relevance of identity at times overshadows its shortcomings. Though identity is largely agreed to be mutable and fluid in its nature, it poses fundamental difficulties to political stability and social cohesion when there exist a number of competing and conflictive identities. From Smith's conceptualisation, particular emphasis within national identity is premised on the 'commonality' of a number of variables. Hence, where the issue of this 'commonality' is under challenge then it is possible to envisage national identity being a problem. More so, where such competing identities hold diametrically opposed aspirations and visions of the state, seek to exclusively control the state apparatus and expropriate national identity for their exclusive symbolism, then the potential for violence and pervasive conflict increases. In his study of the Israel - Palestinian conflict, Kelman has argued that where such competing claims appear, they are perceived as a direct mutual threat to the existence of other identities and by extension their perceived entitlements of land, resources and power.[24] Groups then perceive the situation as zero-sum; for the existence of group A's identity is a direct and real threat and challenge to the existence of group B's identity. Between such groups, conflict and violence becomes inevitable unless there is a redefinition of the groups' identities and in particular their specific relationship first with the formal state and second, with each other. Overall, such identity contention can be seen to be a dynamic outcome of a number of interrelated forces: identity politics of the state, interactive relationship between different identity groups within the state, identity politicisation and assertiveness and sometimes the impact of external forces.

Often, race, ethnicity and language tend to overlap with other aspects of class, gender, sexuality, age and various demographic features to form complex, multiple, dynamic and contingent identities that we all have.[25] At the centre of national politics is national identity and in states with multiple identity groups, fundamental issues like the selection of an official language, the composition of the political elite, symbolic representation of the state, access and control of state resources all seem to create, promote and strengthen identity awareness within subgroups or regions. This, in the developing world in general and Africa in particular, tends to align group competition along identity markers and therefore the potential for group confrontation is more marked if and when the above issues are highly sensitive and contested.[26] For states emerging from identity-based conflicts, one of the short- and medium- term solutions has been to redefine identity boundaries. While it is prudent to treat identity as always in flux, and in a process of redefinition and reconstitution, where this redefinition is done in such a way as to alter the composition of national identity or for purposes of exclusion of competing identities, post-conflict reconstruction is bound to be very problematic.

Perhaps Rwanda within contemporary politics provides a compelling case for analysis of the problem of national identity and its relevance to political stability and post-conflict reconstruction. Composed of three 'ethnic groups', the majority Hutu (85%), minority Tutsi (14%) and Twa (less than 1%), the Hutu redefinition of national identity in immediate post-independence Rwanda was geared towards the eradication of the Tutsi competing identity and its implication, thereby enabling Hutus to stake exclusive claims on the state. The First Republic (1963–1970), which was dominated by the Hutus, ensured that the Rwanda state was not only perceived as a Hutu state but also symbolised and understood as such through symbols, laws and political rhetoric.[27] To the Hutu elite, the Tutsi were unwelcome pretenders to the Rwandan 'national identity' and usurpers of state resources and power. They contend that while the Tutsi could be accommodated in Rwanda, they should be consigned to the nation-state margins and excluded from placing legitimate claims to the real and symbolic representation by the Rwandan state. This attempt at systematic exclusion of the Tutsi from enjoying the full benefits of state membership and their relegation as second class citizens within the social structure bred inter-group violence, instability and the weakening of the state structure.[28] Since the subsequent Second Republic (1970–1993) did not seem to fundamentally alter this logic, the temporal lull in inter-group conflict and modest success of post-conflict reconstruction in the late 1970s and early 80s was illusory and temporary. For as long as the question of national identity was never fundamentally addressed, the Tutsi determination to be part of the Rwandan state and its identity was bound to cause recurrent political problems. Following, it is possible to argue that the 1990 civil war and the subsequent genocide can partly be located within the context of the broader question of national identity and its attendant implication. For the Hutus, they perceived a real threat to their 'national identity' and 'Hutu state' from the minority Tutsi both within and outside Rwanda, while for the Tutsi, recognition of their legitimate claims to the Rwandan state and their subsequent re-integration was non-negotiable. At the time, such claims were diametrically opposed to each other and inevitably bred political instability, social discord and a disputed Rwandan 'national identity' that consequently needed 'deconstructing' and 'reconstructing'.

Up north, the-over-two decade conflict in Sudan has also been reflective of such national identity crisis between the Arabised north and the animist and

Christian black south.[29] Following the zeal within the northern elite to structure the Sudanese 'national identity' as an Islamic Arab state, the north systematically constrained and undermined the southern Christian/animist black identity. In response, the over-two-decade southern rebellion was not so much seek political power but primarily to reemphasise the individual and southern group identities as part of the Sudanese national identity.[30] The faltering of post-conflict reconstruction after the 1972 peace agreement, while addressed the question of national identity and acquiesced to some autonomy of the south, appears to have either left fundamental questions unanswered among the north or to have had weaknesses that created an opportunity for the resumption of hostilities in 1983 that were to last for another 20 years. Currently, while the main crisis between the south and the north has been settled through granting of some political and economic autonomy to the black south, another crisis in the Darfur region is in full throttle. With the *janjaweed* 'Arab' militias terrorising the black populations with purported government backing, the United Nations and the international community claim that some kind of 'ethnic cleansing' is being carried out by these militias with tacit support of the Khartoum government. Once again, at the root of this conflict is identity and the threat perception Darfur represents to the political elite in Khartoum. This problematisation of identity is captured well by Prunier when he quotes a survivor from one of the attacks that had happened:

> The Janjaweed were accompanied by soldiers. They attacked the people, saying: "You are opponents to the regime, we must crush you. As you are Black, you are like slaves. Then the entire Darfur region will be in the hands of the Arabs. The government is on our side. The government plane is on our side, it gives us food and ammunition."[31]

It is possible to argue that while the conflict settlement with the main southern Sudan by far ensured group autonomy as regards its identity, norms, belief systems, territorial integrity and political power, it did not go far enough to embrace the groups in Darfur. Hence, post-conflict reconstruction in Sudan in general was not only made difficult but indeed faltered at the starting blocks.

In the Ivory Coast, debate as to who is 'indigenous' and 'non-indigenous' (elsewhere referred to as èntragères) for the benefit of state entitlements, control or share of political power once again reiterates our argument about the complexity of 'national identity'.[32] Focusing on the identity politics at play, the allegedly 'bona fide' Ivorians seek to lock out and actively exclude the 'non-native,' or those whose 'national identity' is in question, from sharing equitably the national cake. In 2000, a presidential candidate from the opposition party The Rally of Republicans, Alassane Quattara, was blocked from running because he was allegedly not a 'real' Ivorian.[33] The groups that expropriated the 'bona fide' identity rested in part on the negation of 'other identities,' hence taking on an exclusivist and monolithic character. This has resulted in a prolonged ethnic group conflict short of a full blown civil war. It is this either "we are" or "they are" notion that makes existing post-conflict reconstruction approaches broadly inadequate as the case here clearly demonstrates.[34] Hence, I argue, that the development and nourishing of a national identity that overrides the divisive potential of subgroup allegiances would not only help the population to grow together into a collective community of will but its absence will only set the diverse groups on a collision course. Perhaps Doumbia, an Ivorian, effectively captures the extent to which the question of national identity in post-conflict reconstruction discourse has become important when he noted that:

> The day I obtained my nationality card, I killed a chicken to thank my ancestors...that was in 1978. Since then, I've had to renew it twice. The first time, civil servants took a year to investigate my background. The second time, they refused to renew it, saying I was a foreigner...an Ivorian without papers is like a dog without a master.[35]

There is no doubt that the question of 'national identity' is at the heart of the Ivorian conflict as many without papers or official state identification are from the north, whose Ivorian identity has been long under question or contested. For the northern rebels the choice is simply between handing over weapons or a national identity card, with its national entitlements. So, for the successful resolution of this conflict in the short run and post-conflict reconstruction in the long term, renegotiation of issues around national identity and its implication are presumed critical. Hence, it is possible to perceive the on-going (albeit contested) national registration and census as falling within the context of redefining parameters of national identity upon which substantive post-conflict reconstruction will be grounded.

Conceptual Fusing: National Identity and Post-Conflict Reconstruction Theory Reconsidered

There is no doubt that a case has been made that national identity within contemporary politics seems to be problematic for socio-political stability. Likewise, the hypothetical deduction that seems to emerge from the fragile or often incomplete post-conflict reconstruction in multi-identity societies is that the question of national identity when effectively addressed lies at the heart of a successful post-conflict reconstruction approach. Consequently, it is logical to reflect on another complimentary but important debate of whether it is possible to construct or imagine an inclusive 'supra national identity' that supersedes subgroup loyalties and if not, how can reconstructionists contain or mitigate subgroup 'pushes' and 'pulls' to ensure the success of post-conflict reconstruction?

Some identity scholars have long asserted that there exist overlapping individual or group identities that become relevant or otherwise as circumstances dictate. Hence, people may stress certain identities and suppress others when it is in their best interest to do so.[36] But if (national) identity is fluid and multisided it is possible to perceive it as possessing a degree of permeability. This therefore gives rise to the possibility of the waning of certain identities when ideal conditions exist but also creates opportunities for the evolution or 'imagining' of broader sometimes inclusive national identity constructs. Within political interaction, the way groups seek to identify and define themselves and also position themselves *vis a vis* the state is relevant to other groups with whom they occupy socio-political space since each group is directly affected by the other's definition of self. In attempting to establish liberal institutional structures within post-conflict societies, it is crucial to establish who the constituent members of that society are, the nature of their inter-group relationship and group position in relation to each other within the state. Increasingly, faced with the dilemma of dealing with competing identity claims with a history or potential for violence, the issue to reconstructionists has become an option of whether on one hand to recognise and to a degree entrench such diversity within political and constitutional structures or on the other hand seek to nullify or de-emphasise these identities (*de-ethnicisation/de-identification*). This can be pursued primarily along four dimensions: the classic melting pot, assimilation, the salad bowl and the citizenship models.[37]

The melting pot phenomenon describes a model of group relations in which a state's constituent identity groups engage in a process of reciprocal fusion. This can primarily be in two forms: (1) all identity groups acculturate to a universalistic set of values and symbols with no ancestral connotations or (2) there is a two way influence between identity groups in the society such that no group achieves symbolic or actual dominance. Generally within this model, diverse identity groups' belief systems, language, economic and social values are fused together in a broad and continuous process of cultural reformulation and transformation. This then ensures that subgroup identities wane or become irrelevant over time and if they persist ideally become secondary to the universalistic identity. This effectively suppresses subgroup tensions and allows for the evolution over the long term of a national identity and a stable political structure.

To date, ever since the emergence of the melting pot rationale, it is increasingly clear that perhaps the expected gelling and dissolution of particularistic identities was rather unrealistic. What instead has been observed is the evolution of assimilation or what elsewhere is referred to as long-term 'switching'.[38] This describes a process whereby members of a subgroup, usually a minor or subordinate subgroup, take on the cultural and structural characteristics of another subgroup or national community. While there are various strands of assimilation as developed by Gordon Milton, what seem to be particularly relevant in this analysis are two strands of structural and civic assimilation. Broadly, reconstructionists may pursue an assimilationist agenda where it is possible to envisage the absorption and integration of minor or subordinate identities within dominant group identities.[39] While it is true that minority identities are rarely completely subsumed by dominant identities, it is possible for these to internally evolve, be reconstructed, transformed or be selectively retained in response to the environment in which they operate. Kelman has tacitly pointed out that in fact (national) identities are commonly reconstructed sometimes gradually and sometimes radically as historical circumstances change, crises emerge, opportunities present themselves or new elites come to the fore.[40] However, such 'total' integration in this context can only be successful for the transformation of national identity when the minor/subordinate identities are willing to forego their identities for the adoption of a dominant one. More often than not, this will be the case if there are tangible benefits that would accrue to the 'converted'.[41] Elsewhere, Barth's similar understanding of the permeability and flexibility of group boundaries is perhaps grounded on the idea that migrants (normally a minority) come to be assimilated into adjacent or dominant groups.[42] It is evident therefore that pursuing an inclusive and harmonious national identity, political elites and group leaders will seek to 'imagine', socially construct or 'negotiate' a 'new' national identity based however on existing authentic elements sometimes held in common by the competing groups like common history, common language, common religion, common customs, common cultural expressions, common values, common grievances, common aspirations and common experiences. This can be achieved through concerted negotiations with mutually acceptable tradeoffs through a general appreciation of each other's self worth and how they seek to project their identity and its place within the general body politic.

However, when systematic assimilation is unilaterally pursued by dominant groups either through coercion, legal measures or constitutional structures, post-conflict reconstruction success will be less forthcoming.[43] While in the short run this may deliver an ad hoc national identity, it does not guarantee long-term group integration and therefore a cloud of possible resentment, rebellion and outright violence will still hang over post-conflict reconstruction.[44]

Within post-genocide Rwanda, it is clear that part of the post-conflict reconstruction strategy is the reassertion of a 'new national identity', the promotion of 'switching' from subgroup loyalties to an overarching Rwandan identity. Very much aware of the post-independence exclusionist national identity that emphasised the Hutu as the bona fide national identity, the new regime has moved to banish ethnic (group) identification and encourage the nurturing of a 'Rwandan identity' elsewhere referred to as 'Rwandanicity'. As the minister of Good Governance, Protais Musoni argued:

> In the socio-political arena, there is still need to have policies, processes and programs that can create a citizen that is above sectarianism. The historical processes Rwanda has gone through have created a sectarian conditioned Munyarwanda with all the exclusion mentality that goes with it. Such conditioning can not form the basis for the synergetic relationship that is required for social advancement...a new culture of national identity must be forged and nurtured.[45]

Currently, political rhetoric and 'popular discourse' not only frowns upon subgroup identification but also actively champions the promotion of a Rwandan self, thereby relegating subgroup loyalty below loyalty to the state with its attendant obligation of tolerance, co-existence and equality. Symbolically, this pursuit of a new Rwandan national identity is complemented by the introduction of new national symbols, like a new national anthem and court of arms designed to emphasise a new beginning and the death of the old.[46] As Schmitter and Karl have argued, 'the need for prior consensus on overarching national identity and boundaries is an indispensable requirement' for post-conflict states.[47] In this particular context, Rwanda (and to some extent Congo DR) seem to acknowledge that to pursue and safe-guard the two states from regressing into identity-based dissonance, the question of national identity needs to be addressed as part of the post-conflict reconstruction framework. However, construction of a 'national identity' on a deeper psychological and sociological level entails some aspect of a collective memory/myth, and there being a contested 'memory' in Rwanda's case, the results from an ongoing reconstruction of a new national identity are yet to be conclusive.

Despite such systematic state and elite national identity engineering efforts, we should be conscious of the potential difficulty of engineering an inclusive national identity largely evident in the fragmentation of Eastern Europe, India's partition with the creation of Pakistan and the latter's partition to create Bangladesh. Perhaps Hobsbawm put it frankly when he noted that "identity groups are about themselves, for themselves and nobody else...a coalition of such groups that is not held together by a single common set of aims or values has only an ad hoc unity...they break up when they are no longer held so together."[48] When post-conflict strategies failed to harmonise and weave together competing identities into a cohesive national identity in post-war Ethiopia after the fall of Mengistu Haile Mariam, state fragmentation seemed inevitable with the eventual birth of independent Eritrea. Sudan too is presently at a threshold of a fundamental referendum that decides whether it remains part of the Sudan or secedes. Assimilation as a post-conflict strategy seems to have less appeal and bears a lot of practical difficulties. What then would be a viable option one would wonder?

Within multiple-identity states, where there is a two-way influence between identity groups, with no attempt to pursue symbolic or real dominance, national identity transformation for the success of post-conflict reconstruction appears realistic. Quite distinct from the assimilationist approach is what elsewhere has been referred to as the 'salad bowl' phenomenon. Theoretically, it would tend to structure group relationships *vis a vis* each other primarily along equality, co-existence, co-operation and reciprocity. The logic is that a subgroup identity is not necessarily submerged within a national identity but retained and sometimes celebrated within the social arena. This perhaps has its justification from the observation that it is sometimes futile to unilaterally attempt to enforce group redefinition of self. In some cases, it is the realisation that group identity is at times non-negotiable and much deeper than first acknowledged, primordial some would assert. In this context, co-existence within the broader society entails active involvement of diverse groups in institutions, the construction of social ties and horizontal networks, participation in social cultural activities, but most importantly equal access to the rewards that the economic and political systems generate and distribute. Cohen has argued elsewhere that 'when men do fight...fight across ethnic lines, it is nearly always the case that they fight over some fundamental issues concerning the distribution and exercise of power whether economical, political or both.[49] Equitable distribution of economic and political opportunities creates a window for co-operation and co-existence. Hence, boundaries of competing identities are acted upon by forces internal and external to the groups but are perceived to be structurally non-hostile.[50] On the other hand, sectoral or institutional domination by distinct groups within multiple-identity societies presents an opportunity and a basis for bargaining to stabilise and achieve balance of power sometimes through formally acknowledging subgroup spheres of influence or niches.

While the 'salad bowl' espouses co-operation and co-existence, it is also true that some identities are rigid, inherently conflictual and caught up in a complex dysfunctional socio-political structure with limited avenues of dialogue to negotiate an overriding national identity. This may also arise primarily from the nature and structure of society and the position such competing identities occupy in it. Following group dominance models, Sidanius and Pratt have argued that societies tend to be organised as group-based hierarchies with dominant groups enjoying disproportionate shares of positive socio-political values of power, privilege and prestige while subordinate groups suffer disproportionate shares of negative socio-political values.[51] Within this context, where some group identities are perceived as inferior and less worthy, barriers to national identity formation through cooperation will be high, not to mention the remote likelihood of a harmonious 'salad bowl'. Hence, Ake makes an important observation that there is a very real potential of many competing identities within a particular state to pull in many different directions that ultimately causes demand overload, systematic breakdown and ultimately violent conflict.[52]

There has been a more pragmatic approach that builds on the logic of the 'salad bowl' phenomenon, to which this essay particularly subscribes. This essentially redefines and structurally reconfigures the relationship between the state and its constituent individuals and groups. This is what is widely perceived as citizenship. Basically, citizenship defines those who are and who are not members of a common society.[53] According to Waters, it spells out the procedures and sets of practices defining the relationship between the state and its individual members.[54] Consequently, by redefining group boundaries and their collective identity *vis a vis* the state, citizenship divorces subgroup identification from the state and instead confers legalistic obligation to constituent members of a particular state. In the event, it nurtures a sovereign individual emancipated from particularistic solidarities and enhances universalistic identity that supersedes subgroup loyalties. Hence, the resultant national identity while respectful of individual and group particularities stresses universalistic norms and obligation and provides members with an opportunity to participate in the national community. The claim to the existing national identity is validated within the public realm through such legal and bureaucratic instruments as voting rights, identity cards and passports. Crucially, however, this process does not negate group identities *per se* but rather fundamentally dilutes their political relevance and their ability to structure or impact to any meaningful degree group or individual political behaviour. Also, the process helps to realign group positions within the state from a vertical to a horizontal social group structure. Increasingly therefore, it is through the equal access diverse identity groups have to shared structures of power that organize commanding legal, economic, and cultural institutions on the local and national level that give national citizenship great credence. The renegotiation of areas of citizenship for national identity helps to bridge the gap between various identity groups which in turn helps subordinate ethnic, racial, and cultural differences to the assimilating logic of a common culture. Of course, national identity is a social construction that is built upon a series of inclusions and exclusions regarding history, citizenship, and national belonging. As Anderson has pointed out, the nation is an 'imagined political community' that can only be understood within the intersecting dynamics of history, language, ideology, and power. In other words, national identity is neither necessarily reactionary nor progressive politically.[55] Hence, within post-conflict reconstruction discourse it is crucial to redefine national identity not through a primordial notion of ethnicity or a monolithic conception of culture and identity, but as part of post-modern politics of group diversity and differences in which identities are constantly being negotiated and reinvented within complex and contradictory notions of national belonging.

Conclusion

One of the key roles of a viable heterogonous state is overseeing and moderating group relationships and interaction. In principle, within liberal and democratic states, it ensures that none feels dominated or alienated within both the social and political arena. However, (as is often the case) whenever any one group tends to dominate the state, it makes other groups feel excluded, weak, vulnerable and open to manipulation. This is the kind of push factor towards group tension and conflict. While the state normally requires and demands the transfer of primary allegiance from subgroups, it at the same time contains internal inconsistencies as sometimes through its policies and power dynamics it manifests group dominance both politically and culturally. Hence, the state ceases to be a neutral arbiter and actor but an active participant in the resultant conflict. The question then to post-conflict reconstructionists is how to transform the character of the state and its component social units. Can, for instance, a Hutu or Tutsi be at the same time a Rwandan with loyalty both to the Hutu/Tutsi identity and the Rwandan national identity? Can a *Nyamulenge* owe loyalty both to his ethnic group and to his Congolese identity? Are these two levels of allegiances incompatible? Does 'negotiation' and assertion of national identity necessarily negate group identities within post-conflict reconstruction?

Throughout this essay, I have tried to address these questions through a number of analytical contexts. Yes, one can be a Hutu/Tutsi and Rwandan, Nyamulenge and Congolese. The expression of one's subgroup identity need not necessarily negate assertion of national identity, but most importantly, the shift in the way groups identify themselves and how they use this identification within their daily transaction with the state and other groups has become increasingly crucial in determining state stability, inter-group relations and development of a national identity. Primarily however, I have broadly observed and argued that since the existing post-conflict reconstruction theories do not address the critical question of national identity, post-conflict reconstruction has consistently faltered as my empirical cases demonstrate. Hence, a more pressing need to fundamentally restructure or revamp the theory by treating national identity as explicitly integral to post-conflict reconstruction both in theory and practice.

Within many societies, common symbols, cultures, values and beliefs help gel communities together to enhance national identity. However, in some heterogeneous states these can be the very basis of conflict. But as diverse groups continue to interact with each other, through cooperation, co-existence and accommodation, their socio-political conception of self may be exposed to redefinition and adaptation through a number of ways: melting pot, assimilation, salad bowl and citizenship. Contrary to some arguments that identities are rigid, post-conflict reconstruction practitioners should seek to promote a universalistic conception of self and the idea of the individual sovereign in such circumstances. Because many aspects of identity can be construed as constructed and therefore vehicles for pursuing group goals, within reconstruction theory, the strength of integrating national identity lies not so much in its rigidity but ability and potential to be readapted to contemporary challenges like the pursuit of peace and group co-existence.

Increasingly within a more dynamic political world and in the face of pervasive identity-based conflicts, it is imperative that identities or at least their perception have to be seen to shift. They are not necessarily zero-sum and therefore the formulation of an all inclusive national identity that is primarily responsive to subgroup anxieties and needs would bolster long-term social cohesion and political stability. Hence, there is need to have policies, processes and programs that can create citizenship or transcendent identities that are above subgroup loyalties. Likewise, since it has been argued that identities are imagined, deconstructed and reconstructed, it is possible to de-emphasise and dissolve over the long term some contested or problematic aspects of group identities though ideally these should not be core to group identity. It is through this sometimes subtle redefinition of subgroup identities that national identity can be enhanced. Ultimately, the forging of a new national identity preferably through a model of liberal citizenship ought to replace subgroup loyalties and their relevance at least within the political arena.

Within a revamped post-conflict reconstruction framework, faced with similar opportunities and costs, social goods and bads, subgroup identities should not predetermine a group or an individual's potential experiences. In this way, the state structure will accord none advantages and impose on none negative costs on the basis of their particularistic identities but most importantly help stitch all harmoniously together within a unique fraternal bond of national identity. For a revamped theory of post-conflict reconstruction particularly within multiple identity states, an integral theorisation of national identity could fundamentally impact on its contemporary relevance and adequacy in post-conflict analysis.

Notes

1   The use of identity in this essay in particular reference to multiple identities will be similar or close to ethnicity. Smith 1993 (28) establishes this equivalence when he notes that 'to grasp the nature and power of ethnic nationalism today, one must focus primarily on the collective level of identity and community.

2   Michael Brown (1997) in M. Guibernau and John Rex (eds.), 'Ethnicity and Violence' in *The Ethnicity Reader: Nationalism, Multiculturalism and Migration* (Malden: Blackwell). Kevin Quinn, Michael Hechter and Erik Wibbels, "Ethnicity, Insurgency and Civil War Revisited" unpublished paper (2004).

3   M. Renner (1998), in Michael Klare and Yogesh Chandrani (eds.), "The Global Divide: Socioeconomic Disparities and International Security," in *World Security: Challenges for a New Century* (St. Martins Press, 1998), 243.

4   C. Walker, "A Nation is a Nation, Is a State, Is an Ethnic Group Is a...," *Ethnic and Racial Studies* 1 (4) (1978), 377.

5   Abraham McLaughlin, "Push to Limit Ivory Coast Conflict," *The Christian Science Monitor* (Nov 12. 2004). Francis Deng, "Sudan: A Nation in Turbulent Search of Itself," *Annals of the American Academy*, 603 (2006), 155; Jay O'Brien, "Ethnicity, National Identity and Social Conflict," *Nordic Journal of African Studies* 2 (2) (1993), 70.

6   See Rene Lemarchand, *Rwanda and Burundi* (London: Pall Mall Press, 1970); Nigel Eltringham, *Accounting for Horrors: Post-Genocide Debates in Rwanda* (Sterling, Va.: Pluto Press, 2004). Susanne Buckley-Zistel, "Dividing and Uniting: The Use of Citizenship Discourses in Conflict and Reconciliation in Rwanda," *Global Society* 20 (1) (2006).

7   Hurst Hanum, *Autonomy, Sovereignty and Self-Determination: The Accommodation of Conflicting Rights* (Philadephia: University of Pennsylvania Press, 1990), 26.

8   Alex Austin, Martina Fischer, and Norbert Ropers (eds.), *Transforming Ethno-political Conflict: The Berghof Handbook* (Wiesbaden: VS Verlag für Sozialwissenschaften, 2004), 375.

9   The New Partnership for African Development, *African Post-Conflict Reconstruction Policy Framework* (NEPAD Secretariat, 2005), 5.

10 NEPAD, *African Post-Conflict Reconstruction Policy*. Alcira Kreimer, John Erickson, Muscat Robert, Margaret Arnold, Colin Scot, *The World Bank Experience with Post-conflict Reconstruction* (Washington D.C.: 1998). Christopher J. Coyne, "The Institutional Prerequisite for Post-conflict Reconstruction," *The Review of Austrian Economics*, The World Bank 8 (3/4) (2005), 325.

11 See Von L. Mises, *The Selected Writings of Ludwig von Mises*, 2000, 3. Richard M. Ebeling (ed.), *The Political Economy of International Reform and Reconstruction* (Indianapolis: Liberty Fund, 2000). Kreimer, *World Bank Experience*. W. Foote, W. Block, K. Crane, and S Gray, "Economic Policy and Prospects for Iraq" *Journal of Economic Perspectives* 18 (3) (2004).

12 Anthony Smith, *Theories of Nationalism* (New York: Harper and Row, 1971). Anthony Smith, *The Nationalist Movements* (London: Macmillan, 1976). Anthony Smith, *Nationalism in the Twentieth Century* (New York: New York University Press, 1979). Anthony Smith, *The Ethnic Revival* (Cambridge: Cambridge University Press, 1981). Anthony Smith, "Ethnic Myth and Ethnic Revivals," *European Journal of Sociology* 25 (1984). Anthony Smith, *The Ethnic Origin of Nations* (Oxford: Blackwell, 1986). Anthony Smith, *National Identity* (Reno, University of Nevada Press, 1991).

13 Smith, *Ethnic Revival*, 74. Smith, *National Identity*, 143. Thomas Hylland Eriksen, "Ethnic Identity, National Identity and Intergroup Conflict: The Significance of Personal Experiences," in Richard D. Ashmore, Lee Jussim, David Wilder (eds.), *Social Identity, Intergroup Conflict and Conflict Reduction* (Oxford: Oxford University Press, 2001).

14 See David Turton (ed.), *War and Ethnicity: Global Connections and Local Violence* (Woodbridge, Suffolk: University of Rochester Press, 1997).

15 Brubaker Rogers and Fredrick Cooper, "Beyond Identity," *Theory and Society* 29 (2000), 6.

16 Malik Kenan, *The Meaning of Race: Race, History and Culture in Western Society* (Basingstoke: Macmillan, 1996).

17 Smith, *National Identity*, 9.

18 C. Herbert Kelman, "Negotiating National Identity and Self Determination in Ethnic Conflicts: The Choice Between Pluralism and Ethnic Cleansing," *Negotiation Journal* 13 (1997), 171.

19 See also E. Roosen, *Creating Ethnicity: The Process of Ethnogenesis* (Newbury Park, CA: Sage, 1989). G. A. De Vos, "Conflict and Accommodation in Ethnic Interactions," in G.A. De Vos and M. Suarez-Orozco (eds.), *Status Inequality: The Self in Culture* (Newbury Park, CA: Sage, 1990), 204.

20 J. Giordano, *Ethnicity and Mental Health: Research and Recommendation* (New York: Institute on Pluralism and Group Identity, 1974), 16.

21 Smith, *National Identity*, 144.

22 Michael Hechter, *Containing Nationalism* (Oxford: Oxford University Press, 2000), 30. See also Nathan Glazer and Daniel Moynihan, *Beyond the Melting Pot* (Cambridge: Harvard University Press, 1963).

23 William Yancel, Eugene Ericksen and Richard Juliani, "Emergent Ethnicity: A Review and Reformulation," *American Sociological Review* 4 (1976), 400.

24 Herbert C. Kelman, "The Political Psychology of the Palestinian-Israeli Conflict: How Can We Overcome the Barriers to a Negotiated Solution?" *Political Psychology* 8 (1987), 354.

25 Carl E. James and Adrienne Shadd, *Talking about Identity: Encounters in Race, Ethnicity and Language* (Toronto: Between the Lines Press, 2001), 2. Crawford Young, *The Politics of Cultural Pluralism* (Madison: University of Wisconsin Press, 1976), 38. Pierre Van den Berghe, "Ethnicity in the African Experience," *International Social Science Journal* 23 (1971), 512.

26   See Charles Tilly, *Durable Inequality* (Berkeley: University of California Press, 1998). Charles Tilly, *The Politics of Collective Violence* (New York: Cambridge University Press, 2003).

27   Amalia Fawcett, "Becoming Rwandan: A Dialogue of National Identity," *Refugee Survey Quarterly* 22 (4) (2003), 107.

28   See R. Breton, "The Ethnic Groups as a Political Resource in Relation to Problems of Incorporation: Perceptions and Attitudes," in Raymond Breton, Wsevolod W. Isajiw, Warren E. Kalbach and Jeffrey G. Reitz, *Ethnic Identity and Equality* (London: University of Toronto Press), 198.

29   Deng, "Sudan," 2006. O'Brien, "Ethnicity, National Identity," 70.

30   Dunstan Wai (ed.), *The Southern Sudan: The Problem of National Integration* (London: Frank Cass, 1973). W George Shepherd, Jr., "National Integration and the Southern Sudan," *The Journal of Modern African Studies* IV (1966).

31   G. Prunier, *The Ambiguous Genocide* (Ithaca, NY: Cornell University Press, 2005). See also Julie Flint and Alex de Waal, *Darfur: A Short History of a Long War* (London: Zed Books, 2006).

32   Daniel Chirot, "Chaos in Ivory Coast: Roots and Consequences," *The Globalist* online accessed November 17th 2004. Pawson, "Ethnic Split Stirs Ivory Coast," BBC news online accessed 19th June 2006. James Copnall, "Ivory Coast's Cultural Divide," BBC news online accessed 19th June 2006. Mathew Kirwin, "The Security Dilemma and Conflict in Cote d' Ivoire," *Nordic Journal of African Studies* 5 (1) (2006).

33   Copnall, "Ivory Coast," 2006.

34   Copnall, "Ivory Coast," 2006.

35   Assocatied Press, "National Unity Hinges on Individual Identity," *All Africa News* online, August 23, 2006.

36   Eric Hobsbawm, "Identity Politics and the Left," *The New Left Review* 1 (217) (1996), 41.

37   Glazer, *Beyond the Melting Point*. Kim Y. Young, "From Ethnic to Interethnic: The Case for Identity Adoption and Transformation," *Journal of Language and Social Psychology* 125 (3) (2006), 287.

38   Joane Nagel and Susan Olzak, "Ethnic Mobilisation in New and Old States: An Extension of the Competition Model," *Social Problems* 30 (2) (1982), 129. Milton Gordon, *Assimilation in American Life: The Role of Race, Religion and Nationality Origins* (New York: Oxford University Press, 1964). Herbert Gans, "Symbolic Ethnicity: The Future of Ethnic Groups and Cultures in America," *Ethnic and Racial Studies* 2 (1979). Herbert Gans, "Ethnic Invention and Acculturation: A bumpy-line Approach," *Journal of American Ethnic History* 12 (1992). E. Morawska, "In Defence of the Assimilation Model," *Journal of American Ethnic History* 13 (1994).

39   J. Sidanius and F. Pratto, *Social Dominance: An Intergroup Theory of Social Hierarchy and Oppression* (New York: Cambridge University Press, 1999), 19.

40   Kelman, "Negotiating National Identity." "The Role of National Identity in Conflict Resolution," in Richard D. Ashmore, Lee Jussim and David Wilder (eds.), *Social Identity Intergroup Conflict, and Conflict Reduction* (Oxford: Oxford University Press, 2001), 194.

41   See Abner Cohen, *Customs and Politics in Urban Africa* (Berkeley: University of California Press, 1969). Beverley Lauwagie, "Ethnic Ideology, Boundaries and Mobilisation Among the Gypsies in the US and Britain," paper presented at the Annual Meeting of the Mid

west Sociological Society (Des Moines, IA, April 7th., 1982). Nelson Kasfir, "Explaining Ethnic Political Participation," *World Politics* 31 (1979). Cynthia Enloe, *Ethnic Soldier* (Athens: University of Georgia Press, 1980).

42   Fredrick Barth, *Ethnic Groups and Boundaries: The Social Organisation of Culture Difference* (London: Allen and Unwin, 1969).

43   Charles Tilly, *The Formation of Nation-States in Western Europe* (Princeton: Princeton University Press, 1975), 71.

44   See Andrea K. Talentino, "The Two Faces of Nation Building: Developing Function and Identity," *Cambridge Review of International Affairs* 17 (3) (2004).

45   Protais Musoni, "The End of the Transition Period: Prospects and Challenges," Conference paper presented at the workshop on Citizenship and Social Reconstruction in the Aftermath of Genocide, Butare, March 2003, p. 13.

46   Fawcett "Becoming Rwandan," 107.

47   P. C. Schmitter and T. L. Karl, "The Conceptual Travels of Transitologists and Consolidologists: How Far to the East Should They Go?" *Slavic Review* 53 (1994) 143.

48   Hobsbawm, "Identity Politics," 44.

49   Abner Cohen, *Customs and Politics in Urban Africa* (Berkeley: University of California Press, 1994), 94.

50   Wsevolod W. Isajiw, "Definition of Ethnicity," *Ethnicity* 1 (1974).

51   Sidanius and Prato, *Social Dominance*.

52   C. Ake, "Why Humanitarian Emergencies Occur: Insights from the Interface of State, Democracy and Civil Society," *Research for Action* 31 (1997), 8.

53   J. M. Barbalet, *Citizenship* (Minneapolis: University of Minnesota Press, 1988), 1.

54   Malcolm Waters, "Citizenship and the Constitution of Structures and Social Inequality," *International Journal of Comparative Sociology* 30 (1989), 160.

55   Benedict Anderson, *Imagined Communities: Reflections on the Origins and Spread of Nationalism* (London: Verso 1991).

Ethnicity and National Identity Externalized: Impact of Identity on Foreign Policy in Post-Soviet Ukraine

Michael Grossman

With a Russified population in the east and a nationalistic, staunchly Ukrainian population in the west, it has been difficult for the leaders of Ukraine to develop a unified national identity that appeals to all segments of society. The conflict centers around whether to define Ukraine as Ukrainian, a view favored largely by those living in Western Ukraine, or as Eastern-Slavic (Russian-Ukrainian), favored largely by residents of Eastern Ukraine, particularly the Crimea region. The struggle to establish a unifying national identity should have been reflected in the leaderships' efforts to establish a coherent foreign policy, since national identity is directly tied to foreign policy through its identification of the "other." Yet despite the societal contradictions that exist concerning Ukrainian national identity, Kiev was able to establish a consistent foreign policy. This is due in large part to the fact that Ukraine's foreign policy elite did not make any effort to reconcile the different identities that existed in society nor to follow the majority's views on which identity to ascribe to the country. Rather, the government chose an identity that represented the views of the Western minority, since it corresponded to the foreign policy that they believed would benefit Ukraine and that represented the opportunities they saw as available to it internationally. Subsequently, the chosen identity and the preferred foreign policy were mutually reinforcing, with the aim of achieving the ruling elite's international policy goals.

The difficulty many scholars have had in defining identity, not to mention quantifying it, has led most researchers to focus on variables that they see as more promising in explaining a state's international behavior. Nonetheless, the idea that identity does matter in the study of foreign policy has gained some followers in the field and it has grown in popularity. Still many questions remain about how to apply this variable. In particular, while it is easy to argue that identity plays a role in the policy process, questions remain about what that role exactly is and how it is reflected in the final outcome. At a more basic level, a question exists about how identity is determined; is it purely elite driven or does the citizenry have a role in determining a state's identity?

In the case of post-Soviet Ukraine, the issue of identity touches on all aspects of politics within the state, and nowhere is the link between identity and policy more evident than in foreign policy. The formation of a common national identity necessitates the cultural differentiation from a foreign "other." With a divided population this task has not been easy. The conflict centered on whether to define Ukraine as either uniquely Ukrainian, a view favored largely by those living in Western Ukraine, or as Eastern-Slavic (Russian-Ukrainian/Eurasian), largely favored by residents of Eastern Ukraine.

This chapter will examine elite national identity and foreign policy preferences in post-Soviet Ukraine. The questions it will seek to answer are how did the governing elite define identity and what role did it play in Ukraine's foreign policy? The chapter will argue that Ukraine's foreign policy elite did not make any effort to reconcile the different identities that existed in society nor to follow the majority's views on which identity to ascribe to the country. Rather, the government chose an identity that represented the views of the Western minority, since it corresponded to the foreign policy that they believed would benefit Ukraine and that represented the opportunities they saw as available to it internationally. Subsequently, the chosen identity and the preferred foreign policy were mutually reinforcing with the aim of achieving the ruling elite's international policy goals.

National Identity and Foreign Policy

National identity has long been one of the most difficult concepts to define. For every definition proposed, a host of examples appear to qualify or reject it. Just as difficult a task as identifying what exactly is national identity is the task of trying to pinpoint where it originates. Some scholars have argued that national self-perception originates with the masses and is thus an organic expression of commonality. Others have noted that national identity emanates from the ruling elite and is simply a means to a political end (a way to arouse the masses to action). Still others have pointed to a combination of the two, arguing that national identity is organic but its mobilization requires action by the political elite.

Danilo Kis[1] describes national identity in purely organic terms—as collective paranoia. It results from envy and fear and most of all from the loss of individual consciousness. Barrington Moore, Jr. provides a definition of national identity which also reflects its organic nature: "membership in a group that can save an individual from the anxieties of carving out his own meaningful place in the world, especially when the realistic chances of doing so are tiny."[2] In addition, Glenn Chafetz[3] sees national identity as a response to the domestic political needs of each group.

In contrast to the above definitions, Edward Keenan argues that national identity can be wholly inorganic.[4] In looking at Russian beliefs regarding Ukraine, he notes that the identity developed since the reign of the tsars has been completely artificial. The ties that Russians feel towards Ukraine were created by the rulers as a method of justification for policies that otherwise would not have had any support. Looking at the same case, Stephen Velychenko likewise found that the Russian monarchs cultivated a sense of national identity among the population that would not only enable them to pursue a policy of expansion, but also provide a sense of legitimacy to their rule.[5] Ilya Prizel notes: "Since the memories of society...are inconsistent and selective, the national identity is subject to what layer of a polity has the custodianship of the collective memory."[6]

Others have argued that national identity encompasses both of the above definitions. It consists of what the general population sees as its national identity and what the ruling elite defines as such. So it can be manipulated to some extent but not completely. Donald Horowitz notes that national identity is defined as both organic and inorganic, thus subject to manipulation, yet still emanating from the masses.[7] He also points out that national identity is not immutable and can be manipulated in order to fit the circumstances. "As group cohesion grows, cultural deviation and rough edges get smoothed off."[8] Nonetheless, the possibility for manipulation of national identity is limited. Leaders "cannot call into play an identity that is not founded on judgments of relative likeness and differences."[9]

This tension between popularly defined national identity and elite defined national identity is particularly salient for Post-Soviet societies. The Soviet regime tended to define national identity according to political considerations, mixing populations, as was the case with Nagorno-Karabakh, or creating national groups that had no historical roots, as was the case with many of the Central Asian states. "It virtually created nations and nationalities following criteria and purposes that were its own, and in conformity with these it charted out 'national' or 'republic' borders."[10] This process naturally stunted and distorted the process that leads to the development of a cohesive national identity. This was not an inadvertent outcome but rather a deliberate policy aimed at promoting "the creation of Soviet men and Soviet women, members of one Soviet people, living in one Soviet state."[11] Because of this legacy, governments within the post-Soviet space tend to be the primary definers of national identity.

Regardless of who defines it, national identity answers the question of "who are we?" It provides a sense of belonging that is the understanding of a society of themselves and what they represent in the world.[12] In this regard national identity is directly linked to foreign policy. Donald Horowitz argues that national affiliation is "ascription in an ostensibly nonascriptive world."[13] Every definition of what one is begins with an identification of what one is not: the "other." This distinction begins usually through contact and conflict with an outside group.[14] By providing a system that structures the perception of the world, national identity "establishes moral, pragmatic, and cognitive priorities that aid its adherents in distinguishing...which actions are acceptable and which unacceptable...and where lies security and where danger."[15] In addition, national identity structures foreign policy by provoking the actions of other members of the international community. Thus, "national identity serves not only as the primary link between the individual and society, but between a society and the world."[16]

At the same time, a state's international behavior may act to reinforce a specific national identity. Ilya Prizel notes that "the conduct of foreign policy... has a strong dialectical relationship with national identity,"[17] since foreign policy not only can reflect a state's national identity but can in fact be used to strengthen a state's national identity. James Richter adds that: "Competing constructions of national identity...entail correspondingly competing images of the international system. Foreign policy can lend credence to these images by making them concrete, demonstrating through state practices how 'we' distinguish ourselves from 'them' and how 'we' should behave towards 'them.'"[18] Subsequently, the relationship between national identity and foreign policy is not always unilinear. While national identity may help shape a foreign policy, the way a state behaves internationally may also reinforce a chosen national identity.

Externalizing National Identity: National Role Conceptions

National role conceptions provide a useful tool for examining the influence national identity has on foreign policy behavior particularly at the elite level. Whereas national identity prescribes certain characteristics and values to a state and its population in a general sense, national role conceptions ascribe these characteristics and values to the state in the international framework. They assign to the state certain behaviors and expectations. Thus, national role conceptions can be viewed as a bridge between national identity and foreign policy behavior.

The relationship between national role conceptions and state behavior has long been recognized. This connection is premised on the view that foreign policy behavior is, to a great extent, role performance and can be explained by decision makers' national role conceptions that are derived from policymakers' shared beliefs.[19] Simply put, national leaders will behave in accordance with what they perceive as their country's role in the world. Policymakers define their state's role in the stratified international system and this definition has an effect on the types of policies a state pursues by "[imposing] obligations on states and [helping] shape their interests."[20]

Role conceptions can play an important part in the foreign policy process by limiting the policy options the leadership sees as available and structuring the foreign policy culture. By determining the decision makers' perception of their countries, roles necessarily influence the kind of behavior that is expected or seen as appropriate. Charles Hermann points out that "roles are these decision makers' expectations about the pattern or configuration of foreign policy activity that their government will follow in certain situations in support of their beliefs."[21] In more general terms, Jönsson and Westerlund state that rather than determine behavior, roles assume to limit the range of foreign policy behavior, "insofar that certain types of behavior are associated with certain roles."[22]

In this respect roles can function as substantive decision regimes. Charles Kegley introduced the concept of decision regimes after observing that in order to make difficult decisions "policymakers acknowledged the need to reduce the task by placing it in a set of rules."[23] Building on the often used conceptual framework of regimes as a set of norms that govern the function of different systems, Kegley suggests that within foreign decision-making groups there likewise exists a decision regime that functions as "a set of consensually based rules for action which limit a state's range of permissible options in its conduct abroad."[24]

Finding a Place in the World:
The Search for Identity after Independence

As the last nails were being placed in the coffin of the USSR, all of the former Soviet republics were faced with the challenge of creating identities that were unique and separate from the now defunct multi-ethnic state. As noted by Kataryna Wolczuk, this task was not just academic but had practical considerations, since the task of "[defining] the national 'self' not only accomplishes a symbolic break with the previous political community but also sets out the parameters of statehood with regards to language and minority rights."[25] Yet defining a national identity is often a difficult task since "new states tend to be bundles of competing traditions gathered accidentally into concocted frameworks rather than organically evolving civilizations."[26] Nowhere was this truer than in post-Soviet Ukraine.

"The heterogeneity of the titular majority in conjunction with the presence of large contingents of minorities [made] the project of fostering a collective identity a precarious yet pivotal task for Ukraine."[27] The task was complicated by what often appeared to be intractable differences among the population. Disputes, sometimes violent, broke out among the citizens of Ukraine on basic national identity issues such as religion, language, and culture. As late as 1999–2000, violent protests were still occurring in both Western and Eastern Ukraine concerning the usage of the Russian language or its denial in public forums and in the government. The divisions within Ukrainian society are so stark that one scholar noted, rather dramatically, that "one may say that Ukrainians do not know who they are or what kind of national state they want to build."[28]

Census data and public opinion polls clearly demonstrate the divisions that exist within Ukrainian society. While ethnic Ukrainians represent the majority of the population, 77.8% according to 2001 census data, this majority is not uniform across the country. In many parts of Eastern Ukraine, Ukrainians are either a minority as in the Crimea region,[29] where they make up only 24.3% of the population with a Russian majority, or their majority is substantially below the national average, for example in the Donets'k region, where they represent only 56.9% of the population. In total, out of 27 political regions, seven either do not have a Ukrainian majority equal to the national average or Ukrainians are in the minority.[30] Almost all these areas are located predominantly in the Eastern part of the country, have the highest level of urbanization, and largest concentrations of population—representing almost 33% of the total population of the country. The only major large urbanized areas that do have a substantial Ukrainian majority are the western region of L'viv and the city of Kyiv.

While the census shows that a majority identify themselves as ethnically Ukrainian, this identification proves limited in that respondents had to select only one nationality. A long history of intermarriage has resulted in a large percentage of the population having mixed ethnic origins. According to a recent World Bank survey, approximately one-sixth of the population is of mixed Ukrainian-Russian ancestry.

Thus for many Ukrainians the choice of identity on the census is not completely driven by genealogy. This fact is reinforced when compared to the census data from 1989, when a larger percentage of the population (22%) identified themselves as Russian. Stephen Rapawy (1998) notes that this change in identity is due in large part to a process of reidentification among Ukrainians. Pirie (1996) reinforces this point, citing the fact that 39% of

Ukrainians who self identify as Russians believe that personal choice was the most important criteria in determining identity.

Beyond the ethnic divisions that exist within the country, linguistic divisions further contribute to the muddling of a coherent national identity. Several scholars have noted the relationship between language and national identity.[31] Tariq Rahman,[32] looking at identity in Pakistan notes that after religion, language has become one of the primary determinants of identity. National identity develops through interaction with other groups, this interaction, whether oral or written, takes place through language. As a result language is one of the most basic means for differentiating one's group from those who are not part of the group.

While ethnic Russians account for 17.3% of the population, according to the census, nearly 30% identify Russian as their mother tongue. Polls by the Rozumkov Center find an even greater parity between Russian speakers and Ukrainian speakers, with 40.4% noting that they exclusively speak Russian at home and 39.7% Ukrainian.[33] The language division similarly falls along the East-West continuum, with regions in the West and South representing a predominantly Russian speaking population, while the Ukrainian language dominates in the West of the country. Polls conducted by the Rozumkov center[34] in 2003 show the divisions clearly. When questioned on whether Russian should be given an official status in Ukraine, Ukrainians in the West overwhelmingly said no while those in the East said yes in the same percentage.

Table 3.1. Should the Russian Language be Granted Official Status in Ukraine (% of those polled)

	West	East	Central	South
Yes	13.4	68.7	32.6	57.8
No	68.7	14.7	37.6	17.6
I do not care	13.4	14.1	23.3	17.6
Hard to say	4.5	2.5	6.5	7

The hazy nature of Ukrainian mass national identity was further illustrated when the people were asked with which of their neighbors they identify. In a series of surveys conducted by Stephen White et al.[35] Ukrainians were asked whether they perceived of themselves as European or Eurasian. Less than half identified with Europe and the West. Surprisingly, when a similar survey was given to Russians a larger number replied positively to the European self-identification (see table 3.2). A later poll conducted in September 2005, by the Rozumkov center,[36] found similar results (see table 3.3). Again the regional divisions are evident, with participants in Eastern Ukraine identifying with Europe more than those in the rest of the country.

Table 3.2. Perceptions of European Identity (% in each country)

Do You think of yourself as a European?	Ukraine	Russia
Often	8	18
Sometimes	26	34
Rarely/never	57	47
Don't know/no answer	8	2

Table 3.3. Do you consider yourself to be European? Do you feel that you belong to European civilization?

	West	East	Central	South	Total
Yes	19.3	6.9	9.1	7.6	10.4
Probably yes	32.8	15.6	28.7	14.6	22.9
Probably no	23.2	29	25	27.4	26
No	16.7	42.1	30.7	46.9	34.3
Hard to say	8	6.4	6.5	3.5	6.4

The pattern seen in Ukraine concerning the issue of national identity is also reflected in the foreign policy preferences of society. Polls conducted between 1994 and 2001 (table 3.4) show that either a majority or a plurality of Ukrainians supported closer relations with the Commonwealth of Independent States (CIS) and Russia, clearly reflecting a Eurasian orientation. Further-

Table 3.4. Foreign Policy Orientations of the Ukrainian Population (%)

	1994	1995	1996	1997	1998	1999	2000	2001
Closer ties with members of the CIS	41	39	32	24	24	18	15	16
Cooperate with Russia; strengthen East Slavic Union	18	15	14	29	29	29	27	36
Develop the Baltic–Black Sea Alliance	2	1	1	1	1	1	0	0
First of all develop relations with Western countries	13	14	16	14	13	16	17	13
Self-reliance, strengthen independence	13	14	19	16	18	20	26	21
Different regions of Ukraine should choose their own ways	4	4	5	4	5	4	4	3
Difficult to answer	10	11	12	11	9	10	10	9

Source: Cited in Churylov, 2005

more, those who expressed a preference for the West were never in the majority, nor were those who preferred a more independent focus such as creating a Baltic–Black Sea Alliance or focusing more on Ukrainian self-reliance.

Later polls found similar opinions. When asked whether the EU, the US, Russia, or the CIS should be the priority for Ukrainian foreign policy, either a majority or a plurality consistently chose Russia and the CIS as their preferred direction.

Table 3.5. Which direction of foreign policy should be a priority for Ukraine? (% of those polled)

	Feb. 2002	Feb. 2003	Feb. 2004	Feb. 2005
Relations with Russia	31.6	34.2	41.1	38.8
Relations with CIS	20.6	22.6	15.2	7.7
Relations with EU countries	31.4	26	30.8	37
Relations with US	4	2.8	2.4	1.2

Source: The Ukrainian Center for Economic and Political Studies (www.uceps.org)

The foreign policy preferences also followed the regional divisions identified earlier. In particular, Ukrainians living in the Western regions, preferred increasing relations with Europe, reflecting a stronger European identity, in much greater numbers than those living in the highly Russified East and South, who tended to prefer looking to their Eastern neighbors in foreign relations. The more mixed population in the Central region reflected a more mixed view in their preferences.

Table 3.6. Which direction of foreign policy should be a priority for Ukraine? (% of those polled in February 2004)

	East	West	Center	South
Relations with Russia	52.6	16.7	37.5	54.6
Relations with CIS	18.2	10.3	14.1	17.2
Relations with EU countries	19.7	58.9	31.7	18.5
Relations with US	1.5	3.2	3.2	1

Source: The Ukrainian Center for Economic and Political Studies (www.uceps.org)

National Identity Preferences of Ukrainian Foreign Policymakers

In order to determine the national identity preferred by the leadership in Kyiv an examination was undertaken of the national role conceptions expressed by the foreign policymaking elite. To create a more systematic examination, this project relied heavily on the methodology developed by K.J. Holsti[37] and Philippe Le Prestre.[38] In particular, it paralleled their use of content analysis of speeches by foreign policymakers.

This study began with an examination of foreign policy statements by the leadership in Ukraine for the years 1992–2005. The speeches examined were limited to the pronouncements of top foreign policy officials: presidents, prime ministers, and foreign ministers. Exceptions were made for their official spokespersons, ambassadors, or other officials who were obviously expressing the views of their superiors.

It needs to be acknowledged that the author understands that others bore responsibility for shaping how the state as a whole conceived of its role, including parliamentarians, opinion makers, and the population. The survey was limited to top policymakers because these were the only ones about whom it could be confidently assumed that they could speak with authority on foreign and defense policies. In addition, it was assumed that any role conceptions that would have been reflected in the state's behavior would have been reflected in the statements of these policymakers.

In collecting role pronouncements, an effort was made to include a broad range of sources in order to mitigate the possibility of source bias. The statements were collected from Ukrainian media sources as well as foreign sources found primarily through Lexis-Nexis Academic Universe. The types of statements examined were limited to public pronouncements including official speeches, policy briefings, interviews, press briefings and articles by policymakers. Each statement was examined to determine which national role conceptions were being expressed.

Roles were identified by coding the assertions that refer to the conceptions that decision makers hold of the duties and responsibilities of their state in the international system. After the examination of each statement, the expressed roles were coded according to the date of the pronouncement. Since the main concern of this part of the study was to determine if a particular role was expressed and to gauge the intensity of the role, which is measured by the frequency of the role's expression, the specific policymaker was not noted since this information was not relevant to the project.[39]

There was some concern about giving undue weight to roles expressed more than once in a single statement. In particular, pronouncements that address a specific topic, which calls for repeated invocation of a unique role, may make the role appear quite important when in fact this was the only instance, or one of the few instances, when the role was identified. In order to address this concern, roles that appeared more than once in a particular statement were not coded individually. Rather the text was taken as a whole and the roles expressed in the piece were each coded only once.

The survey of speeches by Ukrainian foreign policymakers revealed a total of 12 expressed national role conceptions:

1. Member of CIS. This role identifies the state as an active member of the Commonwealth of Independent States (CIS) and that the main priority for their foreign policy is to develop and strengthen their connection to the nations that make up this organization and in particular Russia. As the name implies, the role reflects a Eurasian identity, linking Ukraine to the Commonwealth of Independent States (CIS).

2. Member of Western world. This identity reflects the view that Ukraine has always been a part of Europe. This role holds that the main priority in Ukrainian foreign policy is to develop close ties to the West and to integrate into Europe and Western international institutions.

3. Regional leader. Similar to member of Western world, this role emphasizes Ukraine's European identity. While this identity ostensibly could include areas of the Former Soviet Union (FSU), it does not reflect a Eurasian orientation in its specific exclusion of Russia. Whenever Ukrainian leaders referenced this role they were referring to relations with nations in Central and Eastern Europe, not including Russia or to its role as a leading European nation.

4. Active Independent. This role emphasized an identity that was neither Eurasian nor European. Identifying Ukraine as unique and independent with connections to both the West and the East, it points to the belief that Ukraine must cultivate relations and develop economic and security cooperation with diverse regions of the world beyond the FSU, Europe, and the US.

5. Independent player. This role emphasizes Ukraine's right for self-determination and noninterference in its affairs as well as an emphasis on national interest as a guiding point in its foreign policy. This role is also related to the maintenance of Ukraine's non-bloc and non-aligned status.

6. Mediator-integrator. This role notes that the main task in the international system is to promote cooperation among different states and to encourage the settlement of conflicts nonviolently.

7. Example. This role places an emphasis on the importance of promoting prestige and gaining influence in the international system by pursuing certain policies. It also emphasizes the need to act as a benchmark for other states to follow.

8. Instrument for changing the state. This role, to a great extent deals with domestic policy more so than foreign policy. When it is applied

to external behavior it emphasizes the need to create favorable conditions to improve the domestic situation both economically and politically as well as the need to make the promotion of internal development a key component of foreign policy.

9. Arms control and disarmament agent. This role emphasizes the responsibility to help reduce the number of nuclear weapons as well as other weaponry worldwide and to help in limiting the proliferation of weapons of mass destruction.

10. Co-patriot protector. This role emphasizes Ukraine's obligation to help their co-nationals living outside the home country and to protect them from violations of their rights.

11. Protectee. This role alludes to the belief that it is the responsibility of other states to defend Ukraine and to ensure its security.

12. Nuclear free state. After the fall of the USSR, on a number of occasions, the Ukrainian government expressed the view that it was a top priority for Ukrainian foreign policy to eliminate the nuclear weapons left on its territory.

After establishing the different national role conceptions expressed by the leaderships, and coding the different statements according to the national role conceptions they represent, the roles were categorized according to whether they represented a pro-Western identity or a Eurasian/CIS-centered orientation or a more independent orientation. Those roles that did not represent any of these identities were noted but not applied in this study.

Table 3.7. Role Types Expressed by Ukrainian Leadership 1992–1999

Role Type	Expressed Roles
European/Western oriented roles	Member of Western world Regional leader
Eurasian oriented roles	Member of CIS
Independent/multi-vectored roles	Independent player Active independent
Not reflected any identity	Instrument for changing the state arms control and disarmament agent Co-patriot protector Protectee Example: Nuclear free state Mediator-integrator

The examination of the roles according to orientation yielded three roles that clearly reflected a predilection for identifying Ukraine with Europe and the West more generally or with Eurasian and the CIS/Russia. Member of Western world and regional leader reflect the view that Ukraine is a European state and the goal of Ukraine's foreign policy should be to integrate into

Europe. Member of CIS reflected the view that Ukraine's primary identity lay with the former Soviet space and that Ukraine was a Eurasian state and consequently the FSU should be the primary focus of Ukrainian foreign policy.

In contrast, two of the roles identified reflected a broader identity and foreign policy outlook, regarding Ukraine as neither Eastern nor Western but as either independent or as multi-vectored. The active independent identity demands a more global and independent outlook for the state, emphasizing that Ukraine must develop relations with all parts of the world. In contrast, independent player reflects an identity that can be described as bordering on isolationist and insular. This identity proclaims that Ukraine should not side with any state but rather maintain its own independence and sovereignty internationally. While these identities did not necessarily reflect a pro-Western orientation, it must be noted that these independent identities necessarily imply an anti-Russian component. After determining the roles expressed, the sample was aggregated longitudinally by year (see table 3.8).

Table 3.8. Frequency (%) of Expression of Member of Western World, Member of CIS, Independent Player, Active Independent, and Regional Leader Roles.

Role	1992	1993	1994	1995	1996	1997	1998	1999
Active independent	6	2.6	3.3	8.1	4.8	11.9	6.9	8.5
Independent player	15.4	20	18.8	21	14.5	13.6	9.7	12.8
Total of independent roles	21.4	22.6	22.4	29.1	19.3	25.5	16.6	21.3
Member of CIS	11.1	20.9	19.6	16.1	22.6	20.3	16.7	23.4
Regional leader	0.9	6.1	1.8	1.6	1.6	6.8	8.3	0
Member of Western world	19.7	13	12.5	30.6	24.2	32.2	29.2	29.8
Total of Western roles	20.6	19.1	14.3	32.2	25.8	39	37.5	29.8

Role	2000	2001	2002	2003	2004	2005	Total
Active independent	7.04	6.5	9	7.5	4.17	6.67	6.66
Independent player	11.3	19.4	13.6	2.5	4.17	3.33	12.87
Total of independent roles	18.3	25.9	22.6	10	8.34	10	19.53
Member of CIS	15.5	22.2	14	17.5	8.33	16.7	17.49
Regional leader	8.45	0	9	2.5	12.5	20	5.68
Member of Western world	30.9	38.9	50	42.5	41.7	20	29.65
Total of Western roles	39.4	38.9	59	45	54.2	40	35.34

As table 3.8 illustrates, for the majority of the years examined, 12 out of the 14 years, the most commonly expressed identities were starkly pro-European. This role was followed by those that indicated an independent identity and finally by the pro-Russia/Eurasian identity.

A more important observation is that the Eurasian identity was never dominant for the leadership. Even when the Eurasian role was expressed more frequently than the pro-Western role, the independent roles repeatedly outnumbered the roles signifying an Eastern identity. This all changed in 1996, when the pro-European/pro-Western roles became the most frequently expressed identities. Consequently, it can be argued that the leadership in Kyiv adopted a decidedly anti-Russia identity, since the independent roles also implied an anti-Russian orientation.

This observation is interesting since it has been observed that Ukrainian society is divided between a staunchly nationalistic population that dominates the Western section of the country and a more Eurasian/Russian-focused population in the Eastern regions with a more mixed view in the Central regions. Thus, it would be expected that the role orientations fighting for the "top billing" would be those that reflected this division. Yet upon closer observation this was not the case. The independent roles and the Western/European roles were the most frequently invoked.

More importantly, as polls have shown, the majority of Ukrainians do not identify themselves as Europeans. It is only in the Western regions where a majority see themselves as part of a European civilization. It appears that the leadership in Kyiv chose an identity that corresponded to a minority view exclusive to only one part of the country rather than trying to reconcile the different identities that exist within the country or adopt an identity that would balance the different views.

Ukraine's Foreign Policy

Several scholars have noted that, since independence, Ukraine's foreign policy has been characterized by confusion, a lack of clear direction, and a great deal of wavering. Mikhail Molchanov argues that "Ukrainian foreign policy is that of oscillation. Sitting uneasily on the porch between East and West, official Kyiv makes no comment to either side." [40] Several scholars have gone further, proclaiming that: "unfortunately, Ukraine has never had a clear defined geopolitical strategy."[41] While there is ample evidence to support such observations, upon closer examination a clear pattern emerges in Ukraine's international behavior consisting primarily of limiting Moscow's ability to influence Kyiv and the goal of firmly rooting Ukraine in European institutions. This was clearly reflected in the national identity adopted by the leadership.

Much of Ukraine's foreign policy, beginning almost immediately after gaining independence and lasting for the first five years, was focused on establishing and relentlessly reasserting its sovereign rights.[42] This was due to the fact that for the governing elite, the main threat to the state's independence emanated from Russia.[43] This concern was not unfounded since Russian governmental officials were not shy in expressing their doubts about Ukrainian independence.[44] Consequently, although it was one of the founders of the CIS, Kyiv never officially joined the organization, preferring to remain an associate member. The government likewise refused to join the unified military command or the Russian-Belarus-Kazakhstan Free Trade Zone.

In their effort to "move away from Moscow and to preserve as much distance as needed to secure state independence,"[45] the leadership worked to expand and diversify the newly independent state's connection to Eastern and Central Europe. Ukraine worked hard to cultivate relations with Poland, Hungary, the Czech Republic, Slovakia and Romania. In the early 1990s, Kyiv took great pains to become more involved in as many regional organizations as possible, unsuccessfully lobbying to join the Visegrad group, attempted to gain entry into the Central European Initiative and the East Carpathian Euroregion, and established military cooperation with Poland and Hungary. It likewise tried unsuccessfully to establish a security belt in Central Europe that would have included Ukraine, Belarus, Poland, the Baltic States, Moldova, the Czech Republic, Slovakia, Romania, and Austria. The group would have included all Central and Eastern European countries except Russia, "effectively shifting the frontier for Ukraine's eastern border."[46]

Ukrainian efforts at establishing itself in Central and Eastern Europe proved only partially successful. For many of the Central and Eastern European states, efforts to create organizations outside the EU or NATO were seen as a hindrance to their future plans for joining these organizations. In addition, many of these states feared that the establishment of any security zones between Russia and NATO would turn the region into a permanent buffer zone.[47] Furthermore, during 1993–1994, Ukraine's failure to implement economic reforms led many Central and Eastern European states to perceive it as a threat to their own security.[48] Nonetheless, Kyiv continued to pursue efforts at developing relations that would ensure its independence from Moscow. It was the leading proponent and continues to be the leading member of GUAM, an anti-Moscow group within the CIS established in 1996, consisting of Georgia, Ukraine, Uzbekistan, Azerbaijan, and Moldova,[49] which seeks to establish closer ties with NATO and the EU, and it was the main proponent of the Black Sea Economic Cooperation pact (BSEC).

In 1995, Ukraine's foreign policy focus shifted from securing its independence from Moscow to more aggressively pursuing relations with Europe and the West as the opportunities for improvements in this relationship began to increase. The change in Ukrainian-European relations actually began in mid-1994 with the signing of the Partnership and Cooperation Agreement (PCA), which intended to establish a strong political link between Ukraine and the EU and to facilitate a free-trade area between them, and with Kyiv joining NATO's Partnership for Peace.[50] By 1995, Ukraine's leadership openly embraced the idea of greater cooperation with Europe. Following a meeting with NATO's secretary general, President Kuchma became a strong supporter of NATO expansion. In the same year, Ukraine applied and was accepted into the Council of Europe, even as Russia was still struggling to be admitted. Soon afterwards, Ukraine and the North Atlantic Council had their first "16+1" consultation at the Political Committee level. By 1997, Ukraine had established a permanent mission to NATO, and by 1998, NATO, had sent a liaison officer to Kyiv to facilitate military cooperation.[51]

The Ukrainian government's pro-Western attitude was clearly reflected in 1998, when the Ukrainian Ministry of Foreign Affairs announced that a priority of Ukrainian foreign policy was to gain associate member status in the EU. Later that year, the National Strategy for Ukraine's Integration into the EU was adopted, proclaiming EU membership as a long-term goal for Kyiv. That same year, the EU-Ukraine Cooperation Council met for the first time and formally adopted the PCA Work Program.

While being hailed as more Western oriented than Leonid Kuchma, the recently elected president, Victor Yushchenko, has basically continued to pursue the foreign policies established by his predecessors. Like Kuchma, and Leonid Kravchuk before him, Yushchenko's foreign policy priority seems to be the continuation of the dual policies of distancing Ukraine from Russia while moving towards integration into European institutions. Yushchenko has stated that he strongly favors Ukrainian membership in NATO and has worked for establishing a free trade zone with the EU with an eye towards eventual membership, an objective he believes can be achieved within a decade.[52] While arguing that he still sees Russia as "strategic partner," he has noted that integration with the West will supersede any integration within the Russian dominated CIS.[53]

Ukraine's behavior within the FSU further exemplifies its efforts to limit its relationship with Russia. While the Ukrainian leadership has gone so far as to suggest that it may actually leave the CIS altogether,[54] it continues increasing its role in GUAM. In 2005, Ukraine proposed turning the informal group into a formal international regional body with its own secretariat, office, and action plan.[55]

Analysis

The question at the heart of this chapter is what role did national identity play in the creation of Ukraine's foreign policy? It has been observed that one of the connections between national identity and foreign policy is that identity influences foreign policy by structuring the choices policymakers see as available or by shaping the foreign policy debate. Yet this was not the case with Ukraine. Although both the identity and foreign policy pursued were clearly Western oriented, to a great extent, the dominant identities expressed by the leadership followed the foreign policy preferences chosen by Kyiv even before the USSR had disintegrated, which were to put as much distance between Ukraine and Moscow as possible.

The leadership in Kyiv clearly understood that in order to develop both politically and economically, the only choice they had available was to move towards the West since Moscow was not in a position to help them out financially. Furthermore, the initial need to guarantee state sovereignty necessarily meant that the leadership would work to limit Russian influence, since many in the Russian government were openly skeptical about Ukrainian independence. In order to do this, it was necessary to espouse an identity that reflected Ukraine's separation from the FSU. Thus during the years immediately following the dissolution of the Soviet Union, the leadership emphasized a strong independent identity.

With the growing global recognition of Ukraine's independence, and more importantly, the West's renewed interest in the country and the success of Ukrainian efforts to enter Western institutions, the leadership saw an opportunity to not only distance itself from the Kremlin but to integrate into Europe. In order to pursue this policy, it was necessary to recast Ukraine as a European state. Consequently, by 1995 we see an increase in the espousal of a pro-Western identity among foreign policymakers.

Thus, we see a dynamic relationship between national identity and foreign policy. For foreign policymakers in Kyiv the priority was to establish a policy that would ensure Ukrainian sovereignty. In order to maintain such a policy, it was necessary to espouse an identity that put Ukraine outside Russia's sphere of influence. At the same time, Ukraine's international behavior reinforced the national identity preferred by the leadership. By working to integrate into Europe, and consequently gaining acceptance into Trans-Atlantic institutions, those in power demonstrated to the population that Ukraine was indeed a European state.

The natural question that remains to be answered is: why was the government able to define the state's identity in a manner that was not supported by the majority of the population? It has become common for scholars to observe that Ukrainian society is divided between a staunchly nationalistic population that dominates the Eastern section of the country and a more Eurasian/Russian/Slavic-focused population in the Western regions. Subsequently, in defining an identity for the entire nation it may be expected that the governing elite in Kyiv would make some effort to reconcile the different views of society. Yet the government tended to ignore the majority views on both national identity and foreign policy. The leadership in Kyiv, whether it was headed by Kravchuk, Kuchma, or Yushchenko, insisted on identifying Ukraine as a European state and as part of Western civilization, as opposed to a Eurasian state.

To a great extent the answer lies in the nature of Ukrainian society. Jennifer Moroney[56] points out that in post-Communist states civil society tends to be weak. Subsequently, "the role and importance of the 'public' in Ukrainian politics are far less than in the West."[57] In addition, for many of the post-Soviet states the institutions of civil society remain weak.[58] Thus, the lack of institutions for popular mobilization means that, after elections, the public is in no position to direct the government to represent their views.

In addition, the nature of the divisions that exist in society also strengthens the government's hand in relation to the general public. The lack of popular consensus on a unified national identity allowed the leadership to define it as they saw fit. In this case, Ukrainian identity was defined away from the threat they saw posed by Russia and towards a more independent and Western-oriented outlook policy necessitated by the need to reform the economic and political system.

More importantly, there is a clear division within Ukrainian society in the level of political intensity which bolsters the government's pro-Western identity. Overall, Ukrainians tend to be rather passive on issues of foreign policy and identity, being far more concerned with economic issues.[59] At the same time, there is a great deal of difference between Eastern Ukraine and Western Ukraine in the level of political motivation. Western Ukrainians tend to have a high level of attachment to their country. In contrast, identities in the East and South tend to be more dispersed. In these regions, Ukrainian identity competes with at least six other potential identities: an ethno-linguistic Russian one, a territorial one, a genealogical or "pure" Russian one, a regional one, a pan-Slavic one, and even a Soviet identity.[60] As a result, Western Ukrainians tend to be more intense in their opinions, more politically motivated, and tend to have a higher amount of efficacy—they tend to elect leaders who share their views of foreign policy and national identity.[61]

The weakness, or even lack, of a unified Russophone nationalist movement also greatly contributes to the general direction taken by the government in defining the state's identity. Although ethno-politics have been important, the political mobilization of the Russian community has not been consistent, primarily occurring during elections when electoral blocs seek to gain the support of their numerous votes in regions such as the Donbas.[62] Consequently, it is only when they are confronted with the most extreme elements of Ukrainian nationalism or when Kyiv tries to remove local powers that Russians and Russian-speakers across the country find common cause.[63]

Thus, the nature of Ukrainian society allowed the government to define the state's identity in non-Eurasian terms. Still, the chosen identities, whether independent or Western, did have their roots in at least one segment of society. So the elite, in searching for an identity which would support their preferred foreign policy options, did not create an identity that was wholly artificial. More importantly, the identities espoused reflected the preferences of the most politically active strata of Ukrainian society—those in the West, for whom identity had the most political salience.

Conclusion

The relationship between national identity and foreign policy has been widely discussed among scholars in the field, yet there are still a great number of questions as to how national identity is determined and what type of influence national identity has on the foreign policy process. In addressing these issues, Ukraine provides an interesting test case.

In determining the state's identity the choices made by the Ukrainian government were contrary to the preferences of the majority of the population. The majority of Ukrainians expressed an identity that was Eurasian in nature. Yet the ruling elite chose an identity that classified Ukraine as a European/Western state. Still, although this identity did not reflect the majority view, it was not arbitrarily created. It did reflect the preferences of the most politically motivated segment of the population for whom the issue of identity was most relevant: those in the Western regions of the country.

It would appear that the choice of identity was conditioned by the foreign policy preferences of the leadership. Early on, the leadership had come together around the ideas that Ukraine had to distance itself from the FSU in order to limit Russian influence and to integrate into European and Western institutions. Once this path was established the government began espousing an identity that supported this goal. Yet the relationship between identity and foreign policy was not unidirectional. Rather, what we see in Ukraine is that the relationship is one of mutual reinforcement. In order to move away from Russia it had to develop an identity that would be non-Eurasian and it needed foreign polices that would demonstrate this fact.

Notes

1   Danilo Kis, "On Nationalism," in Mark Thompson, ed., *A Paper House: The Ending of Yugoslavia* (New York: Pantheon Books, 1992).

2   Barrington Moore Jr., *Injustice: the Social Bases of Obedience and Revolt* (New York: M.E. Sharpe, 1978), 488.

3   Glenn Chafetz, "The Struggle for a National Identity in Post-Soviet Russia," *Political Science Quarterly* 111 (4) (1996–1997), 633.

4   Edward Keenan, "On Certain Mythical Beliefs and Russian Behaviors," in Karen Dawisha and Bruce Parrott, ed., *The Legacy of History in Russia and the New States of Eurasia* (Armonk, NY: M.E. Sharpe, 1994).

5   Stephen Velychenko, *National History as Cultural Process* (Alberta: Canadian Institute of Ukrainian Studies Press, 1992).

6   Ilya Prizel, *National Identity and Foreign Policy: Nationalism and Leadership in Poland, Russia and Ukraine* (Cambridge: Cambridge University Press, 1998), 14.

7   Donald Horowitz, *Ethnic Groups in Conflict* (Berkley: University of California Press, 1985).

8   Horowitz, *Ethnic Groups in Conflict*, 69.

9   Horowitz, *Ethnic Groups in Conflict*, 70.

10 Roman Szporluk, "Statehood and Nation Building in Post-Soviet Space," in Roman Szporluk, ed., *National Identity and Ethnicity in Russia and the New States of Eurasia* (Armonk, NY: M.E. Sharpe, 1994), 4.

11 Szporluk, "Statehood and Nation Building in Post-Soviet Space," 5.

12 Philippe Le Prestre, "Author! Author! Defining Foreign Policy Roles after the Cold War," in Philippe Le Prestre, ed., *Role Quests in the Post-Cold War Era* (Montreal: McGill and Queen's University Press, 1997).

13 Horowitz, *Ethnic Groups in Conflict*, 74.

14 See Ilya Prizel, *National Identity and Foreign Policy: Nationalism and Leadership in Poland, Russia and Ukraine* and Hans Kohn, *The Idea of Nationalism: A Study in the Origins and Background* (New York, Mcmillan, 2005).

15 Charles Furtado, "Nationalism and Foreign Policy in Ukraine," *Political Science Quarterly* 109 (1) (1994), 85.

16 Prizel, *National Identity*, 19.

17 Prizel, *National Identity*, 8

18 James Richter, "Russian Foreign Policy and the Politics of National Identity," in Celeste Wallander, ed. *The Sources of Russian Foreign Policy after the Cold War* (Boulder: Westview Press), 70.

19 See K.J. Holsti, "National Role Conceptions in the Study of Foreign Policy," *International Studies Quarterly* 14, (3) (September 1970); Charles Hermann, "Superpower Involvement with Others: Alternative Role Relationships," in Stephen Walker, ed., *Role Theory and Foreign Policy Analysis* (Durham: Duke University Press, 1987).

20 Le Prestre, "Author! Author!" 6.

21 Hermann, "Superpower Involvement," 220

22 Christer Jönsson and Ulf Westerlund, "Role Theory in Foreign Policy Analysis," in Christer Jönsson, ed., *Cognitive Dynamics and International Politics* (New York: St. Martin's Press, 1982), 133.

23 Charles Kegley, "Decision Regimes and the Comparative Study of Foreign Policy," in Charles Hermann, Charles Kegley, and James Rosenau, eds., *New Directions in the Study of Foreign Policy* (Boston: Allen and Unwin, 1987), 250.

24 Kegley, "Decision Regimes," 225.

25 Kataryna Wolczuk, "History, Europe, and the 'National Idea': The 'Official' Narative of National Identity in Ukraine," *Nationalist Papers* 28 (4), 1.

26 Clifford Geertz, *The Interpretation of Cultures* (London: Fontana, 1993), 240.

27 Wolczuk, "History, Europe, and the 'National Idea'," 1.

28 Mikhail Molchanov, "National Identity and Foreign Policy Orientation in Ukraine," in Jennifer Moroney, Taras Kuzio, Mikhail Molchanov, eds. *Ukrainian Foreign and Security Policy: Theoretical and Comparative Perspectives* (Westport: Praeger, 2002), 228.

29 Crimea is considered for the purposes of this paper as one of the regions of Ukraine, but its official designation is that of an autonomous republic.

30 Other regions where the Ukrainian majority is below the national average are: Zaporizhzhia region (70.8%), Luhans'k region (58.0%), Odesa region (62.8%), Kharkiv region (70.7%), and the city of Sevastopol' (71.6%).

31 See for example: Anna Fournier, "Mapping Identities: Russian Resistance to Linguistic Ukrainisation in Central and Eastern Ukraine," *Europe-Asia Studies* 54 (3) (2002); Viktor Stepanenko, *The Construction of Identity and School Policy in Ukraine* (New York: Nova Science Publishers, 1999); Paul Pirie "National Identity and Politics in Southern and Eastern Ukraine," *Europe-Asia Studies* 48 (7) (1996).

32 Tariq Rahman, "Language and Ethnicity in Pakistan," *Asia Survey* 37, 9 (1997).

33 <www.uceps.org>

34 <www.uceps.org>

35 Stephen White, Ian McAllister, Margot Light, John Lowenhardt. "A European or a Slavic Choice? Foreign Policy and Public Attitudes in Post-Soviet Europe," *Europe-Asia Studies* 54 (2v) (March 2002).

36 <www.uceps.org>

37 Holsti, "National Roll Conceptions in the Study of Foreign Policy."

38 Le Prestre, "Author! Author!"

39 It needs to be acknowledged that there is an implicit assumption being made in choosing to ignore who made which statement. It is assumed that all the foreign policymakers in the

respective countries are of a similar mind in how they see the role their countries should play internationally. This assumption is not unjustified since the foreign policy-making process in Ukraine was extremely centralized and the president tended to appoint foreign and prime ministers who saw things his way.

40 Molchanov, "National Identity," 228; See also Jennifer Moroney, "Ukraine's Foreign Policy on Europe's Periphery: Globalization, Transnationalism, and the Frontier," in Jennifer Moroney, Taras Kuzio, Mikhail Molchanov, eds., *Ukrainian Foreign and Security Policy: Theoretical and Comparative Perspectives* (Westport: Praeger, 2002); Tor Bukkvoll, *Ukraine and European Security* (London: Royal Institute of International Affairs, 1997).

41 Institute for Strategic Studies cited in Molchanov, "National Identity," 240.

42 Paul D'Anieri, "Constructive Theory and Ukrainian Foreign Policy," in Jennifer Moroney, Taras Kuzio, Mikhail Molchanov, eds., *Ukrainian Foreign and Security Policy: Theoretical and Comparative* Perspectives (Westport: Praeger, 2002)

43 Victor Chudowsky, "Limits of Realism: Ukrainian Policy Towards the CIS," in Moroney, *Ukrainian Foreign and Security Policy*; Molchanov, "National Identity."

44 For example in March of 1993 Russian officials were warning other countries not to bother building large embassies in Kyiv because they will soon be downgraded to consular sections in a unified state.

45 Molchanov, "National Identity," 238.

46 Jennifer Moroney, "Ukraine's Foreign Policy on Europe's Periphery: Globalization, Transnationalism, and the Frontier," 78.

47 Moroney, "Ukraine's Foreign Policy"; Stephen Burant, "Foreign Policy and National Identity: A Comparison of Ukraine and Belarus," *Europe-Asia Studies* 47 (7) (1995).

48 Moroney, "Ukraine's Foreign Policy on Europe's Periphery."

49 The organization was initially called GUUAM but Uzbekistan left in 2005 and the name was changed to GUAM.

50 Moroney, "Ukraine's Foreign Policy on Europe's Periphery."

51 Molchanov, "National Identity."

52 Steven Woehrel, CRS Report RL32845, *Ukraine's Orange Revolution and US Policy* (Apri 2005) <fpc.state.gov/documents/organization/45452.pdf>.

53 Woehrel, CRS Report RL32845.

54 "Ukraine and Georgia Mull Leaving Post-Soviet Club," *Spiegel* (May 10, 2006).

55 "Ukraine President Says Regional Bloc Should be Formalized," *Interfax-Ukraine News Agenc* (April 22, 2005).

56 Moroney, "Ukraine's Foreign and Security Policy."

57 Victor Chudowsky and Taras Kuzio, "Does Public Opinion Matter in Ukraine? The Cas of Foreign Policy," *Communist and Post-Communist Studies* 36 (2003), 287.

58 Stephen Kotkin, "Gasputin: All That Stands Between Democracy and Russia is Russia, *The New Republic* (May 29, 2006).

59 Chudowsky, "Does Public Opinion Matter in Ukraine?"

60 Neil Melvin, *Russians Beyond Russia: The Politics of National Identity* (London: Royal Institu of International Affairs, 1995); Jane Dawson, *Eco-nationalism: Anti-nuclear Activism an National Identity in Russia, Lithuania, and Ukraine* (Durham: Duke University Press, 1996 Graham Smith and Andrew Wilson, "Rethinking Russia's Post-Soviet Diaspora: Th

Potential for Political Mobilization in Eastern Ukraine and North-east Estonia," *Europe-Asia Studies* 49 (5) (1997).

61   Chudowsky, "Does Public Opinion Matter in Ukraine?"

62   Chudowsky, "Does Public Opinion Matter in Ukraine?" To a great extent, the de-politicization of the Russophone community has been influenced by Moscow's behavior, which has not been as eager to play the diaspora card in Ukraine as it has in the Baltics

63   Melvin, *Russians Beyond Russia*.

CHAPTER FOUR

The Black Panther Party's Confrontation with Ethnicity, Race and Class

Paul J. Magnarella

In the course of the Black Panther Party's short history, its intellectual leaders displayed a fair degree of flexibility in their conceptualization of socio-political-economic relationships and the place of the Party and Black Americans within domestic and global contexts. They evolved from being Black nationalists to revolutionary nationalists, to revolutionary internationalists, and finally to revolutionary intercommunalists. On the issue of race, however, they were consistently opposed to its belief and practice.

D eep unrest marked the early 1960s in the United States. Resentment against the US involvement in Vietnam fueled riots in major cities and protests at universities. The civil rights movement grew in intensity as African Americans, American Indians, Mexican Americans, and women demanded equal rights and better economic opportunities. Blacks and many other minorities expressed fear and resentment of municipal police departments, few of which had more than a token number of minority officers. On August 28, 1963, over 200,000 people, mostly Blacks, marched on Washington, D.C., to hear Martin Luther King's "I have a dream" oration at the Lincoln Memorial. Despite King's popularity, militant Blacks challenged his non-violent, Gandhian approach to attaining civil rights. In August 1965, the National Guard was called out to help quell six days of protests and riots in Watts, a large Black section of Los Angeles. The very popular Black leader, Malcolm X, was murdered in 1965, and the following year forty-three American cities including Washington, D.C., Baltimore, Atlanta, and Detroit experienced race riots in which over 3,500 persons were arrested, and seven killed.

Within this context of social and political unrest, Huey P. Newton and Bobby Seale founded the Black Panther Party for Self-Defense (BPP) in Oakland, California, in October 1966.[1] They took the black panther symbol from the Lowndes County Freedom Organization and the term "self defense" from the Deacons for Defense and Justice.[2] Huey P. Newton gave himself the title of Minister of Defense of the BPP and Bobby Seale became its Chairman. Seale, the son of a carpenter, was born in Dallas, Texas, on October 22, 1936. During the Second World War his family moved to Oakland, California. After leaving Oakland High School he joined the United States Air Force and served for three years before being court-martialed for disobeying orders. In 1962 Seale entered Merritt College in Oakland, California. Influenced by a Malcolm X speech at the College, Seale joined the Afro-American Association and became active in the civil rights movement.

Huey P. Newton, was born in Monroe, Louisiana, on February 17, 1942. The youngest of seven children, he was named after the Louisiana politician, Huey P. Long. Huey's father was an active member of the National Association for the Advancement of Colored People (NAACP). Huey's family moved to Oakland, California, where Newton met Bobby Seale at Merritt College.

Together, in October 1966, Newton and Seale wrote up the Black Panther Party Platform and Program, entitled "What We Want; What We Believe."

1. We want freedom. We want power to determine the destiny of our Black Community.
2. We want full employment for our people.
3. We believe that the federal government is responsible and obligated to give every man employment or a guaranteed income...if the white American businessmen will not give full employment, then the means of production should be taken from the businessmen and placed in the community.
4. We want an end to the robbery by the white man of our Black Community.
5. We believe that this racist government has robbed us and now we are demanding the overdue debt of forty acres and two mules. Forty acres and two mules was promised 100 years ago as restitution for slave labor and mass murder of black people. We will accept the payment as currency which will be distributed to our many communities.
6. We want decent housing, fit for shelter of human beings.
7. We believe that if the white landlords will not give decent housing to our black community, then the housing and the land should be made

into cooperatives so that our community, with government aid, can build and make decent housing for its people.

8. We want education for our people that exposes the true nature of this decadent American society. We want education that teaches us our true history and our role in the present-day society.

9. We want all black men to be exempt from military service.

10. We believe that Black people should not be forced to fight in the military service to defend a racist government that does not protect us. We will not fight and kill other people of color in the world who, like black people, are being victimized by the white racist government of America.

11. We want an immediate end to police brutality and murder of black people.

12. We believe we can end police brutality in our black community by organizing black self-defense groups that are dedicated to defending our black community from racist police oppression and brutality. The Second Amendment to the Constitution of the United States gives a right to bear arms.

13. We want freedom for all black men held in federal, state, county and city prisons and jails.

14. We believe that all black people should be released from the many jails and prisons because they have not received a fair and impartial trial.

15. We want all black people when brought to trial to be tried in court by a jury of their peer group or people from their black communities, as defined by the Constitution of the United States.

16. The 14th Amendment of the U.S. Constitution gives a man a right to be tried by his peer group. A peer is a person from a similar economic, social, religious, geographical, environmental, historical and racial background. To do this the court will be forced to select a jury from the black community from which the black defendant came.

17. We want land, bread, housing, education, clothing, justice and peace. And as our major political objective, a United Nations-supervised plebiscite to be held throughout the black colony in which only black colonial subjects will be allowed to participate for the purpose of determining the will of black people as to their national destiny.[3]

With few exceptions, the wants stated in the BPP seventeen-point program are universal in nature. All people want: (1) freedom; (2) full employment; (3) an end to their exploitation; (7) decent housing; (8) a true history of themselves; (12) an end to police brutality; (15) trial by a jury of peers; (17) land, bread, housing, education, clothing, justice and peace. Point (9), the exemption of all Black people from military service and point (13), freedom of all Black men held in prison and jails are peculiar to African Americans, who believe that their historic experience of slavery and the injustices in the American criminal justice system justify their claims that involuntary military service and imprisonment are unfairly oppressive. Newton claimed that the Ten Point Program was a survival program, not a revolutionary program. He reasoned, in Marxist style, that the revolution would come when the ruling bourgeois class was overthrown by the proletariat.

In December 1966 Eldridge Cleaver was released from Folsom Prison and paroled in San Francisco. He joined the staff of *Ramparts Magazine*, and in February 1967 he joined the BPP, becoming its Minister of Information. By April 25, 1967, the BPP produced the first issue of its newspaper, the Party's official organ for disseminating news and party ideology.

Although Eldridge Cleaver became one of the Party's most eloquent spokespersons, Newton was regarded as the chief architect of the Party's ideology and goals. Fellow Panther Mumia Abu-Jamal writes that "the intense, driven, acutely brilliant, self-conscious, and mercurial Newton was the [Party's] motivating force."[4] "It was Huey's Party.... We read his words and tried to emulate his resistance.... That meant that Huey's political insights and developments became ours, to the extent that we could follow and understand them."[5] Eldridge Cleaver wrote that "the ideology of the Black Panther Party is the historical experience of Black people...interpreted through the prism of the Marxist-Leninist analysis by our Minister of Defense, Huey P. Newton.... One of the great contributions of Huey P. Newton is that he gave the Black Panther Party a firm ideological foundation that frees us from ideological flunkeyism and opens up the path to the future—a future to which we must provide new ideological formulations to fit our ever changing situation."[6]

Evolving Identities

Given Newton's position in the Party, this chapter will focus primarily upon how he claimed the Party addressed the issues of identity, class and race. This is not to imply that everyone in the Party followed Newton's instructions or agreed fully with his pronouncements. There were often sharp differences between the West Coast Panthers, headquartered in Oakland, California, and the East Coast Panthers in New York. As Eldridge Cleaver writes, "The Panthers were never a tightly run, cohesive national body. Metropolitan groups would spring up, using our name...but their operations were often vague and their motivations puzzling. Discipline was constantly a hassle and enforcement a real challenge for people running the party."[7]

The Beginning: Black Nationalism

Newton explains that "when we started in October 1966, we were what one would call black nationalists."[8] Influenced by the early writings of Malcolm X, Garveyites, and the W.E.B. DuBois Club of America, Newton then believed that the suffering at the hands of others would end when African Americans established a nation-state of their own.[9] He advocated taking land from the Unites States to create a separate state for American Blacks. Later he realized that was impractical. He considered a movement of American Blacks to Africa, but concluded that Africa was too foreign a place for people who had been deprived of their African language and culture. Since all of the earth's livable land surface was already claimed, establishing a new nation-state required the power necessary to take land from others. Realizing that the BPP and African Americans alone would be incapable of doing this, and believing that class not race was critical, in 1969 he changed the Party's identity and goals from those of black nationalism or separatist nationalism to revolutionary nationalism.[10]

Revolutionary Nationalism

Part of the reason for the rejection of cultural nationalism may have been the Panthers' confrontations with other Black nationalist groups. Early in its history, the BPP clashed violently with Maulana Karenga (a.k.a. Ron Everett, b. 1941) leader of US (United Slaves) a self-described cultural nationalist, who advocated for a separate state for blacks and the adoption of African culture. In the late '60s, US and the Panthers vied for control of the African Studies program at UCLA. In their confrontation, two US members shot and killed two Panthers.[11]

David Hilliard, one of the BPP's first members and its chief of staff, commented on the Party's new self-identity as follows: "We call our position 'revolutionary nationalism,' as opposed to 'cultural nationalism.' which limits the struggle for self-determination to appearances—dashikis, African names, talk about 'new nationhood' and the black nation.... Dress and language are definitely not what Fanon has talked about in *The Wretched of the Earth*. Instead he insists that the only worthwhile culture is *revolutionary* culture.... We won't free ourselves through steeping ourselves in an African past and folklore but by aligning ourselves with other liberation fighters..."[12]

Newton reasoned that white racists are able to oppress Black people because they control the means of production and profit from maintaining a Black underclass.[13] Hence, the reigning economic system of capitalism had to be replaced with socialism. Newton realized that capitalists exploited people regardless of color and that many Whites (communists and socialists) also opposed capitalist exploitation and were genuinely concerned about racism. Furthermore, Newton saw that black capitalists exploited poor blacks, just as white capitalists did. Consequently, he changed point three in the Panthers' Ten Point Program to read: "We want an end to the robbery by the capitalist of our black community." The original version had read "robbery by the white man."[14] Newton contrasted revolutionary nationalism to the reactionary nationalism of the cultural nationalists, who viewed Whites as the oppressors, whereas he regarded the capitalist class as the oppressor.

The revolutionary part of the BPP goal and identity was heavily influenced by liberation literature. Newton writes: "We read the works of Frantz Fanon, particularly *The Wretched of the Earth*, the four volumes of Chairman Mao Tse-tung, and Che Guevara's *Guerrilla Warfare*."[15] The goal of the BPP was to overthrow the capitalists and put the people in power. Since the Party was primarily concerned with Black Americans, it called for Black power. Given this Marxist ideology, Newton was willing to ally the BPP with the White communist Peace and Freedom Party, Students for a Democratic Society (SDS) and the Gay Liberation Front. Eldridge Cleaver and several other BPP members ran for political office as Peace and Freedom candidates.

Newton also believed it was important for the Panthers to ally with the Peace Movement that was campaigning against the war in Vietnam. He saw the military-industrial complex as part of the system of class exploitation. "At one time I thought that only Blacks were colonized. But I think ... the whole American people have been colonized, if you view exploitation as a colonized effect. Seventy-one companies have exploited everyone."[16]

These alliances cost the BPP support of Black nationalists, who detested any political associations with Whites. However, alliances with sympathetic Whites proved very beneficial, in terms of money and propaganda, to the Panthers who were orchestrating a "Free Huey Campaign" nationally. In September, 1968, Newton had been convicted of manslaughter and sentenced to 2-15 years in prison for allegedly shooting a police officer. Newton continued to guide the Party from his cell.

While Newton was in prison, Stokely Carmichael visited him and advised Newton that the only way he could get out was by "armed rebellion, culminating in a race war."[17] Newton disagreed with him and explained: "While I acknowledged the pervasiveness of racism, the larger problem should be seen in terms of class exploitation and the capitalist system. In analyzing what was happening in the country, I said that we would have to accept many alliances and form solidarity with any people fighting the common oppressor."[18] Carmichael objected to the Panthers' alliance with the Peace and Justice Party and warned that white radicals would destroy the movement and alienate Black people. Newton later reflected on Carmichael's prophecy and conceded that Carmichael's warning had some validity, although he was wrong in principle. "As a result of coalitions," Newton wrote, "the Black

Panthers were brought into the free speech movement, the psychedelic fad, and the advocacy of drugs, ...All these causes were irrelevant to our work."[19]

Revolutionary Internationalism

In May, 1970, the California Appeals Court, citing an error in juror instructions, reversed the voluntary manslaughter sentence of Huey Newton's 1968 conviction. On August 5, 1970, Newton was released on $50,000 bail; but still had to face another trial in the police shooting. Even before his release, Newton had added a strong international dimension to revolutionary nationalism. He viewed Western capitalism or the Western bourgeois ruling class as being the exploiters of peoples around the world. Evidence of this existed in the colonizing of Third World peoples, economic imperialism, and US opposition to Castro, communist China, North Korea, and North Vietnam. He believed all the exploited peoples of the world had to unite to overthrow the international ruling bourgeois class. "We said that we joined with all of the other people in the world struggling for decolonialization and nationhood, and called ourselves a 'dispersed colony' because we did not have the geographical concentration that other so-called colonies had."[20]

Newton's views concerning colonialism came primarily from Frantz Fanon's *The Wretched of the Earth*. Bobby Seale claims that he had read that book six times before introducing it to Newton, who immediately became enthralled with it.[21] They made the book part of the Party's assigned reading.

Frantz Fanon (July 20, 1925–December 6, 1961) was born on the Caribbean island of Martinique into a mixed lineage that included African slaves. He became one of the preeminent thinkers on the issue of decolonization and the psychopathology of colonialism. His works inspired anti-colonial liberation leaders such as Ali Shariati in Iran, Steve Biko in South Africa and Ernesto Che Guevara in Cuba. He also influenced the Palestinians, the Tamils, the Catholic Irish, the Black Panthers and other people seeking self-determination.

David Hilliard expressed this international position in his November 15, 1969, speech in San Francisco: "Black people should not be forced to fight in the military to defend a racist government that does not protect us. We will not fight to kill other people of color in the world, who like Black people are victims of US imperialism on an international level."[22] Hilliard prefaced his remarks with the following slogans: "All power to the people. Black power to Black people, Brown power to Brown people, Red power to Red people, and Yellow power to Ho Chi Minh, and Comrade Kim Il Sung the courageous leader of 40,000,000 Korean people."[23]

In July 1969 Eldridge Cleaver, a fugitive from the American courts, arrived in Algeria as a guest of the Algerian government to attend a Pan-

African cultural festival. There he made contacts with numerous African, communist and other Third World leaders. By 1970, the Algerian government gave the BPP International Section, based in Algiers, quasi-diplomatic status, with the right to obtain entrance and exit visas for members and guests, a monthly stipend, and official identity cards.[24] The BPP International Section in Algiers functioned until 1972. During this period, Newton, Cleaver and other Panthers visited by official invitation a number of African and communist countries, including Cuba, North Vietnam, China, and North Korea.

While in Algiers, Eldridge Cleaver explained the following to an interviewer: "We [BPP] are a Marxist-Leninist Party, and implicit in Marxist-Leninism is proletarian internationalism, and solidarity with all people who are struggling, and this, of course, includes white people."[25] Cleaver maintained that suffering is colorblind and oppressed people need unity based on revolutionary principles rather than skin color.

Revolutionary Intercommunalism

In a speech delivered on November 18, 1970, at Boston College, Newton explained the final shift in BPP ideology. He explained that revolutionary internationalism would not work because the United States, the world's dominant military and economic power, was not a nation-state, but rather an imperial empire that coerced or bribed the governments of other states to serve its interests. Hence, most states, with the exception of a few, like Cuba, North Korea, North Vietnam, China, the Soviet Union and the East European socialist democracies, consisted of communities of peoples who were exploited by the international capitalist class. He explained that "the world today is a dispersed collection of communities. A community is different from a nation. A community is a small unit with a comprehensive collection of institutions that exist to serve a small group of people....The struggle in the world today is between the small circle that administers and profits from the empire of the United States and the peoples of the world who want to determine their own destinies."[26]

In his 1974 speech entitled "Who Makes U.S. foreign Policy," Newton explained: "The strategic agencies of foreign policy—the State Department, the CIA, the Pentagon, and the Treasury, as well as the key ambassadorial posts— have all been dominated by representatives and rulers of America's principal corporate financial empires."[27] He further explained that the corporate ideology prevails in the U.S., because corporations control the communication media and indoctrinate people into believing that the corporate interest is the national interest to be pursued domestically and internationally.

Newton had originally conceptualized Black Americans as being a colony. Now, he admitted he was mistaken. Because Black Americans originated in Africa, have lived in the United States for generations, and have lost their African heritage through slavery and exploitation, they could not be considered a colony subjugated by others. They are, Newton now reasoned, an oppressed community within the boundaries of the United States.[28] The oppressed communities of the world needed to unite in the common cause of destroying capitalism, making socialism a reality, and bringing the power of local control to communities. Each community should be able to govern and police itself and control the means of production so that it can have the economic resources necessary to enjoy a humane living standard. "Our ultimate goal," Newton wrote, "is to have various ethnic communities co-operating in a spirit of mutual aid, rather than competing. In this way, all communities would be allied in a common purpose."[29] Here, Newton appears to be following a variant of the Marxist dialectical sequence that culminates in the victory of proletariat ethnic communities and the disappearance of the state.

The Panthers on Race/Racism

The Panthers recognized the existence of racism, but refused to become reverse racists. As discussed above, they allied themselves with a number of predominantly White liberal and radical groups. The lawyer they relied on and trusted most was a White: Charles Garry. None of the Panther leaders ever claimed racial superiority. Instead, they recognized that many ethnic communities wanted respect and dignity just as they did. Newton wrote that BPP programs had one goal: "complete control of the institutions in the community. Every ethnic group has particular needs that they know and understand better than anybody else, each group is the best judge of how its institutions ought to affect the lives of its members."[30]

Favoring a materialist analytic methodology for explaining social phenomena, Newton explained racism in terms of material profitability. "The white racist oppresses Black people [because] it is economically profitable to do so. Black people must develop the political power to make it unprofitable....This racist United States operates with the motive of profit; he lifts the gun and escalates war for profit. We will make him lower his guns because they will no longer serve his profit motive."[31]

The Panthers believed that Black policemen could be just as fascist as White policemen. Eldridge Cleaver appreciated that white liberals gave the Party significant amounts of money to help with Newton's legal defense fund and bail for himself. He wrote: "My mother had taught all her children that there were whites you could count on, for they were good and just, and that there were blacks you should avoid, for they were unkind and dishonest. Our family was not fed racism.... I argued this position night and day within the Panthers...we were against police brutality; and some of them were black."[32]

David Hilliard quoted Bobby Seale as saying: "we see ourselves as a nation within a nation.... We don't see ourselves as a national unit for racist reasons.... We don't fight racism with racism. We fight racism with solidarity."[33] During the question-answer period following a talk Newton gave on intercommunalism in February 1971, someone commented that the ideology of intercommunalism and the restriction of BPP membership to Blacks appeared to be a contradiction. Newton agreed, but explained that it was a contradiction the Party was trying to resolve. The Party's first goal, he said, was to help the Black community. The Panthers have to meet the people on the grounds that they can relate to best. Because Blacks relate best to other Blacks, the Party was being pragmatic to get the job done. "When that job is done, the Black Panther Party will no longer be the Black Panther Party."[34]

The Black Panther Party and Class

Newton, Eldridge Cleaver, and other BPP leaders adhered to the methodology of dialectical materialism and the Marxian view of class conflict sparked by internal contradictions. Panther ideology differed from conventional Marxism by regarding the lumpenproletariat as the vanguard revolutionary force that could eliminate capitalism and racism in the United States. In his article "On the Ideology of the Black Panther Party," Eldridge Cleaver credits Newton: "what Huey did was to provide the ideology and the methodology for organizing the Black Urban Lumpenproletariat. Armed with this ideological perspective and method, Huey transformed the Black lumpenproletariat from the forgotten people at the bottom of society into the vanguard of the proletariat."[35] Cleaver explained that Marx never addressed racism in the United States. Hence, American Blacks had to develop their own version of Marxism that was applicable to their unique historic experience. Cleaver maintained that there were major differences between the White proletariat and lumpenproletariat on the one hand and the Black proletariat and lumpenproletariat on the other. Each had different historic experiences and related to society and the means of production differently. Cleaver described the Black lumpen as follows:

> The Lumpenproletariat are all those who have no secure relationship or vested interest in the means of production and the institutions of capitalist society. That part of the "Industrial Reserve Army" held perpetually in reserve; who have never worked and never will; who can't find a job; who are unskilled and unfit; who have been

displaced by machines, automation, and cybernation, and were never "retained or invested with new skills"; all those on Welfare or receiving State Aid.

Also, the so-called "Criminal Element," those who live by their wits, existing off that which they rip off, who stick guns in the faces of businessmen and say "stick'em up'" or "give it up"! Those who don't even want a job, who hate to work and can't relate to punching some pig's time clock, who would rather punch a pig in the mouth and rob him than punch that same pig's time clock and work for him, those whom Huey P. Newton calls "the illegitimate capitalists." In short, all those who simply have been locked out of the economy and robbed of their rightful social heritage.[36]

Cleaver argued that the very conditions of life of the lumpen dictate spontaneous and extreme reactions against the system as a whole. Because the lumpen have been bypassed by the labor unions and even the Communist Parties they are forced to create their own forms of rebellion. "The streets belong to the Lumpen," Cleaver declared, and "it is in the streets that Lumpen will make their rebellion....[they are] the true revolutionaries in the urban centers."[37]

Cleaver and Newton were in full agreement on the vanguard role the Black lumpen could play in the revolution. As Bobby Seale recalls:

Huey wanted brothers off the block—brothers who had been out there robbing banks, brothers who had been pimping, brothers who had been peddling dope, brothers who ain't going to take no shit, brothers who had been fighting pigs—because he knew once they get themselves together in the area of political education (...the ten-point platform and program), Huey P. Newton knew that...once you organize those brothers...you get black men, you get revolutionaries that are too much.[38]

Sundiata Acoli, an East Coast Panther, believes that the media were able to debase the image of the Party by focusing on the members' lumpen tendencies, which he explained "are associated with lack of discipline, liberal use of alcohol, marijuana, and curse-words; loose sexual morals, a criminal mentality, and rash actions. These tendencies in some Party members provided the media with better opportunities than they would otherwise have had to play up this aspect, and to slander the Party, which diverted public attention from much of the positive work done by the BPP."[39]

Some scholars argue that Newton's reliance on the lumpen weakened the Party's potential for effective change.[40] Newton, himself appears to agree. In a 1971 speech, Newton acknowledged that successful revolutions of the past were led by people with bourgeois skills. "They are people who have gone through the established institutions, rejected them, and then applied their skills to the community."[41] He acknowledged that the BPP "is not so blessed....We see that administrators of our Party are victims who have not received that bourgeois training....We have now what we call the Ideological Institute, where we are teaching these skills, and we also invite those people who have received a bourgeois education to come and help us."[42]

Early on, Newton distrusted and maligned the Black bourgeoisie, claiming they had to be eliminated along with white capitalists. In retrospect, Sundiata Acoli regarded this as a Party defect. He writes that "the BPP preached socialist politics.... They often gave the impression that to engage in any business enterprise was to engage in capitalism and they too frequently looked with disdain upon the small-business people in the community.... The BPP failed to encourage the Black community to set up its own businesses as a means of building an independent economic foundation which could help break 'outsiders' control of the Black community's economics, and move it toward economic self-reliance."[43] In June 1971 Newton admitted that he took his original position too hastily. "In the past," he wrote, "the Black Panther Party took a counterrevolutionary position with our blanket condemnation of Black capitalism. Our strategy should have been to analyze the positive and negative qualities of this phenomenon before making any condemnation."[44]

Conclusion

Throughout the relatively short history of the BPP, Newton and his followers displayed a fair degree of intellectual flexibility in their conceptualization of socio-economic-political relationships and the place of Black Americans within the domestic and global context. They moved from being Black nationalists to revolutionary nationalists, to revolutionary internationalists, and finally to revolutionary intercommunalists. In terms of tactics they also varied. Originally they stressed self-defense, the gun and police patrols. They encouraged Blacks to arm themselves. Eventually, however, Party leaders realized that shoot-outs with the police not only reduced their numbers, they also caused many in the Black community to fear the Panthers. Consequently, they dropped "Self-Defense" from the Party name and focused more on "survival programs," that involved serving the community by providing breakfasts for children and medical care and clothing for families. By 1971, Newton had also reconsidered the roles that the lumpenproletariat, bourgeois education and Black capitalism could play in the struggle. On the issue of racism they were consistent in their determination that it should be eliminated in all of its forms.

By the mid-1970s the Party was in shambles. Newton and Cleaver had split the party into rival factions that were at each other's throats; many Panthers had been killed by the police, and many others were in prison. J. Edgar Hoover's COINTELPRO division of the FBI was unrelenting in its determination to destroy of the Party by means of misinformation campaigns, the planting of agent provocateurs among the Panthers, and other illegal tactics.

Eldridge Cleaver would return to the United States from exile abroad to become a conservative Republican and a Born-Again-Christian. He died in 1998. Huey Newton would become a drug addict. On August 22, 1989, he was murdered on the streets of Oakland in a drug dispute. What had begun with high idealism ended in tragedy.

Notes

1   For the history of the Black Panther Party, see David Hilliard, *This Side of Paradise: The Autobiography of David Hilliard and the Story of the Black Panther Party* (Boston: Little Brown, 1993); Bobby Seale, *Seize the Time: The Story of the Black Panther Party and Huey P. Newton* (Baltimore: Black Classic Press, 1991); K. Cleaver and G. Katsiaficas, eds., *Liberation, Imagination, and the Black Panther Party* (New York/London: Routledge, 2001); C.E. Jones, ed., *The Black Panther Party Reconsidered* (Baltimore: Black Classic Press, 1998).

2   The Lowndes County Freedom Organization was an independent political party in rural Alabama, one of whose organizers was Stokely Carmichael, a former Howard University student civil rights activist, who had been involved in Mississippi voter registration activities as a member of the Student Non-violent Coordinating Committee (SNCC). The Deacons for Defense and Justice had been established in Jonesboro, Louisiana, on July 10, 1964 by a group of African American men who were mostly veterans of World War II and the Korean War. Their goal was to combat Ku Klux Klan violence against Congress of Racial Equality (CORE) volunteers who were promoting voter registration. Their stance stood in opposition to Martin L. King's non-violent philosophy.

3   Available at: <http://history.hanover.edu/courses/excerpts/111bppp.html>.

4   M. Abu-Jamal, *We Want Freedom: A Life in the Black Panther Party* (Cambridge, MA: South End Press, 2004), 96.

5   Abu-Jamal, *We Want Freedom*, 111.

6   Eldridge Cleaver, *On the Ideology of the Black Panther Party* (Pamphlet, 1970). Available at: <http://www.etext.org/Politics/MIM/bpp/bppideology1970.html>.

7   Eldridge Cleaver, *Soul on Fire* (Waco, TX: World Books, 1978), 112.

8   Huey P. Newton, *The Huey P. Newton Reader* (New York: Seven Stories Press, 2002), 184.

9   Newton wrote: "Bobby [Seale] had collected all of Malcolm X's speeches and ideas from papers like *The Militant* and *Muhammad Speaks*. These we studied carefully." Newton, *Huey P. Newton Reader*, 50.

10 Newton, *Huey P. Newton Reader*, 185.

11 Hilliard, *This Side of Paradise*, 238.

12 Hilliard, *This Side of Paradise*, 163.

13 Newton, *Huey P. Newton Reader*, 148.

14 Seale, *Seize the Time*, 60.

15 Newton, *Huey P. Newton Reader*, 50.

16 Newton, *Huey P. Newton Reader*, 152.

17 Huey P. Newton, *Revolutionary Suicide* (New York: Harcourt Brace Jovanovich, 1973), 195.

18 Newton, *Revolutionary Suicide*, 195.

19 Newton, *Revolutionary Suicide*, 195.

20 Newton, *Revolutionary Suicide*, 185.

21 Seale, *Seize the Time*, 25–26.

22 David Hilliard, "If You Want Peace You Got To Fight for It," in P.S. Foner, ed., *The Black Panthers Speak* (New York, J.B. Lippincott, 1970), 128.

23 Hilliard, "If You Want Peace," 128.

24 K. Cleaver, "Back to Africa: The Evolution of the International Section of the Black Panther Party (1969–1972)," in C.E. Jones, ed., *The Black Panther Party Reconsidered*, (Baltimore: Black Classic Press, 1998), 230.

25 Eldridge Cleaver, "Eldridge Cleaver Discusses Revolution: An Interview from Exile," in Foner, *Black Panthers Speak*, 110.

26 Newton, *Huey P. Newton Reader*, 187.

27 Newton, *Huey P. Newton Reader*, 298–299.

28 Newton, *Huey P. Newton Reader*, 253.

29 Newton, *Revolutionary Suicide*, 167.

30 Newton, *Revolutionary Suicide*, 167.

31 Newton, *Huey P. Newton Reader*, 148.

32 Cleaver, *Soul on Fire*, 139.

33 Hilliard, *This Side of Paradise*, 121.

34 Newton, *Huey P. Newton Reader*, 198.

35 Cleaver, *On the Ideology*.

36 Cleaver, *On the Ideology*.

37 Cleaver, *On the Ideology*.

38 Seale, *Seize the Time*, 64.

39 S. Acoli, *A Brief History of the Black Panther Party. Its Place in the Black Liberation Movement*, (1995) <http://www.hartford-hwp.com/archives/45a/004.html>.

40 C. Booker, C. "Lumpenization: A Critical Error of the Black Panther Party," in Jones, *Panther Party Reconsidered*, 337–362.

41 Newton, *Huey P. Newton Reader*, 216.

42. Newton, *Huey P. Newton Reader*, 216-217.

43 Acoli, *A Brief History* <http://www.hartford-hwp.com/archives/45a/004.html>.

44 Newton, *Huey P. Newton Reader*, 229.

Centralization Trends in Nigeria's PDP Regime: Addressing Pluralism in Contemporary African Democracies

Rita Kiki Edozie

In examining the politics of ethnicity and national identity in Africa, this chapter responds to critical reflections of Nigeria's PDP/Obasanjo landslide victory in the country's April 2003 elections. It does so by refuting analyses that predict trends toward a reversal of democracy and the re-emergence of 'neo-authoritarianism' reflected in the country's—and the continent's—Third Wave democratic practice. Countering this mainstream 'failed democracy' approach used to evaluate democratization trends in the country, the article argues contrarily that Nigeria's and Africa's Millennium democratic polities and societies are historically and structurally constitutive in a way that inclines democratic practice in these countries toward 'centralism.' In evaluating complex trajectories in Nigeria's re-installed democracy, the chapter illustrates ways in which the PDP regime—and other dominant party-led democratic regimes in the continent— is merely responding to a political context in which centrist democratic politics is once again re-emerging. In Nigeria, centrist politics, reflected in a manifestation of the Third World 'delegative democracy', has the purpose of maintaining the stability of the democratic system in the country's deeply-divided, complexly plural society, as well as its unevenly developed economy.

The chapter concludes, however, with the contention that due to the dominant party's strategy to maintain the stability of the system and nation, the political rights and civil liberties of the highly pluralist, newly invigorated democratic societies of Africa are indeed being restricted. In this respect, the author recommends that the continent's new centrist democrats may need to adjust their political strategies to accommodate an increasingly democratized and globalized social order conveyed by a highly culturally pluralized and activist African civil society—especially in the Nigerian case.

Failed Democracy and the PDP in Campaign 2003

On April 19, 2003, Nigeria held an internationally celebrated 'second election' observed and assessed closely and controversially by domestic and international observers alike. Carrying 61.0% of the presidential electoral vote, 54.5% of the House of Representatives poll, 53.7% of the Senate and about 80% of the gubernatorial seats (28 out of 36 states), the incumbent President Olusegun Obasanjo and his People's Democratic Party's (PDP) 2003 landslide electoral victory drew criticism of Nigeria's Third Wave democratic transition which was seen to be moving toward a one-party state.

At the time, BBC journalist, Joseph Winter's predictive characterization of the Nigerian elections—calling them a fate equal to the return of military rule and a typical trend by African regimes to revert toward a greater authoritarianism—suggests a discourse inclination to characterize processes of democratization in Africa in sweepingly negative terms.[1] It has become fashionable in this respect for Africanists to comment on the legacy of rogue leaders who 'pessimists' claim have and continue to create mitigating prospects for democracy in the continent.[2] Afro-pessimism of this nature has so permeated the Africanist social science lexicon that the 1990s euphoria over Third Wave democratization in Africa is to be silenced by conclusions of 'failed democracy' and 'good governance' paternalism.[3]

Because of these trends, simplistic analyses by democracy scholars of the continent's democratic processes warrant particular attention. Afro-*optimist* scholar[4], Ebere Onwudiwe, for example, was appropriately instantly critical of Winter's analysis, arguing that the BBC News correspondent's commentary fails to reflect an acute understanding of African politics and history.[5] Onwudiwe's criticism is well founded; and as the current chapter hopes to achieve, there is a need to begin to critically examine the negative, 'behavioral' 'caricatures' of the new trajectories in democratic politics in Africa and the developing world. For example, not integrated in the analysis of many Africanist specialists who continue to privilege unique and exceptional negative characteristics of Africa's politics, is the fact that most Third Wave democratizing countries have also been accused of taking on an 'illiberal' or 'neo-authoritarian' posture. Latin American, Asian, and FSU—particularly Russian—third wave democracies seem to also exhibit characteristics of political centrism, delegation and domination. Of course, centralization trends are constitutive of most Third Wave democracies, not only those in Africa.

Hence, utilizing comparative and critical political science theory and an emerging *Africanist* democratic theory (explanations and reflections of democracy on Africa), the analyses herein, the current discussion of democratization in contemporary Nigeria serves to examine the structural premises that foster the tendency for democratic politics in this country to lean toward dominant partyism, strong presidencies and the democratic system's general inclinations away from the normative liberal democracy genre adopted by most advanced industrial countries. The essay especially attempts to underscore the fact that dominant partyism—not necessarily one-partyism—and strong executives are quite consistent with comparative democratic development elsewhere in Africa and the world. [6]

However, my own analysis of democratization will argue that rather than view Nigeria's obvious trends toward dominant parties and strong executives as teleological negative reversals away from democratic consolidation toward 'authoritarian' rule, it is important to identify the structural underpinnings—socio-cultural (ethnicity), economic and institutional—that impinge upon and influence the tendencies for developing world democratic practice and processes toward centralization and a 'suggestive' dominance in politics. Nigeria and several other Third Wave democracies in Africa are indeed 'developing democracies'. In this respect, the country's deeply-divided society—often characterized as the national-ethnic question—is especially internationally renown and has also informed the subject of classic studies in comparative politics that have documented how in the course of democratic development, Nigerian political elites selected institutional structures to generate desired democratic results that would address the nation's multi-nationality.

For example, the country chose to replace a Westminster parliamentary system with an American presidential system's strong executive by adopting a reformed majoritarian electoral system that included proportional mechanisms for alternative voting. As well, Nigerian political elites made several voluntary innovations within their party system that sought to cultivate 'universal' or 'national' parties and alliances while minimizing 'ethnic' or parochial partisanship. I will argue that not only must the discourse of democracy include the aforementioned events in a repertoire of Nigerian democratic history; these transformations in politics constitute the structural institutional underpinnings that have cultivated Nigeria's contemporary inclination toward a dominant democracy.

Yet, while underscoring this important dimension for understanding democratic consolidation in contemporary Nigeria, in addition to identifying the structural and institutional mechanisms that foster centrist politics and dominant partyism in democratizing countries like Nigeria, I advance the analysis of democratic development in Nigeria with an important additional thesis. My own observation of the structural trend toward what is sometimes celebrated as a democratic politics premised on 'oligarchic and hegemonic power'[7] suggests that there is a critical need for even 'optimist' scholar and practitioner proponents of the politics of 'democratic centralism' and 'governance' to recognize contemporary contexts in which comparative democracy is occurring particularly during the Post Cold War globalized, civil-society driven and highly pluralized era of 'people power' democracy.

As with global trends, Nigeria's longstanding, thriving pluralist culture of civil society mobilization and multi-ethnicism are also significantly contributing to new challenges in the functioning of democratic politics. These trends are evidenced by the dynamic trajectories of democratic politics manifested in the country's Fourth Republic including events such as the Sharia question, the expanding Niger Delta resistance movements, and the periodic strikes by the Nigerian Labor Congress (NLC) against global economic reforms.[8] By recommending the development of a pluralist democratic society, my conclusion suggests ways in which 'state-society' regimes in Nigeria, Africa, and the developing world may reconcile to forge more sustainable democratic regimes.

Comparing Democratization Trends: Nigeria and the Developing World

Due to the empirical re-expansion of the democratic mode of politics in Africa, Latin America, Asia and the Post Soviet/Communist regions in the 80s and 90s, comparative democracy as a sub-discipline of comparative and international politics has generated a wide array of theoretical lenses and models for explaining and interpreting democratic political change and performance in these regions. Several classifications of the Third Wave democracy exist, including the most commonly defined illiberal democracy, the neo-authoritarian regime, the re-configuring 'electoral' state and the virtual democracy. However, the attempt to classify democratization trends in the developing world according to the aforementioned categories does little to reveal the more profound complex dilemmas that democratizing countries are undergoing.

Rather than the arbitrary classifications listed above, there are instead just two general typologies for distinguishing 'democracy' in contemporary international politics: established liberal democracies (ELDs) and fledgling neo-democracies (FNDs).[9] Veteran comparative political scientist, Guillermo O'Donnell, whose theoretical models for the analysis of democratic transitions, consolidations and performance I rely on for the ensuing analysis of Nigerian democratization, refers to the ELDs as properly functioning *liberal representative democracies* found in the West and the latter FNDs as *delegative democracies* found in the developing world. In this 'delegative' genre, procedural institutions of democracy such as regular multi-party elections and democratic constitutions, which prescribe to the nominal acknowledgement of 'political rights and civil liberties' do exist. However, the deep social and economic crisis that these democracies have inherited from their authoritarian predecessors reinforces certain practices and conceptions about the proper exercise of political authority that leads in the direction of a different genre of democracy that is not strongly embedded with either liberal values or the long-term historical features of representative institutions.

An important feature of O'Donnell's model thus that deserves greater exposition is his 'structural' analysis of comparative democracies, which distinguishes itself from the aforementioned normative 'behavioral' and 'cultural' explanations of democratization that dominates democratic scholarship in Africa especially. In this respect, the democratizing state is a function of the structural transformations within the society. While socio-economic and institutional political variables are much more commonly used to examine politics in Latin America, Asia and the FSU, the analysis of democratic politics in Africa still tends to emphasize narrow and simplistic leadership variables in explaining democratic trends. The 'behavior'—not the policies or the cleavaged societal conditions of the constituencies in which Presidents Mugabe, Olusegun Obasanjo and Thabo Mbeki oversee—are attributed as the primary causes for the undermining of democracy in their respective countries.

By emphasizing the notion that the core study of democratization has to do with the proper functioning of the democratic regime, O'Donnell minimizes Western cultural (liberalism) and personal leadership factors as main contributing features influencing democratization trends, and instead argues that it is structural factors within developing world societies that contribute to the divergent practices of democracy between Western democracies and those in the developing world. What makes many Third World and 'transitional' world societies structurally different is a historical contingent that includes legacies of colonialism; nation-state building and economic development. These structural factors are the main influencing variables that affect democratization in these regions.

Developing regions' high incidence of cultural pluralism, economic crises, and weak democratic institutions affect the normative functioning and operation of democratic politics in respective Third Wave countries. In effect, the main inhibitive force in these democracies is indeed the low density of certain political institutions that existed before the democratic transition. In this respect, other non-formalized but strongly operative practices, such as 'commandist' leadership, clientelism, patrimonialism and corruption, usually replace the practice of well-functioning liberal representative institutions. Moreover, O'Donnell's thesis offers 'political' variables rather than 'personal' characteristics for explaining the pre-eminence of powerful ruling party executives in Third World democracies.

For example, new democratic leaders (Presidents or Prime Ministers) in delegative democracies tend to believe that whoever wins the election is entitled to govern as he or she sees fit, constrained only by the hard facts of existing power relations and by a constitutionally limited term of office. The president sees himself/herself as the embodiment of the nation and the main custodian and definer of its interests. For such a figure, who also sees himself as overcoming factionalism and conflicts associated with parties, the political base of the presidency is the 'Movement'—the majoritarian populist constituency. That is why winning presidential candidates in developing world democracies derogate political parties and organized interests, seeing themselves as above such horizontal democratic institutions including the judiciary and legislatures. Accountability to such institutions appears as a mere impediment to the full authority that the president has been delegated to exercise.

Related to this point is the fact that unlike the mainstream school, which focuses on procedural dimensions of elections in democratizing nations, O'Donnell explains elections in delegative democracies from the perspective of a 'political' process rather than a 'technical' process. By doing so, there is an opportunity for an analysis that refreshingly ties elections to the structure and play of political institutions and actors. Elections in Third Wave democracies tend to be high-stakes events where candidates compete for a chance to rule virtually free of all constraints save those imposed by naked, non-institutionalized power relations. After the election, voters are expected to become a passive but cheering audience of what the president does.

Personal leadership or regional cultural attributes may not exclusively explain the behavior of Third World democrats. Rather, structural factors in developing world societies—economic crisis, excessive identity movements, and threats to nation's security—tend to explain the centrist, majoritarian trends of these leaders. It is true that delegative presidents/prime ministers govern less *liberally* than representative democracies. However, in reality, this brand of democracy is indeed liberalism though not of the advanced industrialized pluralist kind, but of the majoritarian kind, having the intent of nurturing a collective nationalistic public good for the purpose of healing the nation by uniting its disperse fragments into a harmonious whole. These structural tendencies influencing politics in contemporary developing and transitional nations are consistent with Rousseau's depiction of democracy. In this respect, democracy's goal serves the ends of the masses as a whole in a 'social contract' as opposed to the amalgamation of individual, competitive interests in a liberal democracy.[10]

A revised conceptual analysis for examining democratic transitions, consolidation, and performance in Nigeria and other regions undergoing democratization must extend beyond the mainstream teleological, path-dependent, Euro-centric template that constructs a model developed under historical conditions found in the West. Instead as does O'Donnell's model for explaining the distinguishing features of the development of democracy in the developing world, the appropriate lenses for examining democratization should examine contingent historical, structural and political patterns in the democratizing country. Such a 'political' basis for examining democracy in a developing world country ought to focus upon the country's long-term historical factors, as well as the degree of severity of the socio-economic/socio-political problems that the newly installed democratic governments inherit.

Nigeria's National Parties, Centrist Electoral Systems and Delegative Presidents

Mainstream analyses critical of dominant parties and strong executive presidencies in Nigeria and Africa generally miss the aforementioned more critical discussion that reveals the institutional and structured dimensions that are fostering the 'restrictive' trends of parties and polities in Africa's incumbent democracies. In Africa, socio-economic conditions have in the past and continue in the present to foster political structures conducive to nurturing national unity and socio-economic welfarism reflected in the emergence of 'dominant' parties and centrist executives.

As a case study for normative models in comparative politics, Nigeria's tendency toward political centrism or what O'Donnell has described as a delegative democracy is symbolically cited by studies in international politics. As early as the foundation of modern Nigerian politics, Sir Arthur Lewis referred to Nigeria when arguing in *Politics in West Africa* that the inherited Westminster system of parliamentary democracy was responsible for much of the authoritarianism then emerging in English-speaking Africa. Since then, scholars devoted to comparing presidential and parliamentary systems often cite Nigeria's successive attempts to adopt a presidential system (Second Republic) to mitigate societal divisions.[11]

It is well documented by the same literature that the African party's dominance has since the independence period been based on the structural need by politics in the continent to efface 'corrosive ethnicity' and to nurture 'economic development'.[12] Rather than the ideology of 'left and right' politics engendered by historical class divisions and transformations in the monarchy in the West—the vanguard of Western liberalism—party ideologies in Africa, certainly symbolized in cogent ways in Nigeria, present 'centrist' conditions as the contingent ideology within African politics. In 1999, referring to Nigeria's PDP and South Africa's ANC as 'Big Tent' parties, political scientist, Richard Sklar, predicted that the PDP would become a truly national party, arguing that the 'national question' was the 'issue' that could sustain a genuinely competitive party system in Nigeria.[13]

Donald Horowitz[14] is one scholar who has eloquently elaborated upon the controversy over 'dominant parties' in democratizing states by arguing that in much of Africa in the immediate post-colonial period, the single party state emerged in response to party competition along ethnic lines. In such a context, ethnically based parties threatened a ruling multi-ethnic party who, afraid of polarization and a shrunken base, declared a one-party state, outlawed competitive ethnic parties and sought to represent their interests through a vanguardist centrist mechanism such as the ruling party or a military provisional council (Horowitz, 1991).

More cogent to the contemporary concerns over Nigerian dominant partyism, Horowitz's study has specifically referred to the fact that the parliamentary system inherited by the post-colonial Nigerian state at independence fostered the northern Hausa-Fulani ethnic dominance of the parliament and of the democratic regime by the northern based, ruling Nigerian Peoples Congress (NPC) ruling party. Events resulting from ethno-religious party dominance precipitated ethnic and partisan instability, the ushering in of the country's first military coup and the reversal of the democratic regime. However in the Second Republic, the country's constitutional design consciously chose the Presidential system with its separation of powers and strong executive institutional distinctions, so that one group could be prevented from controlling the entire country through the parliament.

Nigeria's political culture provides historical antecedents for the contemporary behavior of the People's Democratic Party (PDP). In 2003, the successful party ideology of the People's Democratic Party (PDP), like its historical counterparts—the First Republic's Nigerian People's Congress (NPC) and the 2nd Republic's National Party of Nigeria (NPN) (Joseph, 1987) is merely continuing a tradition of a political culture which relies upon consociational/power-sharing mechanisms and policies. These have been expressed in such slogans as 'unity in diversity', in the country's public policy practice of making administrative appointments according to Nigerian 'federal character', in the employing of voluntary practices by political parties, and in designing electoral strategies and policies such as the 'plurality plus' and 'multi-national reach'. As early as 1967—through the promise of federalism and the devolution of ethnic power to the smaller regions—the power sharing political institution reflected the country's commitment to a unified Nigeria threatened by civil war (Ruth First, 1972, Horowitz, 1991).

In 1967, in describing the political manifestation of Third World 'clientilism'—he called it 'prebendalism'—veteran Africanist, Richard Joseph characterized the 2nd Republic's National Party of Nigeria (NPN) as the

"Successful harmonization of the counter-posed themes of national and sectional loyalties including the equal division of social goods"[15]

According to Joseph, the architects of the NPN knew just what it was that enabled a social formation like Nigeria to work. In contemporary Nigeria also, successful political parties, not exclusive to the PDP, are increasingly reflecting an ideology that fosters multi-ethnic, centrist elite coalition building, which while also tending to embody moderate, compromised political-economic ideologies, present as their main strategic campaign feature, the idea of 'political stability'.

As well, documented by the classic studies of both Donald Horowitz and Arendt Lipjhardt, the Nigerian country case study is internationally known as a case that symbolizes the practice of alternate majoritiarian electoral systems in deeply divided societies. Previously having experimented unsuccessfully with PR Westminster Parliamentary democratic systems (the First Republic), Nigeria's 1979 and 1999 Constitutions for the country's Second and Third/Fourth Republics adopted an American-style Presidential system and the plurality (First-Past-The-Post FPTP) electoral system. Avoiding the 'majoritarian-plurality' tendency toward 'permanent ethnic majorities' in Africa, Nigerian democratic designers revised their majoritarian electoral system to require a successful Presidential candidate to have at least 25 percent of the vote in no less than two-thirds of the states; the system ensured that the President would have support from many ethnic groups. As Horowitz has repeatedly explained, the aim was to elect a moderate, centrist President.

Structural incentives inherent in Nigeria's democratic development apply too much of the African continent's culturally plural societies. Alternative Voting (AV) has been experimental within Africa because of this electoral institution's ability to act as a compromise solution to renegade majoritarianism in a First-Past-The-Post (FPTP), winner-takes-all, electoral system. A contemporary study on comparative elections in Africa concluded that Africa's democratic polities rejected FPTP systems because they encouraged majoritarian tyranny and ethnic polarization.[16] This is evident in Lesotho's 1993 and 1999 elections where the adoption of an FPTP majoritarian system caused wholesale victories by the winning party and the total exclusion of other parties from parliament.[17] Alternatively, the study found that PR systems were favored in Africa because they fostered power sharing and interethnic accommodation. Significantly, however, Alternative Voting has also acted as a compromise to a strict system of Proportional Representation (PR) and consociationalism, which as it did in Nigeria's First Republic's Westminster System, tended to restrict individual citizen's voting rights—and hence liberal democracy—with it's focus on ethnic group rights to the exclusion of the center.

It is these institutional structures generated by the party's multi-national reach ideology, not Obasanjo's personal behavior that has generated the PDP's contemporary party dominance in the 2003 election. Indeed, it is Nigeria's experimentation with Alternative Voting Systems (AV), 'Plurality-Plus' voter mechanisms, which distinguish the country's First Republic Northern People's Congress's (NPC) 'Northern' ethno-hegemonic dominance—a negative and destabilizing factor for democracy in the country—from the Fourth Republic PDP's multi-ethnic coalition genre of 'dominance'—at least culturally a more ethnically inclusive manifestation of control and stability.

The same socio-economic and socio-cultural conditions that fostered centrist party politics in Africa in the 60s still exist in the Millennium. For example, reporting on another win for Togo's Eyadema in 2003, New African reporter, Edwin Eboe proclaimed that there is an emerging argument in Togo these days for a strong leadership to hold power at the center in order to maintain national unity, security and stability in view of the specter of political destabilization that continues to threaten the West African sub-region.[18] Moreover, scholars of South African democracy have begun to reveal ways in which the country's highly liberal Constitution has in effect structurally promoted dominant partyism by translating electoral dominance into a preponderance of political power in the executive and legislature. Anthony Butler argues that the 1996 Constitution perpetuates South Africa's traditionally centralized system of executive authority.[19]

Nigeria's experience with democratic development explains why Africa's-and many Third World incumbent democracies are inclined to become 'non-liberal', delegative democracies where ruling parties continue to reflect centrist characteristics of 'guided democracies' rather than the pluralist tendencies of 'liberal democracies'. Because Africa's re-established democracies inherit the contextual sociopolitical divisions from previous regimes, their new democratic institutions and agents are likely to address these conditions 'delegatively' rather than in a liberal democratic format.

Democratic Politics in the Nigerian Fourth Republic

Centrism and dominance in incumbent Third Wave democratic behavior described as delegative democratization is one important factor that explains Nigeria's 'partially-free' (Freedom House, 2004) performance rating during the country's Fourth Republic. In justifying their reasons for the slow progress of Nigeria's democratic consolidation, the international democracy rating body cited continued political corruption, the increase in political and social violence and statist governance. By 2003, Nigeria's fourth experiment with democratic politics again leaned away from the constraints of the libera democracy that it had re-established four years earlier. Moreover, the political patterns that affected the performance of the new democratic regime conveyed the same structural cleavages that had dominated Nigerian politics since the country's inception.

The expansion of Sharia law in northern states and the Niger Delta question once again reinvigorated the challenges of 'consociational' democracy, and with the Obasanjo regime leaning toward the dictates of the country's external patrons, economic technicsm became a pre-eminent governing tactic of the regime, which tried to implement monetarist, neo-liberal economic reform policies despite overwhelming and massive popular resistance.

Earlier sections of this article have established Nigeria's multi-nationality as an important structural feature to consider in understanding the country's contemporary democratic performance. Nigeria is a country that uniquely constitutes at least four distinctive pre-colonial nations, several minority ethnic groups, and two major religious blocs. As a result, the acceleration of ethno-nationalist fragmentation and ethno-politics during the Fourth Republic and in campaign 2003—especially expressed in the Sharia movement in 2000 and the expansion to new levels of the Niger Delta question—have both occurred as an outgrowth of the 1999 democratic transition and a reflection of the reinvigoration of ethno-democratic politics.

What I mean is that the 2000 Constitutional crisis and its attendant fostering of social cleavage and violence in the country is occurring as a result of disputed interpretations of the 1999 constitution as well as the resurgence of ethno-religious identity movements—Islamic and Christian—pushed forward by organizations within the Nigerian civil society. Moreover, the construction of a 'South-South, Greater Ijaw, Niger Delta' ethno-bloc to compete with the traditional tripartite Hausa-Fulani, Yoruba, Igbo ethnic blocs has emerged as a result of democratization trends, more specifically the mobilization of cultural identity as political identity in the country's deeply divided society.

These transformations in ethnic self-determination coinciding with transformations in political structures—democratization—have fostered the crystallization of ethno-nationalist identity in multi-national Nigeria, an occurrence which is underscoring the growing limitations of the country's previous reliance on consociational mechanisms for mediating cultural conflict and enlarging national citizenship. During Campaign 2003, through ethnic political strategizing, the PDP, and other parties (ANPP, UPGA), all continued to make aggressive efforts to accommodate multi-national interests in the country that fostered Nigerian unity at the center. At the same time, however, these processes have been perceived by pluralist actors in the country as constraints on their own political rights, and on individual and group liberty and self-determination, both cornerstones for a successful liberal democracy.

A second feature of the incumbent Nigerian democratic regime concerns the legacy of military vanguardism, an institutional factor that is consistent with O'Donnell's description of delegative democracies. The Nigerian military's legacy in the Fourth Republic is evidenced by the presence of five former generals as presidential candidates in the 2003 election,[20] as well as by the military institution's shadow prospects for repeated intervention to save the country from the 'corrosive forces of democracy'.[21] Many ex-soldiers dominate contemporary Nigerian politics because of their wealth and thus their ability to sponsor expensive campaigns. Their political experience in previous political regimes also facilitates national name recognition in nationwide democratic campaigns.

Structural continuities between the governance cultures of the old military regime and the new democratic regime are reflected in the Fourth Republic which since its establishment in 1999 has been characterized by the tense and often very conflict-ridden relations between the executive branch and the legislative houses. This lead to the ousting of two congressional leaders, three Senate presidents, the scandalous near two-time impeachment of President Obasanjo by Congress, the vulgar careerism and corporatism within most of the political parties' campaigns, and the unprecedented prominence of political assassinations in the country. Significantly, congressional and senate politicians often complained that President Obasanjo, himself, a former military head of state, ruled in a 'commandist' rather than 'liberal' governing style.

A final criterion affecting Nigeria's incumbent democratic regime's performance concerns the country's political economy. Sayre Schatz' 1960s classical depiction of the Nigerian political economy as a 'nurture capitalist' and 'rentier, enclave oil-economy' (Schatz, 1963) remains relevant to date; nevertheless, older more traditional analyses of the political-economy of oil in the country are rapidly adjusting in the contemporary democratic regimes to include new issues of fiscal federalism and equitable resource mobilization among the country's oil-laden regional constituencies in the Niger delta states. Moreover, Nigeria's unevenly developed economy is characterized by a rapidly growing social stratification precipitated by modernization as well as globalization, causing the growth of distinct class sectors. The country remains the largest oil producer in Africa, generating the second highest GNP, the largest population with a hundred and twenty five million—thus reflecting a very low per capita income of $750—and an increasingly skewed GINI inequality coefficient.

Thus with a 2003 budget estimated at $7 billion dollars, Nigeria's democratic opposition has pointed to the failures of the PDP/Obasanjo neo-liberal economic policies. The PDP regime has been unable to deliver on its campaign promise to improve the country's infrastructure—electricity and transportation. Moreover, despite pledges of poverty reduction and an easing on unemployment, unemployment figures in the country continue to surge and rural poverty has not abated. The government's commitments to IMF structural adjustment policies, including cuts in government spending and the introduction of 'cost recovery' privatization initiatives, removal of oil subsidies, and cut-backs in education and healthcare, have fostered increased organized democratic political resistance by urban civil society groups—including repeated strikes by the NLC, NARD, PENGASSAN, ASUU and NANS. Typically of 'delegative democratic' executives in crisis economies, President Obasanjo continued to rely on technocratic strategies like removing oil subsidies to the Nigerian domestic 'petrol' sector, which, according to the Nigerian Labor Congress, threatened to trigger drastic inflation causing only more distress on the Nigerian worker.

Civil Society and Millennium Democracy: Achieving Ideological (Policy) Pluralism

The aforementioned analysis of Nigeria's incumbent democracy has attempted to explain the regime's tendency toward 'centrism', 'dominance' and 'delegation'. I have argued that there exist structural reasons why Nigerian, African and Third World democracies incline toward this different manifestation of democracy compared to Western liberal democracies. Afro-optimist scholar, Ebere Onwudiwe, in criticizing 'quick' and 'sweeping' characterizations of Nigeria's 2003 elections as predicting a return to African authoritarianism, presents a similar criticism. However, the critical analysis of democratic politics in the continent may need to extend beyond the Afro-optimist discourse critique.

The ensuing analysis of democratic politics in Nigeria is therefore less inclined to agree with democratic analyses that argue that the role of the incumbent democratic regime is merely that of 'developer', 'systems builder' and 'consolidator' and hence, in the Millennium, it is argued, such democracies are still seen to be a repository of the 'guided democracy' model of democracy.[22] In Nigeria, Onwudiwe has argued that the most important question regarding the PDP landslide victory is not ruling-party dominance. Instead, the scholar argues that democratization scholarship should address ways in which new regimes can manage the new democratic government in a way that will support consolidation in Nigeria. By implication Onwudiwe views the dominant, party model positively. Its chief features in addition to free elections and the protection of civil liberties are staying in power for long periods of time, an interventionist state, a strong central bureaucracy, and management of the political affairs of the country by means of conciliation and consensus building.

However, I think that even for Africa, this 'benefactor' role of government described by the aforementioned 'governance' model of 'democracy' is not conducive with the dynamic contexts that constitute the contemporary globalist era. In a truly democratic system, the structural factors of the political system should ensure the possibility that power can be shared among as many competitive forces as possible. In an age of the retreating state, the rapid agitation of civil society, rabid cultural pluralism, identity politics, human rights activism, and global democracy, the emphasis of the contemporary politics of the developing world is on 'democratic power' from below articulated by the mobilization and articulation of civil societies and social movements. Having been at the forefront of dislodging non-democratic regimes in the 90s, thereby ushering in an expansion of democracy to the socio-cultural and economic domains of their societies, in incumbent democratic regimes, Africa's many civil associations are playing a pivotal role in fostering democratic governance.[23]

Nigeria, having one of Africa's largest and most diverse repositories of civil societal elements (Edozie, 2002), is no different from the global trend. That is why it may be ill advised for Afro-optimist scholars to minimize the impact of Nigeria's 'dominant party's' (PDP) inclination to be 'restrictive' on pluralist constituencies. It is in this context, therefore, that I disagree with Onwudiwe's empirical observation that the basis for an effective second party in Nigeria does not exist at this time (Onwudiwe, 2000). The scholar wrongly dismisses the political oppositional potential of the ANPP, the AD, and the UPGA describing them as ethnic and/or special interest parties. By almost celebrating the fact that the PDP 'reigned in' these 'ethnic parties' in the 2003 campaign Onwudiwe's characterization of pluralist forces in a democracy sounds like 17th century federalist, James Madison who also debated the need for early America to 'enlarge the Republic' in order to circumvent 'factions', 'special interests'. He—Madison—argued this position in direct contradistinction to the position of his anti-federalist opposition counterpart, Thomas Jefferson, whose own definition charactered of 'factions' as the essence of 'participatory democracy.[24] What I mean is that also, in much more recent characterization of democracy, the post-modern conceptualization of politics as a radical democratic politics (Laclau and Mouffe, 2001) cannot be dismissed as irrelevant to the African cases.[25] That democracy is increasingly being manifested in the form of a loose coalition and network of identity struggle has its implications for the performance of African democracies too.

Behaving very much like Ethiopia's EPDRF-TPLF, which despite the 1990s new ideology of Ethiopian ethnic federalist democracy has come under intense human rights scrutiny for its tendency towards centralization and its disinclination to truly devolve power in the ethnic regions,[26] similarly the PDP's centrism, dominance and delegative features are certainly not good for Africa's modern democracies. Note also events in post-genocidal Rwanda where the Rwandan Patriotic Front (RPF) recently organized a much-awaited democratic transition. During the election campaign, the newly transformed militant movement and incumbent ruling party, the RPF, unabashedly imposed censorships and restrictions on the main opposition party, the MDR, accusing the party of 'divisionist ideology', an ideology according to President Paul Kagame that threatened to undermine Rwandese national unity.[27] Such dispensation, which seeks to forcibly undermine the continent's associational, cultural, national and ethnic diversity, will surely restore a continent ridden with political conflict and social violence as has occurred in the past. The 2003 post-election oppositional rumblings by the ANPP and other acclaimed 'cheated' political parties pose a similar threat for Nigeria.

Yet ironically, the beauty of Nigerian politics is the fact that despite the country's authoritarian legacies, democratic ideals in the complexly pluralized nation continues to lie in a longstanding and persistent zeal for and practice of self-actualization and self-organization. This is evidenced by the lawsuit enacted by civil societal associations against INEC—the country's electoral body—during campaign 2003. In 2002, Nigeria's civil society groups—led by political activist Gani Fahwehimi—rejected the electoral commission's (INEC) restriction of the party system to five registered parties by suing the electoral institution's policy on the grounds that the decision subverted Nigerians' political rights. In winning this claim, Fahwehimi's suit opened up Campaign 2003 to the participation of 23 more political parties.

Pluralized socio-political mobilization of this kind traces its genesis in Nigeria to the early nationalist politics in the Zikist movement in the 40s, in the social democratic ideologies of the South-western Action Group (AG), and in the progressive elements in the Nigerian Middle Belt social movements. By 1999, combining these regional progressive elements with associational political organizations of the 'left'—NLC, ASUU, NANS, NADECO, the CLO, CDHR—a Nigerian pro-democracy movement did create changes in the country's political landscape, significantly affecting civilian party political alignments and the incorporation of broader sectors among civil society into the political process by the 1990s.

Ten years of a dynamic pro-democracy movement by Nigerian plural forces fostered new political issues for the 1999 and 2003 democratic campaigns which included a clamoring for a debate about the socio-cultural constitution of Nigeria and a sovereign national conference,[28] a discrediting of military vanguardism, pressures on political elite leadership accountability, new concerns for human and civil rights, and a shift to concerns for fiscal federalism and wealth re-distribution (Edozie, 2002: 138). Significantly, in the 2003 campaign, it was Gani Fahwehimi's National Conscience Party (NCP), Olisa Agabakoba's Green Party (GP), and the once vanguard pro-democratic force (NADECO) though currently more marginalized Alliance for Democracy (AD), that all represented the hope for sustaining Nigeria's pluralist progressive political agenda.

Also encouraging is the news that the country's main coalition of opposition parties has announced that it will unite to support a single candidate to run for president in the 2007 polls. Justifying its action on similar successful coalition tactics in winning the presidency in Kenya, the Conference of Nigerian Political Parties (CNPP) chairman argued that there was a need for Nigeria's opposition parties to coordinate their efforts to win out over President Olusegun Obasanjo's ruling PDP.[29]

Conclusion

Simplistic analyses of democracy in Africa by pessimists and optimists alike must extend beyond the mainstream conceptual dualisms of 'autocratic democracy' versus top-down democratic capacity building. Dominant party politics and 'delegative democracy' is democratic practice which, while not authoritarian as has been suggested by proponents of 'failed democracy' in Africa, is, however, resulting in Nigeria's lower political classification in international democracy assessments such as Freedom House's political rights and civil liberties ratings.[30] Despite obvious structural limitations impinging upon Nigeria's democratic regime, obstacles that present obvious limitations on democratic performance and consolidation,[31] Nigeria's democracy can extend beyond its current practice of delegation and regime dominance to become a more substantive democracy that respects a fuller range of political rights and civil liberties.

Rather than reverting to 'guided democracy' models where Third Wave democratic regimes continue to rely on paternalistic postures toward their citizens, Nigerian and other developing-world democracies are compelled to perform and address their democratic constituencies' needs in new and complex ways, a reality that is the dilemma of the practice of democratic politics everywhere—including the contemporary US. The conservative-liberal ideological tension between supporters of 'guided' democracy—Onwudiwe—and supporters of 'participatory' democracy—myself—couldn't be more evident in the trends in Nigerian democratic politics.

President Obasanjo, the PDP, Nigeria—and the rest of Africa—are best served in the Millennium with a pluralist democratic agenda that, while nurturing the continent's uneven political and economic development i delegative ways in the interim, in the long run also especially mediates the continent's diverse political interests in the incumbent democratic regimes and polities. By embarking upon models of pluralist democracy,[32] the PDP's success as a democratic regime is not in its strategy to control, subvert, and dominate, but in this democratic institution's ability to govern interactively and collaboratively with political associations—including major opposition and peripheral political parties, civil society organizations, populist classes and ethnic nationalities.

Perhaps Nigeria's delegative democracy is indeed learning pluralist democratic politics from practice. Significantly, in his second term, for example, that President Obasanjo invited Niger Delta militants to participate in a conflict resolution dialogue on the Niger Delta question contrasts with the President's strategy in dealing with similar socio-political violence that erupted in Baylesa state within four months of his first term.[33] In that case, Obasanjo's military option to the crisis, which resulted in the sending in of government troops to quell the resistance, caused not only heavy civilian loss of life, but especially drew sharp criticism from the new democratic congress and senate as well as from civil society constituencies—the media, NGOs—on what they deemed the undemocratic posture of the Obasanjo regime's policy.[34] As well, the fact that the Nigerian Labor Congress (NLC) in collaboration with several civil society NGOs—NASU, NECA, LASCO—have through their nationwide strike mobilizations compelled Obasanjo's delegative democracy to reconsider and mutually deliberate alternatives to Washington Consensus economic policies in addressing economic reform in Nigeria without escalating poverty is also a sign of the mediating regime-civil societal relations required for a viable Nigerian democratic politics.[35]

In the long run, I am optimistic about the prospects for Nigerian democratization. The deep interaction effects facilitated by civil societal interest articulation and public policy dialogue between the democratic regime and the country's democratic constituents is nurturing the country's democratic institutions and facilitating their effort in becoming important democratic decisional points in the flow of political power, thereby furthering the democratic process. In essence, the Obasanjo delegative democracy is increasingly being forced to embark upon a constructive role for democracy, allowing participation from diverse constituents in the Nigerian civil society to prioritize complex, national social needs and public goods.

Notes

1 Joseph Winter, "Analysis: Nigeria's One-Party Creep," *BBC News UK edition* 21 (April 2003) <http://newsbbc.co.uk>.

2 Richard Dowden, "Reflections on Democracy in Africa," *African Affairs* 92 (369) (1993), 607–613.

3 Richard Joseph, *State, Conflict, and Democracy in Africa* (Boulder: Lynne Rienner, 1999).

4 Ebere Onwudiwe, "A Reason for Optimism," *Nigerian Guardian* 4 (May 2003).

5 Onwudiwe, "A Reason for Optimism."

6 Until the 1990s, Japan's Liberal Party singularly dominated the country's democracy. Moreover, the only democracy in Africa that did not suffer a democratic reversal or breakdown–Botswana–has through the Botswana Democratic Party (BDP) maintained a dominant party since its democratic establishment while maintaining a thriving liberal democracy. As well, a third national electoral landslide victory for South Africa's African National Congress (ANC) party in 2004 has drawn some scholars and many domestic civil society sectors in the country to observe in the party similar complaints of one-party dominance; yet Freedom House rates the new South African country with the best ratings for a developing world democracy: free.

7 Onwudiwe, "A Reason for Optimism."

8 Funmi Komolafe, Rotimi Ajayi, Victor Ahiuma-Young and Margaret Odeyemi, "Strike: First Phase to Last 4 Days," *Vanguard* 9 (October 2004).

9 Philip Schmitter, "More Liberal, Pre-liberal or Post-liberal," in *The Global Resurgence of Democracy* (Baltimore: Johns Hopkins University Press, 1996), 328-335.

10 Crawford B. Macpherson, *The Real World of Democracy* (Montreal: CBC Enterprises, 1983).

11 Donald Horowitz, "Comparing Democratic Systems," in Larry Diamond and Marc F. Plattner, eds., *The Global Resurgence of Democracy* (Baltimore: Johns Hopkins University Press, 1996), 143-149.

12 Here, I argue that not only political parties, but also other institutions such as the Nigerian military in politics fostered a 'vanguardist' political strategy based on these reasons. See Rita Kiki Edozie, *People Power and Democracy: The Popular Movement Against Military Despotism in Nigeria, 1989-1999* (Trenton: Africa World Press, 2002).

13 Richard Sklar, "Nigeria: Toward a Fourth Republic," in Toyin Falola, *African Politics in Post imperial Times: The Essays of Richard L. Sklar* (Trenton: Africa World Press, 2002).

14 Donald L. Horowitz, *A Democratic South Africa? Constitutional Engineering in a Divided Society* (Berkley: University of California Press, 1991).

15 Richard Joseph, *Democracy and Prebendal Politics in Nigeria* (Cambridge: Cambridge University Press, 1987).

16 John Daniel, Roger Southall, and Morris Szeftel, eds., *Voting for Democracy: Watershed Elections in Contemporary Anglophone Africa* (Vermont: Dartmouth Publishing Company, 1999).

17 Roger Southall, "The State of Democracy in South Africa," *Commonwealth and Comparative Politics* 38 (3) (November 2000).

18 Ebow Godwin, "Togo: Buy Me, I'm Still the Best; Cote d'Ivoire's Descent into Anarchy Has Frightened the Togolese into Thinking of Voting for "the Devil They Know" Ebow Godwin reports from Lome (Around Africa)," *New African*, June 2003.

19 Anthony Butler, *South Africa's Political Futures: the Positive and Negative Implications of One-Party Dominance* (Cape Town: University of Cape Town Press, 2001).

20 Four retired generals provided the top ranking candidates for the presidential race in April, including Obasanjo, Buhari, Nwachukwu, Ojukwu and IBB (Babangida) who is still a powerful political force behind the scenes.

21 Norimitsu Onishi, "Nigeria's President Fears for His Fledgling Democracy," *New York Times*, 8 (February 2002).

22 In guided democracies, society is perceived as an organic whole with common interests. Leaders claim to know what these interests are. Robert Pinkney, *Democracy in the Third World* (Boulder: Lynne Rienner, 2003), 11.

23 Emmanuel Gyimah-Boadi, "Civil Society in Africa," in *Consolidating the Third Wave Democracies* (Baltimore: Johns Hopkins Press, 1997), 278-295.

24 Alexander Hamilton, James Madison and John Jay, *The Federalist Papers* (New York: New American Library, 1961).

25 Ernesto Laclau and Chantal Mouffe, *Hegemony and Socialist Strategy: Towards a Radical Democratic Politics* (Verso Books, 2001).

26 Kidane Mengisteab, "Ethiopia's Ethnic Federalism: 10 Years after," *African Issues* 29 (1/2) (2001).

27 "Rwanda Preparing for Elections: Tightening Control in the Name of Unity," *Human Rights Watch Backgrounder*, 8 (May 2003). <hrw.org/backgrounder/africa/rwanda0503bck.htm>.

28 Northern hegemony, the south-south minorities question, and ethnic zoning were major issues listed for deliberation.

29 Gabriel Packard "Nigeria: 29 Opposition Parties Back One Man Run Against Obasanjo," *IPS/GIN* 11(December 2004).

30 *Democracy's Century* (Freedom House, 2001) <freedomhouse.org>.

31 Larry Diamond, *Developing Democracy: Toward Consolidation* (Cambridge: Cambridge University Press, 1999).

32 Arletta Norvall, "Rethinking Ethnicity: Identification, Hybridity and Democracy," In *Ethnicity and Nationalism in Africa: Constructivist Reflections and Contemporary Politics* (New York: St. Martins Press, 1999), 91-93. Wamba-Dia-Wamba in CODESRIA Bulletin, 1994.

33 "Why I Held Talks with Dokubo- Obasanjo," *Vanguard* 1 (October 2004).

34 "Why I Held Talks," *Vanguard*.

35 "Strike: First Phase to Last 4 Days," *Vanguard*, 9 (October 2004).

CHAPTER SIX

Identity, Discrimination, and Conflict Among Ethnic 'Minorities at Risk' in the Modern World

Clayton D. Peoples

Over ten million people have been displaced by discrimination or mistreatment related to their ethnic identity since 1990; and since 1945, over sixty million people have died worldwide in ethnic conflicts.[1] These staggering figures highlight the importance of studying ethnic identity, discrimination, and conflict in the modern world to better understand what factors are most salient in leading to mistreatment and violence.

Researchers in the Minorities at Risk (MAR) project have identified over 200 ethnic minority groups throughout the world—numbering around one billion in total population—who are presently at risk of mistreatment and potential violent attack in their respective societies. Past work using MAR data suggests that discrimination may be more important than ethnic identity in predicting ethnic conflict,[2] but more research is needed to parse out these relationships. In this paper, I use data from Phase III of the MAR project[3] to explore more deeply the relationships between identity, discrimination, and conflict among these 200-plus ethnic groups.

Minorities at Risk Project: History and Data

The MAR project began in 1986 with the initial work of Ted Robert Gurr and colleagues. With funding from the National Science Foundation and the U.S. Institute of Peace, the MAR project set out o gather qualitative and quantitative information on ethnic conflicts hroughout the world—and to compile information on the specific ethnic ninority groups who are either engaged in conflict or are at risk of experiencing mistreatment or violent conflict. This marked an important step forward in ethnic conflict research given that most data in existence prior to the project's inception were limited to just a few cases. The MAR data were first published in 1993 ('Phase I') in concert with the publication of "Minorities at Risk: A Global View of Ethnopolitical Conflicts," the first major work coming out the project.

Phase I of the MAR project included data on 227 at-risk ethnic minorities worldwide. By Phase III, which was released in 1999, this number had grown to 275 active at-risk ethnic minority groups globally. The Phase III data track the conditions and experiences of these 275 active groups decennially from the 1940s through the 1980s, biennially from 1990 to 1995, and annually after 1995. The data include variables measuring group distinctiveness, identity strength, experience of discrimination, and engagement in conflict, among other things. Table 6.1 lists the variables I use in this paper, describes how I code them, and provides their basic descriptive statistics. Sixteen of the 275 active groups in the data have a missing value on one of my variables, leaving 259 groups for analyses (the sixteen groups were generally representative of the other groups on the measures, and were from a variety of regions of the world, minimizing the risk of selection bias).

Table 6.1. Variables Used in Analyses

Variables	Description	N	Mean	St. Dev.
Ethnic Identity Strength	Strength of the group's ethnic identity, rescaled 0 to 100	259	45.888	21.692
National Distinctiveness	Dummy: 1 = group distinct from dominant group in national background	259	.853	.355
Cultural Distinctiveness	Dummy: 1 = group distinct from dominant group in cultural practices	259	.591	.493
Language Distinctiveness	Dummy: 1 = group distinct from dominant group in language spoken	259	.822	.383
Religious Distinctiveness	Dummy: 1 = group distinct from dominant group in religious affiliation	259	.548	.499
Appearance Restrictions	Dummy: 1 = group faces restrictions on appearance or behavior, 1994	259	.077	.268
Event Restrictions	Dummy: 1 = group faces restrictions on cultural events, 1994	259	.100	.301
Language Restrictions	Dummy: 1 = group faces restrictions on language use, 1994	259	.174	.380
Religious Restrictions	Dummy: 1 = group faces restrictions on religious practices, 1994	259	.127	.334
Economic Restrictions	Dummy: 1 = group faces restric-	259	.097	.296

	tions on economic activities, 1994			
Political Restrictions	Dummy: 1 = group faces restrictions on political activities, 1994	259	.193	.396
Democratization Score	Democracy score (Bollen 1998) in 1994 from Paxton (2002), scaled 0 to 100	259	59.569	31.991
Violent Interethnic Conflict	Dummy: 1 = group engaged in violent conflict with others sometime 1994–98	259	.394	.490

Ethnic Identity: What It Means, Its Predictors

Ethnic identity is an important factor distinguishing group boundaries. Groups must have at least some recognizable identity setting them apart from other groups to constitute a unique ethnicity. Of course, ethnic identity can take on different meanings depending on whose view is involved: the in-group or the out-group. Moreover, the bases for ethnic identity may vary considerably across groups and societies. As such, ethnic identity strength depends on both the views of those involved and the bases of identity. Presumably, ethnic identity is stronger when the in-group and out-group view themselves and one another as distinct, separate ethnicities. Additionally, ethnic identity is likely stronger when there are multiple bases for said distinction, such as distinctive national heritages, cultural practices, language groups, religious beliefs, etc.

The MAR dataset provides a key indicator of ethnic identity strength. The indicator is similar to the concept of categoriness,[4] tapping the extent to which the ethnic group is a distinct, self-identifying ethnicity. For my analyses, I rescale the variable such that the possible scores range 0–100 (from the original scale of 4–20). The average ethnic identity strength among the 259 minority groups under study is 45.9 (45.888 rounded up), and the distribution of scores is normal. There is some variation, however, in ethnic identity strength across different regions of the world. The averages across different regions range from 39.5 among minorities in Sub-Saharan Africa to 54.6 in Latin America and the Caribbean. The averages for groups in other regions of the world are generally clustered around the overall average, and include 40.6 in Western Democracies and Japan, 43.6 in Northern Africa and the Middle East, 48.8 in Asia, and 49.9 in Eastern Europe and Russia.

To explore the ethnic identity strength variable in more depth, I conduct ordinary least squares (OLS) regression analysis to identify its key predictors. Table 6.2 presents the results of the regression model. Not surprisingly, the distinctiveness of the group relative to other groups in their society is an important predictor of ethnic identity strength. Group national distinctiveness, cultural distinctiveness, language distinctiveness, and religious distinctiveness are all statistically significant in the regression model. In fact, these four variables account for over half of the variation in ethnic identity strength, as indicated by the 0.524 adjusted model R^2, suggesting the ethnic identity strength variable is largely reflecting these important distinctions.

Table 6.2. Unstandardized Coefficients, Standard Errors, and Standardized Coefficients from Ordinary Least Squares (OLS) Regression of Ethnic Identity Strength on Various Measures of Ethnic Group Distinctiveness

	Ethnic Identity Strength		
	Unstandardized Coefficients	Standard Errors	Standardized Coefficients
National Distinctiveness	8.723***	2.815	0.143
Cultural Distinctiveness	20.501***	1.954	0.466
Language Distinctiveness	12.866***	2.626	0.227
Religious Distinctiveness	15.272***	1.925	0.351
Adjusted R^2	0.524		
N	0 259		

* $p < .05$, ** $p < 0.01$, *** $p < 0.001$ (one-tailed tests)

As the results in Table 6.2 show, all of the measures of distinctiveness are significantly related to ethnic identity strength at the .001 level, suggesting less than one in one thousand probability that the relationships are a product of mere chance. The results also suggest that while all of the variables are significant predictors of ethnic identity strength, cultural distinctiveness is the strongest predictor. This is demonstrated by the fact that cultural distinctiveness exhibits the largest standardized coefficient among all the variables. This is further illuminated by the readily interpretable unstandardized effect it has on ethnic identity strength: ethnic groups that are culturally distinct from other groups in their society are, on average, 20.5 points higher in ethnic identity strength than groups that are not culturally distinct from other groups. No other variable exhibits such a pronounced unstandardized effect on ethnic identity strength.

A closer look at the cultural distinctiveness variable reveals that it is similar to ethnic identity strength in its distribution across groups around the world. While 59.1% of the 259 ethnic minorities analyzed exhibit cultural practices and norms distinct from other groups in their respective societies, this varies across different global regions. The regional percentages range from 43.3% in Sub-Saharan Africa to 72.4% in Latin America and the Caribbean. Other percentages include 60.3% in Eastern Europe and Russia, 60.9% in Northern Africa and the Middle East, 63.3% in Western Democracies and Japan, and 67.3% in Asia. So again, just as with ethnic identity strength, the lowest levels are among ethnic minorities in Sub-Saharan Africa, the highest are among groups in Latin America and the Caribbean, and groups in other regions are generally clustered around the average.

The preceding analysis suggests that the indicator of ethnic identity strength in the MAR dataset taps the sorts of factors one would imagine are important in ethnic identity—namely, group distinctiveness indexes. The national distinctiveness of a group, their cultural distinctiveness, language distinctiveness, and religious distinctiveness are all important predictors of ethnic identity. The strongest predictor, as one might predict, is cultural distinctiveness. Moreover, both ethnic identity strength and cultural distinctiveness are similarly distributed across minority groups in different regions throughout the globe. I therefore feel confident that this MAR variable adequately measures what it is supposed to: ethnic identity. I now proceed to examine its relationships with discrimination and conflict.

Discrimination: Type and Importance

In this paper I define discrimination as government-enacted policies restricting members of an ethnic group from access to certain valued goods, services, activities, or opportunities. Such restrictions are in place in many countries throughout the world today.[5] There are different general types of discrimination: (1) cultural discrimination, (2) economic discrimination, and (3) political discrimination.[6] Within each of these types of discrimination, then, are a number of more specific restrictions.

Cultural discrimination is a very broad type of discrimination that can encompass many things related to ethnic identity, and is therefore examined closely in this paper. Cultural discrimination consists of restrictions on some of the same dimensions that make ethnic groups distinct. For instance, some policies of cultural discrimination restrict the ability of a group to behave or appear in a certain way relating to their national background or ethnicity. Other policies of cultural discrimination restrict a group from engaging in cultural events or festivals. Some policies restrict a group from using a particular language in certain settings. Other policies restrict a group from specific religious practices.

In terms of prevalence of cultural discrimination, thankfully a relatively small percentage of minority groups in the MAR dataset face cultural restrictions. Nonetheless, a certain percentage of groups do face such restrictions, which likely has consequences. I use variables tracking discrimination in 1994 as the measures of discrimination in my analyses (the inter-year correlations are above .90, suggesting most years reflect the same general patterns). Approximately 7.7% of minority groups worldwide face restrictions on their appearance in 1994; roughly 10.0% of groups encounter restrictions on cultural events or activities; around 17.4% of minority groups experience restrictions on language use; and about 12.7% of minority groups worldwide face restrictions on their religious practices. But what about economic and political discrimination?

Economic and political discrimination fortunately afflict a similarly small percentage of minority groups worldwide. It is nonetheless a problem that still affects some. Around 9.7% of ethnic minorities in the MAR data set experience economic discrimination, which can include restrictions on land ownership, employment in certain sectors, loans, business opportunities, etc. A larger percentage of groups face political discrimination. Roughly 19.3% of minorities worldwide are subjected to policies of political discrimination, including restrictions on the right to hold office, the right to judicial proceedings, free speech, and the right to vote, among other things.

Distinguishing between cultural, economic, and political discrimination is important because these discriminatory types likely differ in terms of their ineluctability and cumulativeness, which could impact the degree to which they influence interethnic conflict. Cultural discrimination is likely the least ineluctable and cumulative of the three types. Economic discrimination is probably more ineluctable and more cumulative, while political discrimination is likely the most ineluctable and most cumulative in impact.

Cultural discrimination can likely be evaded without significant difficulty. Take, for instance, discriminatory policies placing a restriction on speaking a particular language. While such a restriction can be enforced in the public sphere, it cannot be enforced very easily in the private sphere. As such, ethnic groups are generally free to use the language of their choosing when communicating with family members at home or in other private venues.

Economic discrimination can also be evaded. While we typically think of economic exchange as a more public phenomenon, a significant amount of exchange occurs outside public view. This is particularly true in less developed countries, where significant proportions of their economies are informal, driven by underground markets and exchanges that are never officially reported to governmental agencies.[7] So, for instance, discriminatory policies mandating that certain groups be charged higher rates of interest on loans can be sidestepped through borrowing funds from relatives and fellow ethnic community members. This is a particularly common occurrence among ethnic minorities in certain countries. Within ethnic enclaves in some countries, much business (including borrowing) occurs behind closed doors and goes unreported.[8]

Political discrimination cannot be easily evaded. Because political discrimination places restrictions on political activities, which are very much in the public sphere of life, circumventing these restrictions is very difficult. Take, for instance, policies prohibiting members of a given ethnic group from being a candidate for political office. Unless a person from that ethnic group could convince everyone that he or she is not, in actuality, a member of that group, the person could not run for office. The same holds for other types of political restrictions, such as restrictions on voting rights. Because voting typically involves confirming one's identity and eligibility to vote before actually engaging in the act of voting, members of an ethnic group prohibited from voting would have great difficulty slipping through these checks. Inability to participate in the political process, then, could have a cumulative effect. Ethnic groups who face political restrictions cannot challenge the policies that discriminate against them culturally or economically. As such, political discrimination is highly ineluctable, cumulative in its impact, and, as a result, is generally the most pervasive type of discrimination.

Bringing the discussion back to ethnic identity strength, given that discrimination places restrictions on a group based on their ethnicity it may follow that these restrictions are correlated with ethnic identity strength. This could be especially true of cultural discrimination, which specifically seeks to restrict groups from engaging in the practices or activities that make them unique as an ethnicity. To assess the extent to which discrimination /restrictions are correlated with ethnic identity strength, I perform correlation analysis. Table 6.3 presents the results of the correlations.

Table 6.3. Correlation Coefficients of Ethnic Identity Strength with Different Types of Discrimination/Restrictions

	Ethnic Identity Strength	
	Pearson r	N
Cultural Discrimination		
Appearance Restrictions	.175**	259
Event Restrictions	.128*	259
Language Restrictions	.154**	259
Religious Restrictions	.114*	259
Economic Discrimination		
Economic Restrictions	.119*	259
Political Discrimination		
Political Restrictions	-.048	259

* p < .05 , ** p < .01, *** p < .001 (one-tailed tests)

The results in Table 6.3 show that ethnic identity strength is significantly correlated in a positive direction with cultural discrimination. This means that the stronger an ethnic minority group's identity, the more likely the group will experience some form of cultural discrimination. Specifically, ethnic identity strength has a significant positive correlation with all the forms of cultural discrimination analyzed: appearance restrictions, event restrictions, language restrictions, and religious restrictions. Ethnic identity strength is most strongly correlated with appearance restrictions and language restrictions; it is less strongly correlated with event restrictions and religious restrictions.

In terms of economic discrimination and political discrimination, the findings are mixed. Ethnic identity strength is significantly correlated in a positive direction with economic discrimination, just as it was with cultural discrimination. The stronger an ethnic minority group's identity, the more likely the group will face restrictions on their economic activities. Ethnic identity strength is not, however, significantly correlated with political discrimination. Moreover, the coefficient is negative, suggesting that if there is any relationship, it is as follows: the stronger an ethnic minority group's identity, the less likely the group will experience restrictions on their political freedoms.

The findings in Table 6.3 paint an interesting picture. They suggest that ethnic identity likely forms a significant basis for the enactment of cultural and economic discrimination against a group, but ethnic identity does not form a significant basis for the enactment of political discrimination—in fact, ethnic identity strength may decrease the likelihood of political restrictions. One possible explanation is that group identity strength may (a) make a group a target of discrimination, but may also (b) serve as a source of political strength for the group when necessary to fight political discrimination. It may be that those in control of a government tend to enact policies of discrimination against ethnic minority groups who have strong, distinctive identities. In the case of cultural or economic discrimination, the groups targeted may not fight the policies, perhaps because many cultural and economic restrictions can be evaded in the private sphere. But when faced with a situation in which the government attempts to enact policies of political discrimination against them, members of strong-identity minority groups may mobilize politically and avert the attempted policy enactment. In other words, while ethnic identity strength may make groups a target of discrimination, it may also protect them against the most pervasive type of discrimination—political discrimination. This is important, as research suggests that political discrimination is a highly salient predictor of certain types of ethnic conflict.[9]

Conflict: Its Patterns, Roots, and Relationships

The term "ethnic conflict" can encapsulate a number of different types of conflict. Ethnic conflict can vary not only in terms of who is involved or targeted; it can also vary in terms of severity. As far as who is involved or targeted in an ethnic conflict, there are two general scenarios: mobilization against the state, or interethnic conflict not targeting the state. In terms of severity, ethnic conflict can range from nonviolent protests to violence involving fatalities. In this paper, I focus my attention on interethnic conflict that involves violence. The reason why I choose to examine interethnic conflict as opposed to mobilization against the state is to provide the most conservative analysis possible. Given that political discrimination is one of my main predictors, examining mobilization against the state may result in an artificially inflated effect of political discrimination since we should expect groups experiencing political discrimination to target the state in their collective actions. The reason why I focus on violent interethnic conflict as opposed to nonviolent activities is that violent conflict is arguably more serious given it involves loss of life, and, thus, is more critical to study.

Based on the data from the MAR dataset on violent interethnic conflict from 1994 to 1998 (I include all five years since presumably discrimination in 1994 could have lagging effect on conflict as far out as five years), around 39.4% of at-risk ethnic minority groups worldwide were involved in violent interethnic conflict at some point during the five-year period. This percentage varies across different regions of the world, though, as did the ethnic identity strength numbers. Groups in two regions exhibit percentages well above the global average: 57.7% of minorities in Asia were involved in violent interethnic conflict at some point 1994-98, and 44.8% of minorities in Sub-Saharan African were engaged in violent interethnic conflict some time during the same period. All other groups fall below the global average: 34.5% of minorities in Eastern Europe and Russia engaged in violent interethnic conflict during the period, 30.0% of groups in Western Democracies and Japan, 27.6% of groups in Latin America and the Caribbean, and 21.7% of groups in North Africa and the Middle East. Now that ethnic conflict is defined and its prevalence across the world is clear, it is worth discussing the roots of conflict.

The conflict paradigm in sociology lends useful insights into conflict between groups. According to this paradigm, the roots of many intergroup conflicts are objective inequalities between groups—regardless of the group type (class groups, ethnic groups, etc.). More recent work within sociology, however, has begun to also consider the role of subjective perceptions of inequality in creating conflict. For instance, distributive justice research[10] and new ethnic competition research[11] both suggest that subjective inequality is important. According to this new work, groups who subjectively perceive that they are disadvantaged are most likely to ultimately engage in conflict. The degree to which objective and subjective inequality underlie ethnic conflict depends on which form of ethnic conflict is studied—mass mobilization against the state or interethnic conflict.

Research on social movements suggests that inequality (or 'relative deprivation/ structural strain' in the movements literature) may be a necessary, but not sufficient, condition leading to mass mobilization against the state. Drawing on evidence from a number of major movements, this work suggests that political opportunities and resource mobilization are key factors that may explain the emergence of mass mobilization against the state better than inequality alone.[12] But what about mobilization that is less well-organized? Social movements, according to most standard definitions, are organized collectivities working together toward some goal—often a specific policy goal or change in the political power structure.[13] This fits mass mobilization against the state quite well.

But interethnic conflict is frequently less organized; interethnic conflict is generally characterized by sporadic violence, not targeting the state directly (as noted earlier in my definition), that may in fact be more likely when resources are scarce and political opportunity is restricted. This suggests that the objective and subjective inequalities so central to the conflict perspective are vital to explaining the onset of interethnic conflict.

Much of the work in sociology dealing with the connection between inequality and interethnic conflict falls within the ethnic competition literature.[14] This important body of work shows that there is a key relationship between the inequality emerging from competition over desired resources and the development of interethnic conflict. While this work tends to focus on economic competition, recent research suggests that political competition is important in interethnic conflict as well.[15] What may be most important, though, is not political competition per se, but, instead, the degree to which political competition is perceived as unjust.

Relatively recent work in the competition literature shows that competition needs to be perceived as unjust to create interethnic conflict. For instance, in one study of ethnic conflicts in Quebec, researchers demonstrate that conflict is most likely to occur when a group perceives that other groups are violating the rules of fairness in competition.[16] Applied to political competition, this suggests that interethnic conflict is most likely in situations where political competition is perceived to be unjust. Which situations would be perceived in this manner? Situations of political discrimination would most likely be perceived as very unjust, potentially resulting in interethnic conflict. This is confirmed in recent research showing that political discrimination is one of the most salient factors predicting interethnic conflict—ethnic groups who encounter policies of political discrimination are much more likely to be involved in interethnic conflict than groups who do not encounter such policies.[17] In fact, political discrimination is stronger in its impact on interethnic conflict than cultural or economic discrimination. This makes sense in light of the discussion in the last section about how these types of discrimination differ. Given that political discrimination is generally the most pervasive type of discrimination, it logically follows that it would be the most salient type of discrimination in the precipitation of interethnic conflict.

In the next analysis, I explore the relationship between ethnic identity strength, different types of discrimination, and interethnic conflict, controlling for country-level factors (namely democracy). Prior work suggests that ethnic identity strength may not be as important in interethnic conflict as discrimination,[18] so this next analysis will examine whether or not this is true. I use logistic regression in this analysis as opposed to OLS regression because the dependent variable, interethnic conflict, is coded as a dichotomous dummy variable with values 1 and 0. Table 6.4 presents the findings of this logistic regression. In the following paragraphs, I interpret the results. I then proceed to discuss the meaning of the results (in combination with results from earlier tables) for better understanding the relationships among ethnic identity, discrimination, and interethnic conflict.

Table 6.4. Unstandardized Coefficients, Standard Errors, and Odds Ratio Scores from Logistic Regression of Violent Interethnic Conflict on Ethnic Identity, Discrimination/Restrictions, and Country-Level Control Variable

	Violent Interethnic Conflict		
	Unstandardized Coefficients	Standard Errors	Odds Ratios
Ethnic Identity			
Ethnic Identity Strength	0.001	0.006	1.001
Cultural Discrimination			
Appearance Restrictions	-0.081	0.534	0.922
Event Restrictions	1.128*	0.611	3.088
Language Restrictions	-0.322	0.392	0.725
Religious Restrictions	-1.069	0.545	0.343
Economic Discrimination			
Economic Restrictions	-0.254	0.519	0.776
Political Discrimination			
Political Restrictions	1.062**	.391	2.891
Country-Level Control			
Democracy	-0.001	0.004	0.999
N	259		

* p < 0.05, ** p < 0.01, *** p < 0.001 (one-tailed tests)

The results in Table 6.4 show that two of the eight variables have a significant effect on the likelihood of violent interethnic conflict: event restrictions (one of four cultural discrimination variables) and political restrictions (the political discrimination variable). Ethnic minority groups in the MAR dataset who experience restrictions on their ability to hold important cultural events and activities are significantly more likely to engage in interethnic conflict than groups who do not face similar restrictions. The odds ratio score suggests that these groups are in fact around two times (3.088 minus 1 rounded to the nearest whole number) more likely to engage in conflict than groups not experiencing events restrictions. In the case of political restrictions, the relationship is similar: groups who face political restrictions are significantly more likely than groups not facing political restrictions to be involved in interethnic conflict. And again, these groups are around two times more likely to engage in conflict than groups not encountering political restrictions. Overall, these findings suggest that cultural discrimination may bear some relationship with interethnic conflict, but this depends on which specific restrictive policy is examined; economic discrimination has no relationship with conflict; and political discrimination has a strong relationship.

Importantly, the results in Table 6.4 show no significant relationship between ethnic identity strength and interethnic conflict. In fact, the coefficient is very near to 0, suggesting virtually no relationship at all. Groups with stronger ethnic identities are neither more nor less likely than groups with weak identities to engage in interethnic conflict. This is an interesting finding. In the very least, it suggests that contrary to the notion that strong ethnic identity increases the odds of conflict, strong ethnic identity does not make a group more likely to engage in conflict. But why is this? Based on the findings from this analysis and earlier analyses in this paper, I speculate that ethnic identity strength helps protect a group against political discrimination (or in the very least, it does not increase the odds of experiencing political discrimination), and, thus, identity does not increase the odds of conflict given that political discrimination seems to be the key path to interethnic conflict. Additionally, while ethnic identity strength does not protect a group against cultural or economic discrimination—in fact, it is correlated with these types of discrimination, as shown earlier in Table 6.3—since these types of discrimination generally do not increase the odds of conflict (with the lone exception of events restrictions within the broader umbrella of cultural discrimination), again ethnic identity strength fails to increase the risk of conflict via these avenues.

Conclusions

In this paper, I set out to explore the relationships among ethnic identity strength, discrimination, and violent interethnic conflict using data from the MAR project on over 200 ethnic "minorities at risk" throughout the world. My findings show that ethnic identity strength is, as one might expect, largely a function of group distinctiveness. Groups who are distinctive in terms of national background, culture, language, and religion exhibit stronger ethnic identity than groups less distinctive in these realms. Ethnic identity strength is significantly correlated with the experience of cultural and economic discrimination such that the stronger a groups' identity, the more likely they are to face cultural or economic discrimination. The same is not true, however, of political discrimination, as groups with stronger identities may be less likely to encounter political discrimination. This, then, likely has importance for the relationship between ethnic identity strength and violent interethnic conflict. There is no statistically significantly relationship between ethnic identity strength and conflict, but there is a significant relationship between political discrimination and conflict whereby groups experiencing political discrimination are significantly more likely to engage in conflict than groups not experiencing political discrimination. It may be, then, that since ethnic identity strength may serve as a protection against political discrimination, it also serves as a protection against engagement in conflict since political discrimination appears to be the key path leading to violent interethnic conflict. My findings therefore shed a positive light on ethnic identity in that strong identity does not increase the odds of interethnic conflict, contrary to the concerns of some, suggesting that strong ethnic identification should not automatically be viewed as a risk factor for intergroup violence.

Notes

1   Wilma A. Dunaway, "Ethnic Conflict in the Modern World-System: The Dialectics of Counter-Hegemonic Resistance in an Age of Transition." *Journal of World Systems Research* 9 (2003), 26.

2   Ted Robert Gurr, *Minorities at Risk: A Global View of Ethnopolitical Conflict* (Washington, D.C.: United States Institute of Peace Press, 1993). Clayton D. Peoples, "How Discriminatory Policies Impact Interethnic Violence: A Cross-National, Group-Level Analysis," *International Journal of Sociology* 34 (2004), 71–96.

3   Minorities at Risk Project, *Minorities at Risk Dataset*, version MARv899 (College Park, MD: Center for International Development and Conflict Management, University of Maryland, 1999).

4   Charles Tilly, *From Mobilization to Revolution* (Reading, MA: Addison-Wesley, 1978).

5   Donald L. Horowitz, *Ethnic Groups in Conflict* (Berkeley, CA: University of California Press, 1985).

6   Ted Robert Gurr and Barbara Harff, *Ethnic Conflict in World Politics* (Boulder, CO: Westview Press, 1994).

7   Thomas Bailey and Roger Waldinger, "Primary, Secondary, and Enclave Labor Markets: A Training System Approach," *American Sociological Review* 56 (1991), 432–45.

8   Alejandro Portes and Alex Stepick, "Unwelcome Immigrants: The Labor Market Experiences of 1980 [Mariel] Cuban and Haitian Refugees in South Florida," *American Sociological Review* 50 (1985), 493–514.

9   Peoples, "How Discriminatory Policies Impact Interethnic Violence."

10   Guillermina Jasso, "Analyzing Conflict Severity: Predictions of Distributive Justice Theory," *Social Justice Research* 6 (1993), 357–82.

11   Lawrence Bobo and Vincent L. Hutchings. "Perceptions of Racial Competition in a Multiracial Setting," *American Sociological Review* 61 (1996), 951–72.

12   Steve Barkan, "Legal Control of the Civil Rights Movement," *American Sociological Review* 49 (1984), 552–65. J. Craig Jenkins and Charles Perrow, "Insurgency of the Powerless," *American Sociological Review* 42 (1977), 249–68. Doug McAdam, *Political Process and the Development of Black Insurgency, 1930–70* (Chicago, IL: University of Chicago Press, 1982). John McCarthy and Mayer N. Zald, "Resource Mobilization and Social Movements: A Partial Theory," *American Journal of Sociology* 82 (1977), 1212–41. David S. Meyer and Suzanne Staggenborg, "Movements, Countermovements, and the Structure of Political Opportunity," *American Journal of Sociology* 101 (1996), 1628–60. Anthony Oberschall

Social Conflict and Social Movements (Englewood Cliffs, NJ: Prentice-Hall, 1973). Charles Tilly, "To Explain Political Process," *American Journal of Sociology* 100 (1995), 1594-1610.

13 J. Craig Jenkins and William Form, "Social Movements and Social Change," in Thomas Janoski, Robert Alford, Alexander Hicks and Mildred Schwartz, eds., *The Handbook of Political Sociology* (New York: Cambridge University Press, 2005), 1447.

14 B. E. Aguirre, Rogelio Saenz, and Sean-Shong Hwang, "Discrimination and the Assimilation and Ethnic Competition Perspectives," *Social Science Quarterly* 70 (1989), 594-606. E. M. Beck, "Guess Who's Coming to Town: White Supremacy, Ethnic Competition, and Social Change," *Sociological Focus* 33 (2000), 153-74. Sean-Shong Hwang and Steve H. Murdock, "Ethnic Enclosure or Ethnic Competition: Ethnic Identification among Hispanics in Texas," *The Sociological Quarterly* 32 (1991), 469-76. Susan Olzak, *The Dynamics of Ethnic Competition and Conflict* (Stanford, CA: Stanford University Press, 1992).

15 Rima Wilkes and Dina G. Okamoto, "Ethnic Competition and Mobilization by Minorities at Risk," *Nationalism and Ethnic Politics* 8 (2002), 1-23.

16 Sarah Belanger and Maurice Pinard, "Ethnic Movements and the Competition Model: Some Missing Links," *American Sociological Review* 56 (1991), 446-57.

17 Peoples, "How Discriminatory Policies Impact Interethnic Violence."

18 Gurr, *Minorities at Risk*. Peoples, "How Discriminatory Policies Impact Interethnic Violence."

Ethnicity in Liberia and Democratic Governance

Edward Lama Wonkeryor

In Liberia, a nation whose population consists of 16 distinct groups, ethnicity has shaped the structure and development of its political, social, and cultural institutions for its entire history. While ethnic diversity has enhanced the lives of its 3.5 million people, differences between ethnic groups also have fostered both minor tensions and major warfare. In the latter 20th and early 21st centuries and like other societies with heterogeneous populations, ethnic conflict at its worse destroyed or nearly destroyed Liberia's government, infrastructure, academic institutions, corporations and small businesses, and other elements. This conflict led to the death or displacement of many Liberians based on their ethnic origin. After its civil war ended with the simultaneous removal of its president by foreign intervention in 2003, Liberia renewed its commitment to democratic governance that would overcome its negative history of ethnicity.

Societies in Africa, Eastern Europe, Latin America, Asia, and elsewhere in the world have witnessed and continue to experience the disastrous consequences of ethnicity gone awry. In his 1998 essay, Bruce J. Berman writes that, "Ethnicity is the product of a continuing historical process, always simultaneously old and new, grounded in the past and perpetually in creation."[1] He argues further that in African societies:

> Colonial states were grounded in the alliances with local 'Big Men', incorporating ethnically-defined administrative units linked to the local population by incorporation of pre-colonial patron-client relations. This was reinforced by European assumptions of neatly bounded and culturally homogenous 'tribes' and a bureaucratic preoccupation with demarcating, classifying and counting subject populations, as well

as by the activities of missionaries and anthropologists. African ethnic invention emerged through internal struggles over moral economy and political legitimacy tied to the definition of ethnic communities—moral ethnicity; and external conflicts over differential access to the resources of modernity and economic accumulation—political tribalism. Ethnicities were, in particular, the creations of elites seeking the basis for a conservative modernization.[2]

Liberians and other Africans see the solution to the tribulations of ethnicity in democratic governance. For Professor Okwudiba Mnoli, democratic governance is the process by which an elected government provides adequate "regular constitutional opportunities for peaceful competition for political power to different groups without excluding any significant sector of the population."[3] Hinged on this perspective, the concern that is openly proclaimed today is democracy, stated as a precondition for the observance of human rights. This observance may take a variety of forms. Hence, J. J. Linz notes that we consider a government democratic if it supplies regular constitutional opportunities for peaceful competition for political power to different groups without excluding any significant sector of the population by force.[4] R. A. Dahl suggests that modern democratic regimes are distinguished by the existence, legality and legitimacy of a variety of organizations and associations that are relatively independent in relation to the government and to one another.[5] Contextually, democracy not only implies institutions guaranteeing freedom of political choice, it also requires the pre-existence of social interests that can be represented.

For Larry Diamond et al., democracy is a system of government that meets three essential conditions:

1) meaningful and extensive competition among individuals and organized groups, especially political parties, for effective positions of governmental power at regular intervals, and excluding the use of force;

2) a highly inclusive level of political participation in the selection of leaders and policies, at least through regular free, fair and peaceful elections;

3) a high level of civil and political liberties.[6]

All four authors articulate that contemporary democratic theories emphasize a multiparty political electoral system, the institutionalization of the opposition, including the respect for its role, and the utilization of the principle of political accountability, specifically through the electoral process. In view of this, Guy Hermet contends that a democratic regime may be seen as a political system that offers to all its citizens the regular and constitutional possibility of replacing the government by peaceful means should they decide to do so by a sufficient majority. It allows them to avail themselves of non-violent, freely established parties and associations of their choice, with none debarred, with a view to playing their roles as citizens, and which allows them in practice to enjoy really all the commonly accepted civic rights, safeguarded by legal guarantees written into a body of law that has higher authority than the government and is submitted in the event of complaints to a judicial organ which operates independently and exclusively of government's involvement. From this perspective, democracy cannot exist if a public sphere or political society (civil society) is not recognized.[7]

Hermet argues that the proliferation of democracy is the result of struggles by committed individuals and organizations, with successes in one part of the globe affecting those in other areas. It is clear, for example, that the struggle for democracy in Eastern Europe greatly influenced the success of the struggle in Africa for democracy. It represents the highest achievement of humanity so far in its struggle for progress in social and political relations.

Liberia's founders, who were Africans formerly enslaved in the United States, knew what democratic governance should be and they embraced the American version. But the actions of government exacerbated ethnic tensions and made ethnicity a problem, leading to the emergence of ethnic nationalism. From its founding each administration made public policies that favored the Americo-Liberians and maltreated the indigenous African population. These actions were contrary to the best tenets of the American version of democracy. While the U.S. version of democracy—a pure, unfettered democracy—was a viable form of government for Liberia,[8] but the framers of the Declaration of Independence and the Constitution did not intend to include the poor, the landless, African Americans, Native Americans, women, or any other group that was not just like them-white males. Likewise Liberia's earliest inequities between ethnic groups stemmed from the founder's engaging in similar behavior. The freed Africans who emigrated from America starting in 1821 saw a democracy that created inequality among people in the United States. Although liberated from bondage, the settlers had limited education and did not fully understand the function and constraints of democracy. A lack of autonomy also hampered their ability to implement the nuances of democratic governance in Liberia. Hence, they replicated the less than ideal system of democratic governance of 19th century America in Liberia and used ethnicity as the measure of an individual's worth and ability to access democracy.

Manipulation of ethnicity has contributed to Liberia's national identity problem and created a vitriolic enmity between the ethnic groups and between the free Africans and the ethnic groups during successive administrations. The challenge that the democratically elected government of President Ellen Johnson Sirleaf (2005) faces is a need to promote ethnic harmony and Liberian national identity as precursors to fostering effective democratic governance. Finding this solution is essential to Liberia's economic development, political reforms and full recovery from civil war.

American Acculturation and Its Effect
on Ethnicity in Liberia

Freed Africans who founded Liberia embraced America's democracy by adopting a constitution modeled on the U.S. constitution and achieved the nation's independence in 1847. The earliest reference to the settlers as Americans is to be found in the Dukor Contract, the document that transferred the Dukor or Monrovia region to the American Colonization Society. The Dukor Contract states, among others, that as "certain persons/citizens of the United States of America" have expressed the desire to settle on the Western Coast of Africa, they have accordingly "instructed Captain Robert F. Stockton and Eli Ayres with full powers to treat with and purchase land" for their settlement. Guannu provides an example that, when Liberia affixed her signature to the Brussels Convention of 1890, which, among other things, forbade the sale of firearms and other weapons to black Africans, the Liberian Legislature immediately enacted a clarifying law. In the words of Guannu, the clarifying law states that:

> Any persons violating Articles 9 and 10 of the Brussels Conference of 1890 shall be imprisoned for a term of one year with hard labor, and shall be fined the sum of five hundred dollars and the arms and ammunition in the possession of such person shall be confiscated by Government. But nothing in this section shall prevent the civilize inhabitants [Americo-Liberians] of this Republic from carrying arms as provided in the Constitution of Liberia.[9]

Between 1822 and 1980, the settlers and their descendants along with elites from the indigenous ethnic groups and other naturalized Liberians referred to themselves as Americo-Liberians. Determined to perpetuate hegemony over the Liberian political system, they used the expression "Americo-Liberian" to establish their perceived superiority to other Liberians. The first Africans from the United States and the Caribbean arrived on the *Nautilus* in March 1821. They were four in number. The next group of 15 came with Jehudi Ashmun on the *Strong* in 1822. Between 1822 and 1904, 17,239 persons with origins in the United States and Barbados immigrated to Liberia.[10] Joseph Saye Guannu (1989) maintains that "In Liberian history the term "Americo-Liberian" refers to the settlers who came from North America and constituted the upper echelon of the ruling elite in the Liberian political kingdom."[11] He went on to argue that this is the elite which, according to one school of thought in Liberian politics, was dislodged in the coup of April 1980. Historically, the nomenclature is misleading, as no Liberian could have been politically an American at least before 1868, when the Fourteenth Amendment to the United States Constitution was ratified. The amendment provided, among others, that "all persons born or naturalized in the United

States, and subject to the jurisdiction thereof, are citizens of the United States and of the state wherein they reside."[12]

In the Liberian context, the term "Congo" also refers to Liberians who were not of indigenous ethnic background. Historically the "Congoes" were descendants of Congolese who arrived in Liberia as people who were recaptives taken from slave ships. Perhaps the earliest of this group, a majority who were of Congolese origin, arrived in Liberia on the *Pons* in 1845. Their number was a little over 700. They were recaptured off the coast of Kabinda in present day Angola by the American cruiser, *Yorktown*. In Liberia they were encamped in what is called today Oldest Congo Town.[13] All recaptives numbered 5,457. The Congoes came to play a major part in the growth and development of the Liberian nation, especially since they served as traders and government officials in the interior.

Eventually, both "Americo-Liberian" and "Congo" were used interchangeably to describe Liberians of non-indigenous ethnic groups. Persons from Monrovia and the general coastal region were more Westernized. Another mark of identification was the light complexion of many Americo-Liberians. As these people migrated into the Dukor Corridor, intermarriage with indigenous Liberians exposed the indigenous groups to Western culture and traditions. By the first half of the 20th century, with the natural growth of the population in the territory, one could hardly distinguish between the physical features and cultural practices of Americo-Liberian and the indigenous populations.[14] But language, religion and the geopolitical location (the county of residence) contributed to the demarcation of ethnic groups and the Americo-Liberian population and prevented a strong national identity.

Liberia's National Identity Problem-Impedes Democratic Governance

Ethnic conflict and lack of a cohesive national identity have prevented the peaceful co-existence of its diverse ethnic groups and fostered weak democratic governance. While conflicts existed between indigenous Liberians prior to 1821, major conflicts between Liberia's ethnic groups developed due to the political, military, and cultural dominance of freed Africans over the remaining ethnic groups.

In Liberia, the settlers encountered 16 ethnic groups with various cross-cutting linkages. Many of the indigenous Liberians are multi-lingual and Vai, Mandingo, Kpelle and Krahn are the most widely spoken languages.[15] The people are the Kpelle, Bassa, Gio, Kru, Grebo, Mano, Lorma, Krahn, Gola, Kissi, Mandingo, Vai, Gbandi, Belle, Dei, and Mende.[16] They had longstanding contacts through trade, migration and shifting political alliances. Similarly, The Poro society (male) and Sande society (female) connected most indigenous Liberian ethnic groups, especially the Gola, Dai, Kissi, Vai, Gbandi, Kpelle and Loma. Various ethnic groups participated in common rituals. For example, the Poro in certain Kpelle, Mano vicinities, depended on Gola and Loma elders for the commencement of the ceremonies. In the Gbandi ethnic group, officials of Poro spoke Kpelle instead of their own language. The above examples show the extent of flux between ethnic identities. Indigenous Liberians were fluid and flexible, depending on their perception of situations in which they were located.

Coming from North America, the free Africans or descendants of enslaved Africans opted for a republican form of government. They wanted to form a government patterned after that of the United States with all the assortments of Western civilization (i.e., traditions and Christianity) and the ethos of governing. In a correspondence to the American Colonization Society (ACS) about the formation of government dated December 31, 1825, during the colonial provincial stage of Liberia, Jehudi Ashmun, agent of the ACS, writes:

> The system of government drawn up and adapted in August 1824, as an experiment of the agent of the American Colonization Society in Liberia has, "proved itself, in its principles, entirely sufficient for the civil government of the Colony; and still as liberal and popular as the republican prepossessions of the Board would describe."[17]

Forming a good government was a daunting task for the Founding Fathers, but they were determined to succeed in building a democratic country along with its attendant institutions. To do so, they had to overcome the impediments (i.e., social, economic and ideological [i.e., Poro, Sande societies] fracas) of the numerically superior indigenous Africans among whom they settled. In order to control such populace or convince them to accept them and their Western ways of life, the settlers had to communicate with these diverse ethnic groups through their leaders, by using rhetoric with more sternness, vehemence, and intimidation and consistent with their social norms and beliefs.

Once fully in control of the government, Americo-Liberian policymakers of the First Liberian Republic (1847–1980) promoted policies of ethnic hatred that culminated in the longstanding divisions between the non-indigenous Liberians (freed Africans) and the indigenous Liberians (Africans). Successive administrations imposed harsh tax laws, practiced forced labor and enslavement, seized land, and failed to develop schools and infrastructure thus creating a mass of impoverished indigenous people. By promoting ethnic hatred and inflicting inequalities in social, political, cultural, and economic spheres the Americo-Liberian policymakers laid the seeds for disunity—a trek that shattered the country after the violent demise of the First Republic in 1980.

The Americo-Liberian or settler model of governance was the total concentration of power only in the hands of members of the Americo-Liberian or settler community and safeguarding their economic, political, and social interests at the expense of the indigenous majority. In the process, they marginalized and inhibited the general welfare of all Liberians. The Americo-Liberian policymakers guaranteed the survival of their constituency by advocating evasive behavior, ethnicism, nepotism, corruption, and immorality. For example, the Americo-Liberian policymakers used the Free Masons as an undisputed, sacred institution that served as an arbiter for their community, and a mediating anchor for the government. In other words, major educational, social, political, economic, and cultural decisions for the state were made at the Masonic Temple, without the benefit of the masses of the Liberian people—indigenous Liberians. In his piercing volume, *Ethnic Hatred in Liberia's National Identity Crisis: Problems and Possibilities*, Emmanuel T. Dolo argues that:

> Politicizing ethnic identity and exploiting ethnic difference to serve political ends may well be Liberia's most serious and costly problem. Over the 159 years of existence as a nation state, Liberia has been deeply mired in interethnic strife, intermittent conflict, and full-scale warfare, attributed in part to politicizing ethnic identity or infusing it with hatred. In many communities across Liberia, interethnic tensions have impeded cross-ethnic civic engagement and social development.[18]

Indigenous Liberians also had a form of democratic governance in their communities prior to the arrival of the settlers. For example, chiefs or kings ruled with governing consensus. Decisions pertaining to inter-ethnic conflicts were solved with collective deliberation by respectable elders in a given geopolitical area. The group's decision was submitted to the ruling chief or king who would use it as his final ruling in arbitrating matters between people or communities. Indigenous ethnic groups retained this aspect of self-governance within the overall structure of Liberia at the local level, in the clan or chiefdom. But the appointed representatives of the national government superseded chiefs and kings at the district and county level, thus infusing ethnicity into governance. The resulting cleavages within clans, chiefdoms, districts, and counties contributed to lack of social cohesion, which resonated into uncontrollable political, economic, and ethnic problems in Liberia.

The administration of President William R. Tolbert, Jr. (1971–1980) used the Americo-Liberian hegemony to frustrate efforts to initiate political reforms and build democracy for all Liberians. In this regard, he elevated members of his own Americo-Liberian constituency to prominent government and corporate positions at the expense of the indigenous Liberian majority. He labeled the Progressive Alliance of Liberia (PAL), SUSUKU, among others, as "thugs" who were determined to breed and engage in subversive activities to destabilize his government. Tolbert also referred to members of these groups as "a bunch of misfits." One may project that once a negative label is placed on a group or a person as was done in the cases of PAL or SUSUKU, they become *persona non grata* in their own communities and elsewhere in the country; people then scorn and alienate them.

During the military interregnum in Liberia (1980–1990) that brought the indigenous rulers to state power for the first time, the military rulers recognized that without expansive and deliberate use of ethnicity they could not consolidate their power bases, create inter-ethnic solidarity or obtain support for their so-called development programs from the people. Accordingly, they relied on promoting ethnicity through intra-ethnic cooperation to shatter the political and economic strengths of opposition groups, which normally evolved from other ethnic groups, including the Americo-Liberian community. After indigenous Liberians assumed political power through a coup d'etat, the government was controlled predominantly by one ethnic group (Krahn)—the least educated and experienced ethnic group in the country. They marginalized other ethnic groups in the political and economic arenas, while elevating themselves to national prominence, just as Americo-Liberians did in the regimes of the First Republic. Consequently, actions by Liberians of Krahn ethnicity exploded into uncontrollable ethnic and political warfare during the military interregnum (1980–1989), the civil war (1989–2006) and the regime of Charles G. Taylor (2003–2005).

Dolo notes that ethnic tensions and conflicts since 1980 engendered multiple coups identified with specific ethnic groups and counter coups by ethnically-based insurgent groups. Military leader turned president Samuel Kanyon Doe represented the former and rebel leader turned president Charles G. Taylor represented the latter. Ethnicity enjoined to demagogic politics and failed governance by both leaders propagated a more hostile posture in interethnic relations than had been during the settler ruler. During the Doe and Taylor regimes they used ethnicity as a basis for killing people whom they considered as threats.

The military government of Samuel Kanyon Doe successfully practiced ethnocentric nationalism to protect its own interests. As Dolo writes,

> Ethnocentric nationalism provides expansive rights to one group and constricts the rights of others, which engenders distributive inequality and social injustice. In turn, it fosters mutual recrimination. Ethnocentric nationalism emerges out of intolerance, which is a "closed system" that forces adherents to show little or no interest in "learning about those they purport to despise" (Ignaetieff, 1999, p. 96). In response, Ignaetieff (1999) has warned: "Breaking down stereotypical images of others is only likely to work if we also break down the fantastic elements in our own self-regard. The root of intolerance seems to be found in our tendency to overvalue our own identities; by overvalue, I mean we insist that we have nothing in common,

nothing to share; it is the fantasy of purity, of boundaries that can never be crossed" (p. 98).[19] Ethnocentric nationalism is institutional and not personal, and in that sense, it functions like racism. It is privilege that those who have ethnic ties with the people who hold political power receive exclusively because of the ethnic relationship. These people have more power and access to resources in society than others who come from different ethnic background.[20]

Charles G. Taylor targeted sites of interethnic schisms and fissures that emerged under the Doe regime, intensified the hostilities, and institutionalized *ethnonational* cleavages. The misuse of fundamental ethnic differences in Liberia contributed to the problem of national identity in the country, during the civil war. First, he recognized the sensibilities of Nimbaians considering their disaffection with the Doe military government and transformed them into a war machine. He invoked the memories of legendary heroes and heroines of Nimba County to achieve his diabolical aims: the violent overthrowing of Doe and his continual use of violence to maintain state power, pitting one ethnic group against the other (i.e., Mano and Gio versus Krahn and Mandingo, among others. Einar Braathen, Morten Boas and Gjermund Saether affirm that

> Moreover, there is little doubt that one of the main reasons why people kill each other is who they are and the identities they represent. We are all to some degree still tied to the identities around which ethnic and national conflicts are fought.[21]

During the ensuing civil war many Gio, Mano and Krahn people denied their own ethnicity and claimed membership as Kpelle, Bassa, Kru, or Vai people in order to avoid victimization. Taylor's use of ethnocentric nationalism was evident during his tenure as elected president (1997–2003) and contributed to his removal from state power by foreign intervention.

Ethnocentric nationalism has caused ethnic polarization in Liberia. People have used ethnocentric nationalism to enforce stereotypes, prejudice, and hatred that divides and foments sociopolitical tensions and conflict.[22] Alternatively, the term refers to the use of various apparatuses of the state: power, money, military, and other human resources to enforce the prejudices and hatred of one ethnic group toward another. Another variation of the term is the misapplication of state resources to accumulate personal wealth and use the resources to maintain an ethnic hegemony. It was legalized when settlers denied citizenship rights to indigenous people for a prolonged period and hoisted upon the indigenous people an inherent disadvantage. Equally so, ethnocentric nationalism, settler-style, was codified in Liberia's institutions, customs, and law. Finally, internalized ethnocentric nationalism may imply acceptance by members of the stigmatized ethnic group of the negative messages about their own abilities and intrinsic worth.[23]

One must add, that ethnocentric nationalism also takes on a form of egotism by the educated elites to guarantee their strong clasp on power and privilege by spewing meaningless and divisive rhetoric, which keeps the illiterate or minimally informed in a state of perpetual ignorance and apathy. Such acerbic rhetoric can incite false trepidation, increase anxiety, even spur extreme dislike and translate into desires for vengeance, luring the most vulnerable in society into violence, especially youth who are not anchored sufficiently in their self-worth and family ties. Ethnocentric nationalism is used for the personal benefit of individuals and groups and also as a force that affects the lives of others, within and outside one's ethnic group. One's experience of the presence and absence of power in Liberian society is based principally, although not solely, on their ethnic affiliation and/or proximity to members of the dominant ethnic group with political power. Ethnocentric nationalism is also a factor in professional relationships, particularly in the public sector. For the most part, ethnic identity is used by professionals or government employees to further personal interests.

In African societies the traditional concern for consensus, collective interest, collective identity and emphasis on personal-informal relations contradicts individualism, intense competition, impersonality and formal relations associated with democracy.[24] From this worldview, one should examine ethnicity and democratic governance in Liberia, illuminating both positive and negative aspects. Bruce Berman et al. state that "In many African countries, by contrast, state construction is still incipient and incomplete. There is an urgent need to build state capacity, democratizing political systems and liberalizing economic institutions."[25]

In their individual works, R. Wolfinger and M. Parenti drew consensus arguments that in Africa, democracy promotes sub-national ethnic demands capable of pitting ethnic groups one against another in strife that can destroy the country. This is because of the difficulty of an African opposition political party to justify its separate existence from the ruling party on the basis of some important and visible socioeconomic program. Ethnicity provides one of the most convenient and appealing alternatives to such a program. Political constituencies are often geographical in nature and quite often ethnically homogeneous. Therefore, to win the support of an ethnic group is to win a political constituency. Thus, ethnically salient parliamentary candidates tend to emerge and persist because of gains likely to accrue from appeals to ethnic sentiments.[26] They argued that it is believed that socioeconomic competition among ethnic groups is fueled by multi-party political competition to create waste in the use of resources for development because of the political need to balance ethnic interests. Also, ethnicity is seen as promoting the use of violence in multi-party competition because of the absence of restraints within the group against the expression of hostility and violence toward 'out-group members.' At the same time, in order to ensure group solidarity individuals connive at injustices committed by co-ethnics and are unwilling to accept equity for other ethnic groups out of fear of being left behind in the inter-ethnic scheme of things.

For these reasons, it is often argued that multi-party democracy is inappropriate for the multi-ethnic societies of Africa. The impact of ethnicity on democracy is deemed to be essentially negative. In order to overcome these negative effects analysts have suggested one-party regimes of the type that prevailed in many African countries: "Union government" of General Acheampong in Ghana, no-party state, Afrocracy that is based on the principles of traditional, African life, African socialism that varies from Ujamaa in Tanzania to African welfare capitalism purveyed by Sessional Paper No. 10 in Kenya, military rule modeled on the experience of Turkey under Kemal Atarturk and the two-party political system imposed by the Nigerian dictator, Ibrahim Babangida.[27]

On the one hand, ethnicity does not have negative impacts on democratic regimes alone. In one-party states ethnic politics is transferred to exercises within the party. For example, one way by which the True Whig Party of Liberia managed to disempower indigenous Liberian opposition to its rule was to selectively admit indigenous Liberians into the party and ensure that only those who were willing to play second fiddle climbed high in the party.[28] In fact, the occasions when ethnicity created serious difficulties for African societies have occurred during non-democratic regimes. In Nigeria, the civil war was precipitated by the military during their rule. Marcias Nguema's rule in Equatorial Guinea, Jean Bedel Bokassa's in Central African Republic, Idi Amin's in Uganda, the various military regimes in Rwanda and Burundi, Eyadema in Togo, Mobutu in Zaire, the civil wars in Angola, Sudan and Ethiopia, and the ethno-racial massacres in Mauritania were all characterized by the worst forms of ethnic violence perpetrated in extremely authoritarian political systems.[29]

Nnoli notes that, although the tendency is for the negative impact of ethnicity on social life to come to the fore of people's consciousness, there are also positive impacts. First, the political demands of many ethnic movements concern liberty and justice. They express fears about the oppression of their members by other groups and about the distribution of public service jobs and social amenities based on nepotism, and the imposition of the culture of the dominant ethnic group on the others. In this way, ethnicity contributes to democratic practice by its emphasis on equity and justice in its sociopolitical relations. Second, it leads to the appreciation of one's own social roots in a community and cultural group, which is essential, not only for the stability of the individual and ethnic group but that of the country as a whole. Third, it provides a sense of belonging as part of an intermediate layer of social relations between the individual and the state. Fourth, ethnicity provided a local mobilization base for the anti-colonial movement for national freedom;

Fifth, ethnic identity has been instrumental in the promotion of community development in the rural areas. For example, in the 1970s rural-based ethnic unions emerged in Liberia. The best known of these was the Susukuu, a militant rural protest organization established by the Putu Development Corporation of Grand Gedeh County as work societies or cooperatives. Its radical opposition to incompetent governance had effects far beyond Putu Chiefdom. It contributed to the popular consciousness of the 1970s that dealt a death blow to the hegemony of the Americo-Liberians. Another exceptional ethnic union in Liberia was the Kru Corporation of Monrovia which was registered in 1916 as a property-owning body. Apart from its judicial function of settling disputes among the Kru and the usual welfare functions, it participated actively in dock work affairs since most Krus in Monrovia were dockworkers. In fact, the shipping companies placed a share of job assignments though the corporation. In 1958 it acted as a trade union in disputes with shipping companies. Sixth, the mobilization of the various ethnic groups behind the various factions of a nation's ruling class contributes to the decentralization of power in the country, which is healthy for democratic freedoms.[30]

This tendency of ethnic identity to change indicates that ethnicity is not the primordial force which proponents of fixed identity imply. Barth observes that this shifting of ethnic boundaries is closely associated with changes in the set of mutual identification and communications fields in the society.[31] Holloman correlates it with the pattern of access, or lack of it, to political and economic resources at the macro level, and at the micro level with internal structures which simultaneously guarantee rewards adequate to sustain member support and provide for control of change-related deviant behavior.[32] He claims that, ethnic identity is not fixed. It shifts with the shifting alignments of individuals as they seek to better their lives. But ethnic identity is a group identity and, as such, involves group factors. Therefore, both individual and group elements are blended in ethnic identity. In this way the positive impacts of ethnicity on democracy based on individual dynamics are blended with the negative impacts based on group dynamics. This is because the cultural sphere within which democracy can establish itself is defined by a combination of the universal principle of rationalism and an appeal to personal identity which itself has a double aspect: a) the right to choose an individual life, and b) respect for the roots and heritages from which each individual must freely build his or her particular personality, which is community-based.

As such, Liberia has found it difficult to build political democracy or practice transparency in democratic governance, since its inception as an independent country in 1847, all because of practices of ethnicity or ethnocentric nationalism, which foster inequalities in all aspects of life in the country.

Conclusion

Ethnicity has contributed to a national identity problem and impaired democratic government in Liberia from the First Republic, to the military interregnum, as well as during the Charles Taylor regime. With the election of a democratic government in Liberia in 2005, Liberia faces challenges in overcoming its ethnic divisions while trying to rebuild the country's paralyzed economy and democratic rule. President Ellen Johnson Sirleaf needs to promote ethnic harmony and Liberian national identity as precursors to fostering economic development and political reforms. How will President Ellen-Johnson Sirleaf's government address the issues of ethnicity, national identity and democracy? Prof. Nnoli notes in his volume that, "Ethnicity is also seen as one of the main obstacles to democracy because it leads to the substitution of ethnic interests for the national interest, favoritism, nepotism, and the accentuation of social inequality."[33]

Given this challenge, the Sirleaf government was faced with solving the problems of ethnicity through legal and political measures at their disposal. They also had to convey their intentions for creating a more diversified government by choosing members of government from different ethnic groups. Although they made initial steps in this direction, a comprehensive evaluation of their success or failure will not come until their term expires.

The Liberian government may also improve the relationship between the ethnicity and democratic governance by addressing these areas: (1) preventing inter-ethnic chauvinism while promoting inter-ethnic harmony, a precursor to uplifting Liberian nationalism; (2) creating opportunities for Liberians to do business with the Liberian government that is not based on one's ethnic origin; (3) providing basic services, including education, housing, health, and cultural facilities; (4) guaranteeing individual and group rights; (5) bolstering multi-party democracy.

Liberians still need to resolve the problems they face to provide an environment where people tolerate difference and even encourage it, where peace is possible and prosperity for all is a reality. If Liberians embrace social, cultural, institutional, and economic reforms, the country may appreciate and use the positive aspects of ethnicity to achieve the best of democratic governance.

Notes

1 Bruce J. Berman, "Ethnicity, Patronage and the Africans State: The Politics of Uncivil Nationalism," *African Affairs* 97 (1998), 305-341.

2 Berman, "Ethnicity, Patronage and the Africans State," 305.

3 Okwudiba Nnoli, *Ethnicity and Democracy in Africa: Intervening Variables* (Lagos: Malthouse Press Limited, 1994), 2.

4 J.J. Liz, cited in Okwudiba Nnoli, *Ethnicity and Democracy in Africa Intervening Variables* (Lagos: Malthouse Press Limited, 1994), 4. Also see Guy Hermet, "Introduction: The Age of Democracy," *International Social Science Journal* (May 1991).

5 R.A. Dahl in V. Bogdanor, ed., cited in Nnoli, *Ethnicity and Democracy*, 4. Also see Hermet, "Introduction."

6 L. Diamond, J.J. Linz, and S. Lipset, eds., cited in Nnoli, *Ethnicity and Democracy in Africa*, 4-5.

7 Hermet, "Introduction," 249-255.

8 Edward Lama Wonkeryor, et al., *American Democracy in Africa in the Twentieth-First Century?* (Cherry Hill: Africana Homestead Legacy Publishers, 2000), 18-22.

9 Joseph Saye Guannu, "The Perennial Problems of Liberian History," *An Occasional Paper* 2 (1) (1989), 1-19.

10 Charles Henry Huberich, *Legislative History of Liberia* (New York: Central Book Company, Inc., 1947), 41-42; J. Gus Liebenow, *Liberia: The Quest for Democracy* (Bloomington and Indianapolis: Indiana University Press, 1987), 19. The origin of 68 persons was not known.

11 Guannu, "Perennial Problems," 1-19.

12 Guannu, "Perennial Problems," 1-19.

13 Guannu, "Perennial Problems," 1-19.

14 Guannu, "Perennial Problems," 1-19.

15 E. Osaghe, "Ethnicity, Class and the Struggle for State Power in Liberia," paper presented at Conference on Ethnic Conflicts in Africa (CODESRIA), Nairobi, Kenya (1993), 18-19.

16 Liebenow, *Liberia*, 35.

17 Jehudi Ashmun, cited in *The African Repository and Colonial Journal* 1 (1825-1826), 74.

18 Emmanuel T. Dolo, *Ethnic Hatred in Liberia's National Identity Crisis: Problems and Possibilitie.* (Cherry Hill: Africana Homestead Legacy Publishers, 2007).

19 Dolo, *Ethnic Hatred.*

20   F.E. Kendall, *Understanding White Privilege: Creating Pathways to Authentic Relationships Across Race* (New York: Routledge, 2006).

21   Einar Braathen, Morten Boas and Gjermund Saether, "Ethnicity Kills? Social Struggles for Power, Resources and Identities in the Neo-Patrimonial State," in Einar Braathen, Morten Boas and Gjermund Saether, *Ethnicity Kills? The Politics of War, Peace and Ethnicity in SubSaharan Africa* (New York: St. Martin's Press, 2000).

22   M.M. Gordon, *Assimilation in American Life* (New York: Oxford University Press, 1964.)

23   Dolo, *Ethnic Hatred.*

24   C. Ake, "The African Context of Human Rights," *Africa Today* 3 (1, 2) (1987).

25   Bruce Berman, Dickson Eyoh and Will Kymlicka, "Ethnicity and the Politics of Democratic Nation-Building in Africa," cited in Bruce Berman, Dickson Eyoh and Will Kymlicka, eds., *Ethnicity and Democracy in Africa* (Oxford: James Currey, 2004), 15.

26   R. Wolfinger, "The Development and Persistence of Ethnic Voting," *American Political Science Review* LIX (4) (1965). Also see M. Parenti, "Ethnic Politics and the Persistence of Ethnic Identification," *American Political Science Review* ixi (4) (1967); Nnoli, *Ethnicity and Democracy.*

27   Nnoli, *Ethnicity and Democracy.*

28   Osaghae, "Ethnicity, Class and the Struggle," 38.

29   Nnoli, *Ethnicity and Democracy.*

30   Osaghe, "Ethnicity, Class and the Struggle," 38.

31   F. Barth, cited in Nnoli, *Ethnicity and Democracy.*

32   R.E. Holloman, cited in Nnoli, *Ethnicity and Democracy.*

33   Nnoli, *Ethnicity and Democracy.*

Politicized Ethnicities Versus Tribal Ethnicities: Examples from Liberia, Rwanda and Sierra Leone

Abdul Karim Bangura

Ethnic conflicts, which are the most enervating of the many intrastate conflicts with which Africa is grappling, have engendered enormous human and material destruction on the continent. Applying qualitative methodology, this essay examines the causes of ethnic divisions in Liberia, Rwanda and Sierra Leone, and determines whether ethnicity in itself or the politicization of ethnicities is the actual cause of ethnic conflicts. The results of the qualitative analysis demonstrate that ethnic conflicts are actually the consequences of both the old rivalries of values between ethnicities and the will of political leaders to oppress some ethnicities while providing power to others. On account of the complexity and peculiarity of these conflicts, analysis must be done on a case-by-case basis with the employment of a combination of theories.

The period following the fall of the Berlin Wall on November 8, 1989, marking the end of the Cold War between the United States and the Soviet Union, has witnessed unprecedented internal violence in most Third World countries, due to the ideological vacuum that was filled by the emergence of ethnic conflict. Africa is one continent that has been most severely hit by this development. The political, economic and social ramifications of this new development are phenomenal. For a continent inhabited by the poorest peoples of the world, development aspiration, which occupies the center stage of Africa's agenda, is again confronted with a formidable obstacle. A genuine attempt to contain this situation presupposes an intimate knowledge of the causes. This essay is a critical examination of some of the causative factors in the framework of various theories that have been advanced to explain ethno-political conflicts.

Although not new, ethnic conflicts have presented the most daunting challenge to regional and international security in the recent times. It is not uncommon for analysts to simply characterize most conflicts today as ethnic conflicts, particularly those taking place on the continent of Africa. Debate about the conflicts in Africa is replete with numerous causes that have been blamed for these convulsive eruptions. A practical approach in dealing with this debilitating problem entails getting to understand the wellspring of this unravelling situation. Although considerable efforts have been made in that direction, donor fatigue is evident and the problem continues to grow by starting in other states or overflowing the weak borders of already devastated ones. To a great extent, the magnitude and complexity of contemporary intrastate conflicts have rendered the region's collective security mechanisms more of toothless bulldogs. The human toll of these conflicts is enormous to overlook in an era when the dignity of humankind has assumed a high place in the priorities of the international system. The simple characterization of these conflicts as ethnic carries with it serious policy implications. This essay sheds more light on conflicts in Africa, using Liberia, Rwanda and Sierra Leone as case studies. It also makes the suggestion that not all conflicts that have ethnic fault lines are ethnically motivated. And the final section suggests what the crux of this ongoing phenomenon is all about.

This essay adopts the qualitative, multiple-case-study method. It is qualitative in the sense that the analysis of the various theoretical explanations is based on non-numerical data. It is a multiple case study because it delves into the particular cases of Liberia, Rwanda and Sierra Leone in a reasonable depth using secondary data sources. In the view of Robert K. Yin, case studies become useful tools in the following instances: (1) to investigate a present-day phenomenon in the context of real life, when (2) the demarcation line between the phenomenon and real life is blurred, and (3) when a variety of sources are employed.[1] And in terms of methodology, the case-study approach proceeds in three different, but interrelated, ways: explanatory, exploratory, and descriptive. When it is explanatory, it devotes itself to the "how" and "why" of a given situation. In the case of the exploratory, it is an attempt to go into greater depth about a given situation, while the descriptive seeks to answer the question "what happened?"[2] This study is exploratory because it takes an in-depth look at the Liberian, Rwandan and Sierra Leonean conflicts.

In the analysis, the appropriateness of ethno-nationalist approaches in explaining the three cases is scrutinized. The aim at this juncture is to determine whether these postulates provide an acceptable explanation for these conflicts. The technique employed to marshal the data was document analysis, because it is not only a study of various references but also an analysis of their content.

This technique comes in handy when the researcher is not the original collector of the data used, and the phenomenon does not consist of personal beliefs and attitudes that are collected by means of interviews. Also, the other factors that influenced this choice of technique in collecting the data were the availability of information, time, and the relative cost involved in using alternative techniques of data collection.

Theoretical Reverberations

Two major approaches have been used to examine ethnic conflicts. One approach focuses on the role of ethnicity in ethno-regional conflicts. The other approach is the employment of a particular theory to examine one conflict or multiple conflicts.

Analysts have tended to have one of two views of the role of ethnicity in ethno-regional conflicts. Some of them see ethnicity as a source of conflicts, and others see it as a tool used by political leaders to reach personal or a particular group's goal(s). Before discussing these two views, a definition of the key term, ethnicity, will be helpful in understanding them.

According to Ian Robertson, "ethnicity refers to cultural features that may be handed down from one generation to the net. These features may include language, religion, national origin, dietary practices, a sense of common historical heritage, or any other distinctive cultural trait."[3] And as Le Vine points out, ethnicity remains the embodiment of deeper values in institutions and patterns of behavior representing a people's historical experience.[4]

Defining the term ethnicity provides a clearer understanding of what is at stake in the competing two views over the causes of ethno-regional conflicts. Those who view ethnicity as the cause of those conflicts generally invoke three reasons for this causal relation. First, like Patterson, they argue that the experience or the sense of exclusion from a wider social entity can determine the upsurge of ethnic groups.[5] This exclusion can be the result of a defeat in a civil war, or it can take the form of a feeling of oppression when an ethnic group feels that another ethnic group of the wider social entity is economically or politically advantaged. Second, the supporters of this proposition cite fear as a reason. Fear takes place when ancient ethnic or religious rivalries reemerge and create a will to protect oneself from possible attackers. The third reason for this upsurge of ethnic groups is explained by the feeling of loss: i.e., the damage, trouble, disadvantage, deprivation, etc. caused by losing something.[6]

Contrarily, analysts who believe that ethnicity is a tool used by political leaders to achieve ambitious goals argue that the real cause for ethno-regional conflicts finds its root in modern politics, and more specifically in colonialism, the building of the nation-state, and its conflicts over power and resources.[7]

Indeed, they argue that colonizers, eager for power, are those who, as John Bowen points out, "declared that each and every person had an 'ethnic identity' that determined his or her place within the colony or the postcolonial system."[8] Bowen also adds that colonial and post-colonial states "created new social groups and identified them by ethnic, religious, or regional categories."[9] The defenders of this perspective, thus, come to the conclusion that fear and hate find their source in the modern state's demand that people make themselves heard as powerful groups, not in ethnic differences, but altogether in a nation-state framework.[10]

Many scholars have attempted to explain ethnic conflicts from a variety of theoretical perspectives. The competition theory, which is one of them, posits that conflict between ethnic groups is more than likely to be violent when they interact. Ted Robert Gurr supports this view, although from a different angle.[11] He believes that since modernization engenders more interaction and competition among cultural groups, and also contention between cultural groups and the state, it is a source of ethnic conflict. In essence, ethnic competition or interaction leads to ethnic conflict.[12] Implicit in this theory also is the suggestion that desegregation has some association with ethnic tension. This line of argument is also supported by Olzak, who demonstrates that, among many other things, that ethnic desegregation has some association with ethnic conflict.[13] In Douglas Dion's view, this is a spurious relationship that is associated by selection bias.[14]

There is also the primordial perspective which presents the "ubiquity of ethnocentrism." It frames "ethnic conflicts as irrational and blood feuds that cannot be eliminated."[15] The argument here is that aggression of in-groups directed at out-groups has its basis in primordial desire, which attempts to connect group identity and certain features of ascription, normally ethnicity and race. This notion of in-group versus out-group was first introduced by Sumner.[16] Samuel Huntington, in his controversial book, *The Clash of Civilizations*, also embraces the primordial perspective.[17] The main theme of this book is that the prevalent wars of the post-Cold War era will be fought along ethnic, religious and linguistic borders.

Contrary to the primordial view, instrumentalists postulate that ethnic conflict is not a function of the natural division of groups into nation states, but rather a product of elite machination of nationalist sentiments for their political ambition.[18] In fact, Merton buttresses this point by citing instances of positive gesture of in-group toward non-group members in social interaction.[19] Against this backdrop, Merton eschews the notion that in-groups have the propensity to go to conflict with out-groups.[20] The empirical support for this perspective has been provided by Singer in a study of the cultural factors on prolonged rivalries.[21] According to Singer, instead of culture being a causative factor, it is elite manipulation of cultural differences that is the culprit.

Furthering the debate is the world systems theory. According to this school of thought, the multitude of economic links among states has engendered the creation of a hierarchy of more and less powerful states. This division has put the countries of the world into three categories: (1) core, (2) semi-periphery, and (3) periphery.[22] Core states are those that have dominance in trade and military power, and also command diplomatic information and exchanges. On the other hand, peripheral states are those that are the lowest on the scale, if measured against the same yardstick for the core countries. The semi-peripheral states are those that occupy the middle ground between the more central and less dominant states. Consequently, ethnic differences seem to be more pronounced in peripheral countries where economic opportunities are very limited and their natural resources are exploited by the core and semi-peripheral states.

Olzak and Tsutsu explore the centrifugal effect of the integrative process on specific ethnic groups.[23] In core countries, it has the effect of encouraging multiplicity of movements that will use conventional means in voicing grievances, lobbying, and protesting. On the contrary, most peripheral countries clamp down on even the mildest form of protest.[24] Gurr, however, cites modernization as the main culprit motivating ethnic conflicts.[25] He says that in understanding why minorities rebel, "modernization sets the larger context." Gurr points at three major and separate changes that have occurred: (1) the growth of modern states and state systems, (2) economic development, and (3) the communication revolution. According to Gurr, these are not new, except for the rate at which these developments have been taking place. What is, however, important about modernization is that it has increased interaction and competition not only among culturally distinct groups but also between cultural groups and the center. Classical modernization theorists believe that since the process is uneven, certain groups (including ethnic groups), feeling marginalized, tend to mobilize and rebel or revolt against the power elite.

The majority of the literature on post-Cold War conflicts considers culture as the precipitant factor of these conflicts. Indeed, 50 major ethnic conflicts that occurred in 1993 and 1994 are estimated to have driven more than 26 million refugees and each conflict to have caused the death of about 80,000 people.[26] In fact, Maynes even equates ethno-nationalist conflicts to the spread of nuclear weapons.[27]

Although primordial, instrumentalist, modernization and competition theories are the dominant in ethno-nationalist studies, they approach the topic from different perspectives that are sometimes ambivalent. That notwithstanding, they have made tremendous progress getting to the genesis of this complex subject of ethnic conflicts. However, they cannot account for some of the conflicts that have occurred on the continent of Africa. In dealing with the diversity of conflicts in today's world, a healthy caution has to be exercised in attempting to use a single theoretical framework to explain them.

Liberia

Since the settling of freed slaves from the United States in Liberia in 1847, the Americo Liberians, as these freed slaves are known, have dominated every aspect of the Liberian political, social and economic life. For an uninterrupted period of 150 years, the Liberian political realm was reserved only for Americo Liberians.[28] The Americo Liberians imposed a colonial situation over the natives. On account of the tenuous legitimacy enjoyed by the settlers and the shallow penetrative capacity of the government, they relied on powerful institutions like the Masonic Lodge and their True Whig Party to suppress and enslave the indigenes.

The enslavement of the indigenes by former slaves caught the attention of the international community in 1929 when the League of Nations investigated allegations of slave labor in Liberia. That notwithstanding, in 1930, the settlers continued to sell natives to Spanish slave traders on the Atlantic Ocean Island of Fernando Po.[29] Both the United States and the United Kingdom expressed their indignation over this matter by severing diplomatic relations with Liberia for five years.

Furthermore, although Liberian history has been characterized by repression of the indigenes, there was a gradual shift from this tendency in the period following World War II. Although President William Tubman and his successor, William Tolbert, did make reforms, they were too little and too late. But even worse, Tolbert's lack of the necessary leadership skills only aggravated the situation.[30] It was against the backdrop of these grim circumstances that a protest was staged against a 50 percent increase in the price of the staple food, rice. The wrong handling of the protest by the police resulted in rioting, looting, and other acts of vandalism. Hundreds of people, predominantly students, were wounded and killed, while the soldiers and police joined the looting spree that ensued.[31]

In light of this situation, Tolbert's decision to strengthen his grip on power by containing the opposition also came too late. Strike leaders and politicians became the target of his security forces. Many were sent to jail, and press freedom was severely curtailed. And because of the instrumental role of the students in the protests, universities were also closed. In this regard Tolbert was at the mercy of Master Sergeant Samuel Kanyon Doe and his soldiers, a mercy that was never granted him. He was killed and his mutilated body displayed at the John F. Kennedy Memorial Hospital before burial with

27 others in a mass grave.[32] An estimated number of 200 people also lost their lives in the wave of killings that ensued.

Led by Doe, a group of noncommissioned officers of the Liberian army were behind this violent, but successful, coup d'etat in 1980. Doe's record on repression and ethnic monopoly over power proved to be even worse than his predecessor. Despite the massive support enjoyed by this military government at the outset, the euphoria was quick to disappear. Instead of departing from the past, Doe institutionalized tribalism. His lack of vision, coupled with his desire to strengthen his hold on power, aggravated the political as well as the economic situation of the country. Doe's ruthless handling of the attempted coup by Quiwonkpa from the Mano ethnic group brought rancor into the Liberian polity. Members of the Krahn tribe (the ethnic group of Doe) and their allies, members of the Mandingo ethnic group, were appointed to all positions of importance in government, irrespective of qualification. In effect, all Doe accomplished was to crush the Americo-Liberian dynasty and replace it with a Krahn one. The same client-patron relationship that characterized the old order was active and alive again, with the difference being that Doe and his kinship and social network occupied the patron seat. What all of this spelled for the Liberians was disillusionment. The eagerly expected revolution had not happened, due to the lack of vision on the part of Doe and his lieutenants to improve the general well-being of the nation and liberate the indigenous population. As the regime's tenuous legitimacy quickly faded away, the Krahn-dominated army became Doe's instrument of coercion. It was with this instrument that he effectively sought to curb all signs of opposition, except for the National Patriotic Front of Liberia (NPFL, Charles Taylor's military organization).

Notwithstanding Doe's poor human rights and governance records, the United States maintained close ties with Liberia. In fact, according to Funmi Olonisakin of the Center for Defense Studies at King's College in London, Liberia received $500 million between 1980 and 1985.[33] The continuation of United States-Liberian ties could be associated with the Omega navigation station and the Voice of America's largest transmitter station, which were of strategic importance due to the Cold War. The withdrawal of this vital support by the United States severely undermined the ability of the government to maintain a hold on power.

With square pegs in round holes, corruption and inefficiency became the order of the day. With every indication that a violent change was imminent, the United States forced the leadership to conduct an election. This hope was dashed away when a massively rigged election returned Doe to office. The campaign leading to this election was mired in unprecedented repression of all forms of opposition.[34] In light of this, by 1989, trouble could be sensed looming over Liberia.

On December 24, 1989, Charles Taylor attacked Liberia from the border with the Ivory Coast. This became a full-fledged guerilla war, with large-scale massacre of civilians and a complex humanitarian catastrophe. In fact, this struggle represents one of Africa's most violent eruptions in the contemporary era, with a human toll of alarming proportion (150,000 deaths).[35] While Doe's nine years of rule and the civil war dismantled the old order of things, "it left in its place a more corrupt government, interethnic hatreds, rule of the gun and fear and physical destruction."[36] The conventional rules of war were violated with impunity. The savage brutality with which Charles Taylor prosecuted this war, coupled with the humanitarian crisis that ensued, left the neighbors with no alternative but to abandon the old and sacrosanct policy of non-intervention into the internal affairs of a sovereign nation.

The ethnic domination of the Americo-Liberians is not an immediate cause of the Liberian conflict; yet, it is the genesis of the ethnic politics in Liberia, and it provided the background against which Doe rose to power. The role of ethnicity was glaring during the Americo-Liberian rule. The Americo-Liberians denied political and civil rights to natives by using the ethnic line of demarcation. In this regard, one is tempted to jump to the conclusion that ethnic differences were the motivating factor. However, this reveals only half the truth; to be sure, the underlying motivation for interethnic violence is more than just cultural differences and traditional hostilities.[37] Mobilization along ethno-linguistic lines in most cases provides the most viable option when demanding recognition or share of wealth and power. This explanation tends to give credence to the primordialist claim, but only to the extent that ethnicity provided the fault line for domination and suppression. In short, it would be a gross misrepresentation to infer that Americo-Liberian treatment of the natives in the manner they did was a function of just distinctiveness in their cultures. It is reasonable to infer at this juncture, however, that the Americo-Liberian motive was limited to the desire to continue to rule. But as Clapham views it, when governments deliberately limit political participation to small cliques, while subjecting the significant remainder of their nationals to exploitative and brutal rule, they lay the basis for insurgency.[38]

Doe's ethnic division of Liberia only goes to buttress the primordial perspective once more. In a deliberate and calculated move, Doe's government cautiously planned and executed the imposition of ethnic monopoly over state power while at the same time dealing with all other ethnic groups in a ruthless manner. It is worthy of note that ethnicity and repression were clearly stated as reasons for Doe's overthrow of the Americo-Liberian dynasty. Again, the ethnic fault line forms the basis along which Doe had divided the country. It was his desire to maintain a hold on power and the threat perceived by other ethnic groups that intensified ethnic entrenchment. The Krahn ethnic group before Doe's government was indeed at the bottom of the Liberian social stratum. The Krahn were "the-one-at-a-time cigarettes sellers, prostitutes and enlisted men."[39] But with state power in their hands, they quickly became the political elite. The enjoyment of the benefits of governance to a once deprived group was seen as an opportunity never to let go. With the awareness that other ethnic groups were also competing for the same power, Doe sought to entrench his ethnic group and also the allies—the Mandingo. In essence, the ethnic configuration of the government was a move to maintain the hold on power. The decision was not a product of ethnic differences; it was a calculated move to maintain a strong grip on power. At this juncture, the competition perspective may have become the explanatory factor. With the fall of the Americo-Liberian dynasty, other deprived indigenous groups suddenly realized that they too could develop their own dynasties.

Rwanda

In pre-20th-century Rwanda, the terms *Hutu* and *Tutsi* did not carry the same political meanings they do in today's Rwanda. The pre-colonial history of Rwandan Tutsis and Hutus is a complex series of events. The date when the Tutsis arrived and conquered the Hutu entity is unknown. In fact, the two groups lived in perfect co-habitation: Hutus were cultivators and Tutsis were pastoralists. Also, Hutus who accumulated sufficient wealth could become Tutsis, while Tutsis who lost their economic power became Hutus.

From the 7th century until 1916, Rwanda was a highly monarchical polity. The state was organized, centralized, and hierarchical. It is fair to say that Tutsis were the dominant group who formed the warrior-aristocracy of traditional Rwandan society. However, while controlling and ruling Rwanda, the Tutsis did not monopolize the power over Hutus. In fact, traditional Rwanda was a mutually accepted organization of power. Moreover, the social cohesion of the society is illustrated by the fact that large-scale ethnic killings do not seem to have occurred.

Another aspect of Rwandan history is the existence of a strong militia tradition in the country. First playing a role of self-defense against enemies, militias then had a more economic and social role. Second, the militias had a lively cultural life with poetry, music, and dance. Also, both Hutus and Tutsis could be members of these militias. It was even not rare for a Hutu to be in command.

Colonizers of diverse horizons, the Germans and then the Belgians, transformed Rwandan society in its deepest meaning, since they came with firmly held convictions about race and racial hierarchy. Whites were obviously considered as being superior; but among Africans, certain ethnic groups were designated more worthy than others. This is how the Tutsis became superior to

Hutus in the social hierarchy. Westerners had indeed a preference for the Tutsis' facial features. The Tutsis were in general taller and had more "European-like features." Thus, colonial authorities were largely responsible for exacerbating ethnic schisms between the Tutsis and Hutus. Therefore, the proposition that ethnicities are politicized is confirmed here.

However, this postulate is not the only one to be applicable to the Rwandan case. Indeed, wanting to make Rwanda more rigid and more controllable, in 1926 the Belgians decided that the population should be classified as Hutu and as Tutsi, with no possibility of one changing his/her group classification. All citizens were then given national identification cards which included the names of the ethnic groups to which they belonged. Thus, the complicated hierarchy of pre-colonial Rwanda was simplified, with more power concentrated to those at the top, the Tutsis, and fewer benefits for those at the bottom of the hierarchy, the Hutus. The colonialists then eliminated the Hutus' autonomous territories, reducing the status of the group and enhancing Tutsi domination under European control. The postulate that ethnic conflicts find their cause in the feeling of loss and oppression is also validated by the Rwandan case. Indeed, Hutus had lost their land and were politically as well as economically oppressed. Moreover, they also could experience and feel that the Tutsis were advantaged because of physical differences.

The 1994 genocide that occurred in Rwanda also confirms the proposition that ethnicities can be politicized from the top. Indeed, the slaughter that occurred in the 1990s "stemmed from efforts by the dictator-president Juvenal Habyarimana to wipe out his political opposition, Hutu as well as Tutsi."[40] In 1990–91, Habyarimana began to transform an armed gang into a militia called Interahamwe. This militia launched its series of massacres in a village in March of 1992, and in 1993 began systematically to kill Hutu moderates and Tutsis. Throughout 1993, the country's three major radio stations were broadcasting messages of hate against Tutsis, the opponents, and against specific politicians, setting the stage for what followed. Immediately after the still unexplained plane crash that killed President Habyarimana in April of 1994, the presidential guard began killing Hutu opposition leaders, human rights activists, journalists, and others critical of the state, most of them Hutu. Only then, after the first wave of killings, were the militia and soldiers sent to organize mass killings in the countryside, focusing on Tutsis.

Why did people obey the order to kill? For sure, as Bowen affirms, "leaders were able to carry out a plan, conceived at the top, to wipe out an opposition group. They succeeded because they persuaded people that they could survive only by killing those who were, or could become, their killers."[41] Indeed, by broadcasting radio messages conveying hate and portraying the Tutsi led Rwandan Patriotic Front as a group of bloodthirsty killers, organized Hutus turned into killing groups. Bowen sums up the situation by saying that "the killings of 1994 were not random mob violence, although they were influenced by mob psychology."[42] The analysts who support the idea that ethnicities can be politicized would surely agree with this interpretation of the events that occurred during the massacres, and especially with what led to these events. Indeed, negative stereotyping, fear of another group, killing lest one be killed are what the so-called leaders led the people to do. Believing that such conflicts are natural or inherent to specific ethnicities is problematic. However, these negative stereotypes, this fear of another group, and killing to prevent being killed are typical causes said to precipitate ethnic conflicts by those who believe that there are real ethnic triggers and mechanisms in conflicts. This suggests once again that neither politicized ethnicities, nor behaviors and reactions inherent to ethnicities, are the unique variables in the Rwandan case. These two perspectives are actually intertwined.

In sum, the ethnic conflict in Rwanda is the consequence of old and entrenched rivalries of values between ethnicities and the manipulation of these ethnicities by colonizers and contemporary political leaders. Indeed, as the case of Rwanda exemplifies, the greed of these leaders led them to build a nation-state by oppressing minorities. This created and intensified some feeling of oppression, fear, and loss that then launched the multiple genocides that Rwanda experienced.

Sierra Leone

On March 23, 1991, the Revolutionary United Front (RUF) attacked a small military outpost stationed at Bomaru. The RUF, supported by the National Patriotic Front of Liberia (NPFL), quickly routed the Sierra Leone troops manning the post and also killed the two officers in charge. With this initial success, the RUF quickly opened another front in the southern province. In the following months, the RUF advanced rapidly against very little resistance in most of the encounters. For the next eight years, this situation evolved into a full-fledged war, causing untold suffering to the people of Sierra Leone. The rebel war was a product of the cumulative effects of several years of malaise that had befallen the country. So acute were these anomalies that by the late 1980s, rice (the staple food), gas and other essential commodities became luxury items. Long queues for these essential commodities were a common scene in Freetown. When they were available, these products carried exorbitant prices. In effect, the many years of bad governance, declining social and physical infrastructure, and wrong policy choices under the one-party rule of the All People's Congress (APC) were clearly beginning to take their toll. And with no genuine indication that the government was ready to institute remedial political, economic and social reforms, a violent outburst was inevitable. The ultimate question then is the following: What social, economic and political factors precipitated the civil war in Sierra Leone?

When Sierra Leone attained independence in 1961, it had already been integrated into the global world economy by the British. However, this enmeshment only confined it to the exportation of raw materials to the industrialized world.[43] Hence, Sierra Leone was heavily dependent on a narrow range of cash crops such as cocoa, coffee, and palm oil. In addition, the exploitation of the country's vast minerals, which were also sources of revenue, was dominated by transnational corporations from the West that had the technology and wherewithal to undertake such ventures. This extroverted nature of the economy had ramifications for the prices of these minerals and agricultural products. Their prices were not only determined by external forces, but also susceptible to fluctuations. Due to poor performance in this sector, Sierra Leone was in the throes of serious fiscal problems by the end of the 1970s. In the late 1980s, the fiscal deficit accounted for nearly 15% of GDP, while inflation had gone above 100%.[44] Furthermore, international reserves were dangerously low, the "parallel market premium was substantial," and the economy was in shambles.[45] As it did many other African states, Structural Adjustment made Sierra Leone more dependent on social networks rather than building institutions as a means of economic survival.[46] With poverty on the rise, anti-government demonstrations and coup attempts became more frequent. The government's response was brutal, which sent most of the radical opposition in search of alternative means of effecting change. Little wonder that some members of the RUF were students and other people who suffered under the APC.

As the state continued on its downward spiral, so did the social fragmentation that divided Sierra Leone. Even before independence, the society had already been polarized along several lines. The first line of division was between the well-educated and pro-Western settlers and the then less educated communities in the interior. Friction between these two groups was common towards independence, as the Creoles, who constitute only 2% of the population, took over most of the professional jobs and played a preponderant role in the administrative sector.[47] Second, ethno-regional politics divided the country into northern (Temne, Limba, Susu and other groups) and southern elements (mostly Mende). This ethnic division has persisted as a common denominator for political allegiance after independence. Third, the Lebanese who first migrated to Sierra Leone in the 1880s, became the dominant economic power, wielding enormous unofficial power in political circles. This prominent role naturally attracted the hostility of less influential indigenous groups. Fourth, the British resorted to the use of the local chiefs on account of administrative prudence. This heavy reliance on chiefs for control put into the hands of these local authorities more power pitting them against members of the educated elite who were craving a more prominent role in politics. In the absence of a strong state to bridge these cleavages, social fragmentation has continued unabated since independence.

The immensity of Sierra Leone's economic problems, coupled with political malaise and social fragmentation, constitute the underlying causes of the war. The ethnic dimensions of this conflict, if any, are not clear. Indeed the Mende and Temne ethnic groups have had bitter and recurring wars before the advent of colonialism. But, in this particular instance, although the insurgency started in the eastern and southern regions of the country, its leader, the late Foday Sankoh, was a Temne from the north. And although Mende account for a greater majority of the RUF membership, there also exist a considerable number of other ethnic groups. But even if the Mende factor was anything to contend with, it should be understood against the hollowed nature of the Sierra Leone state that lost control over the political and economic space in the eastern and southern provinces. The Liberian dollar was more common than the Sierra Leone currency in these areas, and NPFL forays and the eventual incursion by the RUF met with little or no resistance. In fact, this alienated part of the country quickly joined the rebellion.

However, six years into the war, ethnic tendencies began to creep into the conflict after the victory of the Sierra Leone People's Party (SLPP, an eastern- and southern-based party) in the 1996 multiparty elections. Fortunately, this did not gain currency. In that regard, ethnicity becomes the wrong lens through which the war in Sierra Leone could be viewed. The permeating propensity of ethnic affiliations in a divided society like Sierra Leone had reached the threshold like most issues, including development, education, trade unions, and even politics. But to blame the schisms in Sierra Leone on ethnicity would be a misrepresentation of the reality. The instrumentalist and the warlord theories may help to explain the civil war in Sierra Leone. The RUF's decision to stop hostilities in order to share power gives credence to the instrumentalist perspective as a better explanation for understanding the Sierra Leone conflict. The organization of the RUF and the manner in which Sankoh executed the war led some observers to characterize it as warlord insurgency. According to Clapham, such wars are characterized "by personal leadership, generally weak organizational structures, and still weaker ideological motivations."[48] In short, the main motivation was self-aggrandizement on the part of Sankoh. Even in Liberia where the war started with clearly defined groups fighting against the government (Gio and Mano ethnic groups fighting against the Krahn-based government), things had started to change by 1992. From this point onwards, and more specifically in 1994, the ethnic fault line disappeared, giving way to factional fighting.[49] Although Outram asserts that the reason for this shift is not known, he contends, that evidence is compel-

ling and clear that the configuration of the war changed from ethnic to factional.

Conclusion

It is quite evident from the preceding case studies that not all conflicts in Africa can be explained by a single theoretical perspective of ethnic conflict. Indeed, the three case studies amply demonstrate this point. Ethnic competition
accounts for ethnic conflict and violence in Liberia before and after President
Doe came to power in 1980. In Rwanda, colonial and post-colonial authorities
were responsible for worsening ethnic divisions between Tutsi and Hutu and
contributed to the 1994 Hutu massacre of Tutsi and Hutu moderates. Finally,
the case of Sierra Leone shows that ethnic conflict was not decisive in precipi-
tating the civil war. The instrumentalist approach and warlordism help to explain the break out of civil war in Sierra Leone.

Indeed, most of the newly independent states of Africa are multi-ethnic.
In that respect, the primary view carries with it a gloomy and bleak future for
the continent. And in a world where resources are scarce, there is bound to be
competition and interaction between various demand-bearing groups which,
unfortunately, are usually along ethnic lines in Africa. The problem of scarcity
has been compounded by the unfair distribution of such resources. But even
more dreadful is that Africa has been the most prolific producer of dictators
and authoritarian regimes. This has encouraged self-aggrandizement tendencies among elites and warlords. For a long time to come, socio-economic and
political problems will continue to be a major preoccupation of the African
leaders as has been since independence. It is with this scary scenario of near-
dooms-day that the continent finds itself in the new millennium.

However, Africa should not be consigned to the trash bin on account of
this scenario. What has been discovered in this study may give inkling as to
the direction of further research that could help to get to the nucleus of ethnopolitical conflicts. In the three case studies, it was discovered that none of the
theories is a competent tool by itself to explain any of the conflicts. If anything, the explanation of these conflicts hinges upon a combination of factors
that have collectively brought these countries to their knees under the weight
of war. More important, the three governments were ethnic based; and in
their bid to maintain this status quo and in the fear of strong competition
from other groups, they accumulated power in their hands and became oppressive. But even more disastrous, there is an extension of ethnic monopoly
into the public service sphere and other realms of society, much to the detri-
ment of effective governance and to the exclusion of the others.

The result has been a neo-patrimonial system, anchored mainly on kinship and social networks. The employment of unbridled power led to economic mismanagement, corruption, and social unrest. In effect, government provides the larger context in which the origins of these wars can be traced. Whether it is competition between or among groups, or cultural differences that lead to war, the quality of governance could be a determinant factor. Be it a civil or military government, good governance is about "handling conflicting demands in a way that retains the allegiance and participation of the demanders in the national political system."[50] The need for good governance is, therefore, imperative for Africa to move beyond its current crises. Good governance in the case of the three countries examined in this chapter (and, of course, the rest of Africa) would include the redistribution of wealth and the promotion of democracy, human rights and the rule of law.

Notes

1   Janet B. Johnson and Richard Joslyn, *Political Science Research Methods* (Washington, DC: Congressional Quarterly/Government Printing Office, 1991), 121.

2   Johnson, *Political Science Research Methods*.

3   Ian Robertson, *Sociology* (New York: Worth Publishers, Inc, 1987), 286.

4   Victor T. Le Vine, "Conceptualizing 'Ethnicity' and 'Ethnic': A Controversy Revisited," *Studies in Comparative International Development* 32 (2) 45-76.

5   Orlando Patterson, The Nature, Causes, and Implications of Ethnic Identification," In C. Fried, ed., *Minorities: Community and Identity* (Berlin, Germany: Springer-Verlag, 1983).

6   Mohamed Rabie, *Conflict Resolution and Ethnicity* (Westport, CT: Praeger Publishers, 1994); R.A. Schermerhorn, *Comparative Ethnic Relations* (New York: Random House, Inc, 1970).

7   Yahya Sadowski, "Ethnic Conflict," *Foreign Policy* 111:12 (Summer 1998.); John Correy. "A Formula for Genocide," *The American Spectator* (September 1998).

8   John R. Bowen. "The Myth of Global Ethnic Conflict," *The Journal of Democracy* 7 (4) 3-14 (1996), 99.

9   Bowen. "The Myth of Global Ethnic Conflict," 99.

10 Philip Mason, *Race Relations* (London: Oxford University Press, 1970), 83.

11 Chester Crocker et al., eds. *Managing Global Chaos: Source of and Responses to International Conflict* (Washington, DC: United States Institute of Peace Press, 1996).

12 Edna Bonachi, "A Theory of Ethnic Antagonism: Split Labor Market," *American Sociological Review* 37, 547-59 (1972); Roberts H. Bates, *Ethnicity in Contemporary Africa: East African Studies XIV* (Syracuse, New York: Syracuse University Press, Maxwell School of Citizen and Public Affairs, 1973).

13 Susan Olzak, *The Dynamics of Ethnic Competition and Conflict* (Stanford, CA: Stanford University Press, 1999).

14 Douglas Dion, "Competition and Ethnic Conflict. Artifactual?" *Journal of Conflict Resolution* 41 (5) (1997).

15 Donald L. Horrowitz, *Ethnic Groups in Conflict* (Berkley, CA: University of California Press, 1985).

16 William G. Sumner, *Folkways* (New York: Ginn, 1906).

17 Samuel P. Huntington, "The Clash of Civilizations," *Foreign Affairs* 72, 3:22-49 (1993).

18 V. Gagnon, "Ethnic Nationalism and International Conflict," in S. Lynn and S. Miller, eds., *Global Dangers: Changing Dimensions of International Security* (Cambridge, MA: MIT Press, 1995).

19   Robert K. Merton, *Social Theory and Social Structure* (Glencoe, IL: Free Press PFAFF, 1957).

20   Sumner, *Folkways*.

21   J. D. Singer, "Accounting for International War: The State of Discipline," *Journal of Peace* 98, 1:37-48 (1981).

22   Immanuel Wallerstein, *The Modern World System: Capitalist Agriculture and the Origins of the European World Economy in the Sixteenth Century* (New York: Academic Press, 1974).

23   Susan Olzaks and K. Tsutsui, "Status in the World System and Ethnic Mobilization," *Journal of Conflict Resolution* 42 (6), 691-720 (1998).

24   Johan L. Olivier, "Causes of Ethnic Colectivity and Action in the Pretoria-Witwatersrand-Transvaal Triangle," *South African Sociological Review* (2), 89-108 (1990); Ronald A. Francisco, "The Relationship Between Coercion and Protest," *Journal of Conflict Resolution* 39, 263-82 (1995); Karen Rasler, "Concession, Repression, and Political Protest in the Iranian Revolution," *American Sociological Review* 61, 132-52 (1996).

25   Crocker, *Managing Global Chaos*.

26   Ted R. Gurr, "Peoples Against States: Ethnopolitical Conflicts and the Changing World Sstem," *International Studies Quarterly* 38, 347-377 (1994).

27   J. Maynes, "Invitation to War: Conflict in the Balkans," *Foreign Affairs* 73 (3), 97-109 (1993).

28   *Africa South of the Sahara* (Year Book) London (2005).

29   George Ayittey, *Africa in Chaos* (New York: St. Martin's Press, 1999).

30   I. William Zartman, *Collapsed States: Disintegration and Restoration of Legitimate Authority* (Boulder, CO: Lynne Rienner Publishers, 1995).

31   Zartman, *Collapsed States*.

32   Ayittey, *Africa in Chaos*.

33   Olonisakin Funmi, "African 'Homemade' Peacekeeping Initiatives," *Armed Forces and Society* 23 (3), 349-71 (1997).

34   Lawyers Committee for Human Rights, *Liberia: A Promise Betrayed* (a report on human rights) (New York: LCHR Publications, 1986).

35   Ayittey, *Africa in Chaos*.

36   Zartman, *Collapsed States*.

37   Richard Sandbrook, "Patron, Clients, and Factions: New Dimension of Conflict Analysis in Africa," *Journal of Political Science* 5 (1), 104-119 (1972).

38   Christopher Clapham, *South Africa and the International System: The Politics of State Survival* (Cambridge: Cambridge University Press, 1996).

39   I. William Zartman, *Governance as Conflict Management: Politics and Violence in West Africa* (Washington, DC: Brookings Institution Press, 1997).

40   Bowen, "Myth of Global Ethnic Conflict," 3-14.

41   Bowen, "Myth of Global Ethnic Conflict," 100.

42   Bowen, "Myth of Global Ethnic Conflict."

43   Max A. Sesay, "Civil War and Collective Intervention in Liberia," *Review of African Political Economy* 67, 35-52 (1996).

44   World Bank, *Special Report on Sierra Leone* (Washington, DC: World Bank Publications, 1998).

45   World Bank, *Special Report on Sierra Leone*.

46 Christopher Clapham, *South Africa and the International System: The Politics of State Survival* (Cambridge: Cambridge University Press, 1996).

47 Sesay, "Civil War and Collective Intervention in Liberia."

48 Sesay, "Civil War and Collective Intervention in Liberia," 212.

49 Quentin Outram, "Liberia: Roots and Fruits of the Emergency," *Third World Quarterly* 20 (1), 163–173 (1999).

50 Zartman. *Collapsed States.*

CHAPTER NINE

Saharan State-building and Ethnicity: The Social Context

Santosh C. Saha

There are 1500 distinct ethnolinguistic groups in sub-Saharan Africa and civil conflicts for various reasons are numerous. The vast portion of the current literature on ethnic conflict claims that in-group prejudice, the tendency to judge, evaluate, and act so as to favor one's in-group over an out-group is common. Disputing the thesis that ethnicity is a prime cause for serious conflicts, I examine how ethnicity shapes the cross-cultural encounters and the making of a familiar social and political order, helping the process of state-building in sub-Saharan Africa. My contention is that derivative modernization and Westernization theories, putting disproportionate blame on negative ethnicity, represent many social and political unrealities. The question, as set up by Antonio Gramsci (1971) about consciousness that accepts or challenges cultural hegemony, is different from my core question posed in this chapter: what is the nature of a given line of discourse in sub-Saharan state-building? Is there any internal moral coherence in the African arguments in positive ethnicity? I conclude that the politics of social autonomy and presentation of varied social views should not be viewed as anti-state in terms of state-building. The empirical question is who can take initiatives and reestablish social control of state?

The state is different from the nation because the state is a political organization, an independent power externally and a supreme power internally, whereas nationalism is constructed by social action and reaction by both the elites and the masses, as Hobsbawm argues, countering Gellner's emphasis on "high culture" as the exclusive origin of nationalism. Although states can generate the nation-building process, at times with coercive power as in Africa, state-construction is about the elaboration of technologies of governance as well as the incorporation of social background, including emotional, cultural, and moral ethics derived from the broad social contexts that include religion and environment. My essay is about the structural and philosophical aspects of state-building in sub-Saharan Africa and defends the traditional African conviction that an alternative to the current system in state-building is not only desirable but also feasible. Genuine state building should largely be informed more by African local cultural traditions rather than by derivative Western political culture for both stability of state and social cohesion. Here, the discourse is about the historical problems of power, of good and evil, and also the people's relationship to the political world. Where does the ultimate legitimate source of power lie?

Admittedly, cultural relativism encourages an uncritical acceptance of atrocities, but many social scientists, still unduly, find sufficient leeway to impose external ethics on issues such as African religion and environmentalism. In this respect, sub-altern methodology offers a suitable analytical framework. Subaltern theorists relied in the 1970s on Marxism, heavily influenced by French theory of post-structuralism as well as of the Italian Marxist Antonio Gramsci, all of them practicing sound research methods including extensive primary source work. One can dislike the theoretical component of the sub-altern historiography, but most scholars will probably learn a lot about the history of traditional means of administration, a debatable subject that demands some clarification and attention. Of course, my analysis does not preclude the possibility that social movements quite different from those considered here may have a major role in constituting a future state.

Communitarianism and State

The sub-Saharan worldview of state-building is shaped by being in community with other people, not only the living, but also former members of the living community and new generations to come. In this context, the Western-style individual rights, such as the absolute freedom of choice and the right to exclusive forms of dissent, make little sense because they tend to isolate the individual from the community. Communitarianism, as opposed to Western liberalism, is built through mutual support and group action, not atomic choice and individual liberty. In its extreme form, communal national ideology resembles feudal relationships where rights exist, but obligation to the whole seems to predominate so strongly as to make rights secondary. The community attachment is most likely to bring social pressure on the state to uphold valued moral traditions to build an integrated territorial state that takes into account the relevancy of the existing state structures.[1]

First, the African worldview emanates partly from the current acknowledged deficiencies in state reconstruction. Azarya and Naomi observe that the state-centered societies in Africa are the weakest among the developing countries.[2] It is common knowledge that the state political elites use culture for ideological purposes, as was the case in President Julius Nyerere's ujamma system, to assert their identification with the masses.[3] In postcolonial African societies, fragmentation of social control and the practical difficulties in political mobilization for better governance have created a pathological style at the center of the state. Populist state leaders maintain the environment of conflict by pitting their rhetoric, legislation, and formal policies against the continuing social control of strongmen at the local level (e.g., President Kaunda's "African Humanism"). From the current debates waged in mass media and from the opposition voices, it is clear that state formation remains an open-ended question. As Kelley M. Askew observes, in Tanzanian cultural politics, power comes in several forms—some visible, others invisible, just as some music and dances are more "performative" than others, but the state elites emphasize the visible, even "flamboyant" and the "performative" features only. The marginalized cultural ministries in Tanzania and elsewhere have ignored a continuous stream of negotiations among citizens—citizens who might prefer *taarb* to the officially sanctioned *ngoma* or prefer working their own fields to those of a public cooperative.[4] Obviously, the African view does not conform to populism.

Second, modernization theory makes too many optimistic assumptions about societal change and the role of the intellectual and political elites vis-à-vis the state. The state-centric approach in political science presupposes the autonomy, coherence and effectiveness of the modern state. Occupying an oppositional relationship to civil society, the state takes on "human form" as a rational individual, acting always in its best interests. All cultural variations, competing visions, and socioeconomic differences "are erased in favor of uniformity." When considered at all, culture figures primarily as "an effect of and not a determinant of the state."[5] The state paradigms overstate the effectiveness of state construction in sub-Saharan Africa, but the current literature does not relate to assumptions about where national identities originate from. Ranger (1983) and others argue that the power to imagine communities and invent traditions lies with political and intellectual elites. However, how can the ordinary citizens and economically depressed sections of population in Africa be configured under the existing frameworks in state? These issues are connected to location of power.

Can traditional ways and means yield insights and approaches that may enrich the working process in state building? Assuming that the power basis has been the rural masses and believing that African consensus formula creates a meeting point, it is argued here that African moral, legal, and ethical principles are based on amicable and practical compromises that are being evaluated in this study. Africans believe that Western state paradigms and economic modernization have broken down some of the main social tissues on a broader scale. Since the 1990s, many realistic African political leaders, East and West African novelists, and Western and African analysts have expressed their solidarities with the ethnic components but rejected the harmful ethnic identities of communities. Despite many contradictions, communities, of course, do not give up. Thus, a normative judgment is needed.

Third, the African socio-political identity is a "project identity," a process that has been drawn and needs to be implemented. This is resistance identity: building "trenches of resistance" and trying for survival on the basis of principles different from those permeating the failing current state institutions.[6] Recognizing that the African traditions have a spilt personality—hierarchical order and communal brotherhood—it is acknowledged that the claims to the relevance of old traditions and social ethics, especially culturally valorized cultural values, are problematic and may tend to be an oversimplification of a complex issue of state-building. My point is that a derivative idea of state reconstruction is not accepted with the same enthusiasm as the program of reconstruction which emerges from the grass-roots of most of the local communities. It is about the identity formation. How, from what, by whom, and for what is it constructed? In summary, it is admitted that people are not programmed by the history of their communities to act in specific ways only. Nevertheless, the past offers a huge variety of principles and keys to action, some of which flatly contradict one another. After the protracted civil war in Liberia, many analysts have argued that there is a need for a "national psychic conversion" to adopt a different attitude toward power and a new moral rigor in tenure of public office. There must be a new means of bestowing legitimacy on those who hold power, and possibly to heal the deep-seated feelings of inferiority among the indigenous people such as the Kpelle or Mano, of Liberia, where Americo-Liberians have held some Western state values to their political advantage.[7] Now, in their quest for unified statehood, some African leaders contemplated "creolizing" borrowed Western cultures. The state apparatuses are likely to produce new mixed culture by inserting selected indigenous meanings and symbols into an imported matrix to which Africans are now adapting.[8]

Sub-Saharan Concepts of State

The idealist concept of MacIntyre in *After Virtue* has some similarities with the African stance. In a radical alternative to liberalism, he argues that the mode of moral-political association available in liberal democracy compares poorly with the ethos-inculcating shared life noted in the ancient Greek "polis."

Although his position is impractical in this age of controversial cultural globalization, McIntyre's standard has a point when he claims that ancient forms of moral and political life offer an acceptable standard for African state builders as well.[9] In the 1990s, South African anthropologists such as J. Clyde Mitchell and associates at the Rhodes-Livingston Institute pioneered an anthropological approach for Africa, suggesting that the theory of the plural society is likely to be a solution. Although his influence declined in South Africa in subsequent decades, his version as social and political "systems," meeting in a "common market-place," is viable. His reference to "market-place" is interesting in an African context.[10] Many political scientists argue against Max Weber's concept of the state as a corporate group that has a compulsory jurisdiction over a territory and its population. Weber does not overlook the juridical aspects of statehood and clearly warns us that his definition is only a means, and not an end. He finally suggests that his means is a force, a motivating power.[11]

First, despite their rejection of the liberal label, many African intellectuals and politicians have never failed to incorporate liberal values into their arsenal of political ideas. Jomo Kenyatta of Kenya, who conformed to Malinoski's teachings of community attachments as foundations of the state, gave an early indication of the role of Kikuyu political traditions in moral compromise which, however, preserved the Kikuyu's political dominance. Kwame Nkrumah of Ghana and Leopold Senghor of Senegal called for social relationships between state elites and chiefs, minimizing the influence of modern public institutions. All these statements point to the Confucian formula in which less encompassing communities—families, neighborhoods, small ethnic groupings—are to be nestled within more encompassing ones—local councils, villages, towns, provinces, and the state, sitting within political communities under a national territorial government in the fashion of a "concentric circle."[12] In the African theory of state, the competing ideals of post-modern individualism and old collectivism, as well as those of negative and positive freedom, arise together at the same time. The African state system demands that benefits derived from state should trickle down from the middle classes to the uninitiated masses. Thus, Benedict Anderson's modern state's "armies of clerks"—bilingual and educated elites—should eagerly conform to this spirit.[13] The African view refutes the argument of Anderson, who cites that traditional ideologies and symbols have only secondary place in the construction and operation of modern nationhood. Indeed, ideology-based rationality, using deductive reasoning, often ignores the fundamental basis for human action.

At the same time, Liberalism's positive aspect is appreciated. In recent years in South Africa, the fight against apartheid convinced many black leaders, opposing apartheid to call for the sanctity of the rule of law and representative government. In opposing the ANC party and government after 1994, the Democratic Party, successor to the Progressive Party, stressed the human rights abuses of the central government, portraying the party as the most consistent defender of just laws and competitive open markets.[14]

Second, as stated earlier, the basic issue is identity formation. Gellner and Hobsbawm argue that success in state reconstruction depends on rationalization and implementation of a modern liberal agenda in which the state-builders invent a national identity and propagate the idea by propaganda. Others such as Rubert de Ventos et al. suggest a more complex theory of state reformulation that is a combination of four factors including primary factors (ethnicity, language), generative factors (communications), induced factors (national education), and reactive factors (collective memory), all of which lead to state building.[15] Despite these differences and varieties in arguments, most theories recognize that national identity, both theoretically and practically, is formed by culture as well as politics, the cultural aspect taking a secondary role. The political scientist Richard Sklar is nearer the truth, when he analyzes the complex relationship between traditional authority and the state to argue that that both the modern sovereign state and traditional authorities are legitimate mediums on which local communities have struggled to sustain institutions of governance, moral authority and legitimacy. Pursuing the same argument, Barbara Oomen, a legal anthropologist, also maintains that South Africa's powerful chiefs, as evident from the ethnographic study of "Sekhune," a community in Northern Province, continue to maintain important social, economic, and judicial roles in the evolving political dispensation in the 1990s, affirming that realistic collaboration with the state is possible. Mamdani also argues that a healthy development of a "bifurcated state" with polarization of power between the urban power and the customary rural power may not be a bad idea.[16] In fact, the conflict between chiefs and the successful political party, Botswana Democratic Party (BDP) in Botswana reflects the growing divisions between rural and urban populations, between a growing professional class and the mass of the urban and rural poor.[17]

Third, the African conviction demands that there should be a possibility of shared sovereignty to sustain moral commitments of joint responsibilities. In pre-modern Africa, the state system was not unitary with little scope of pluralism. Control of state boundaries was vague and unclear in the past. In the Sokoto Caliphate, "the area within its perimeter did not wholly come under its jurisdiction" as there were still "pockets of enemy states and people."[18] The early Yoruba kingdom of Oyo was among the "large internally autonomous kingdoms whose rulers were said to derive their crowns from Oyo and were vassals of Alafin."[19] There were possibilities of shared sovereignty. Thus, instead of developing a "template that all states had to fit," state systems were, in fact, diverse in precolonial Africa, which was appropriate to difficult economic and geographic conditions in Africa. It was not simple "primitivism" and pure simplicity.[20] The Afro-centric romantics have earlier explained the Zulu state formation in Southern Africa after 1818 as a demonstration of power and coherence of African initiative. Recent scholarship, justifiably, concludes that Shaka's sovereignty and enactments of power defy any neat categorization because it is not clear what is "African."[21]

It is legitimate to argue that Kwame Nkrumah and Leopold Senghor did not acquire their charismatic qualities in the 1960s from chiefs or from the unchanging traditional side of Africa. Recent African scholarship affirms that they did not base their rule on tradition because that would bring in traditional rulers whom many of the early leaders had fought for control in the last stages of colonialism.[22] A cosmopolitan vision of politics and nationalism was well articulated by Kirwa and the Kampi Nandi squatters in Kenya to overcome President Moi's violent politics. The Kirwa ethnic group claimed that what they wanted was a fair price for their land and that rich individuals supported by the central government must not be given priority. Like many other local movements in East Africa, Nandi nationalists defined civic virtue as a willingness to combat land accumulation from the center.[23] Here, as Kymlicka argues, community should be seen as the source of principles of justice which should be based on the shared understandings of society, not on the universal and historical principles.[24] Rights of citizens require that conflicting demands of various groups are reconciled. The current political order fails to take account of the fact that in many African countries, pastoralists and hunter-gatherers are located at the margins of political life. Formal political institutions are of little use to them as instruments of redress. Intoxicated with pride and political ambition and guided by existing Western institutions, the first generation of African leaders aimed to establish their unequivocal rule over societies. Social control is power of the infrastructural kind that can increase state capabilities by interaction with one another and can incorporate ordinary citizens.[25] The African states have increased military and police power and increased their capabilities by foreign aid and support and yet the social control remains today highly fragmented.

Fourth, some of the Western federal systems intended to mitigate the negative intensity of ethnic identity, have been implemented with some success in several states. The federal solutions are sought to adjust local and regional interests in the spirit of consensus, which is a political concept. The Nigerian federation was built on a triangle of ethnic groups, the Igbo, the Yoruba, and Hausa-Fulani, each at the core a region. It came to appear that Nigeria had only three groups, when in fact, more than 40 percent of Nigerians identified with none of these three. The story of Nigerian constitutional reorganization is one of accommodating ethnic aspirations and reducing dominance of the larger ethnic groups. Its subtext is the important influence that institutional forms, the jurisdictional structures of government, have in shaping ethnic consciousness. In Africa, a solution to ethnic aspiration requires new notions of the state do not depend on one form.[26] No doubt, in every country one or two cultures and languages receive hegemonic support. Consociational and ethnically diverse Belgium has developed national unity based on two languages.[27]

Obviously there are differing experiments. In contrast to revolutionary regimes in neighboring Mozambique, the ANC government has pursued a conservative policy. It has not dismantled rural political structures, although it is by necessity preserving structures that were seen by the black majority as illegitimate. Recently, the government has embarked on a comprehensive program of developing "a vision which will harmonise the indigenous institutions of traditional leadership with our evolving system of democratic governance." But will this compromise erode democracy and encourage the patrimonialism that has afflicted the continent? [28]

Fifth, the African concept gives a priority to civil associations as helping factors. Anthonio Gramsci, the intellectual father of the ambiguous concept of civil society, suggests that a positive democratic social change can be arrived at by the work of civil society that is formed by a series of apparatuses. These include: churches, unions, parties, cooperatives, and civic associations. These, on the one hand, prolong the dynamics of the state, but on the other hand, are deeply rooted among people, and thus it has a dual character. Civil society may seize a state without launching a direct violent assault. This is an important type of identity-building in society. An investigative report by Jonathan Moyo claims that civil society in Zimbabwe—bar associations, so-called independent press and agricultural unions stand for the rights of property rather than for the right of the poor.[29] Nevertheless, Ethiopian intellectuals, many of whom are uprooted exiles, are shaping and nursing a new process of state-building in which the old Ethiopian national symbols such as the Coptic Church, the royal institution, and ancient myths are irrelevant.[30] With no dissent, twenty-seven organizations, nineteen of them based on ethnicity, declared in July 1991 that general democratic political rights of individuals would be affirmed by all the parties including civil organizations. Many civil organizations in Ethiopia have non-traditional civil roles. In Ethiopia, the central government was earlier dominated by one group, the Amhara elite. It was realized that the Amhara and the Tigre peasants also suffered from the inefficient monarchical and socialist regimes. The noted scholar of Ethiopian politics, Christopher Clapman, argues that the Ethiopian political system "is not ethnically exclusive." Concerned groups of citizens calculate that "there can be rewards for staying together as a united Ethiopia." [31]

In sum, we have to examine empirically the historical development in which different groups contested the meaning of citizenship. In this context, concepts are not cultural artifacts but what Durkheim called "natural objects" or facts, and as such, the cultural infrastructure of analysis is not a claim for the discursive constitution of the social world but rather part of a strategy of analysis.[32]

Ethnicity and African Attitude

The rediscovery of ethnicity in African intellectual discourse owes much to the presence of ethnicity as a political reality in the wake of the failures of political states. Once stigmatized by neo-Marxist and modernization paradigms, ethnicity has regained its dominance from the 1990s because of the spread of novel ideas and experiments in different parts of the world.

If otherness implies distance from us, not living in the same moral universe, then it is unacceptable in traditional Africa. Africans do not claim to have a homogenous unit in a particular place with an exotic culture. Nor is there any claim that all the contemporary ethnic groups descended from some kinds of "tribes." While some precolonial African societies, such as some of the small Akan states of southwestern Ghana and southeastern Ivory Coast, did come close to such a model, most did not. Even where they did approach this model, it was often a quite recent development. Because national politics requires people to collaborate with one another to compete for resources, political leaders often mobilize these ethnic groups to create voting blocs or organize sides in civil conflicts.[33] Moreover, professional interests, such as those of doctors or civil servants, have become important bases of political mobilization. Likewise, peasant farmers of many different ethnic groups that live together in a particular region of a country are subjects of political mobilization for many non-emotional reasons. In some countries, such as Kenya and the Ivory Coast, large farmers are powerful interest groups, cutting across ethnicity, although ordinary peasants as a class are not part. When large peasant organizations exist, as in Ethiopia between 1975 and 1991, they are likely to become instruments of government control over the peasants rather than channels through which peasants express their demands.[34]

Ethnicity is not based on "mysticism and myths;" its negative elements come from social injustice.[35] Insightfully clarifying the issue, Thomas Scheff argues that ethnic conflict is potentially a soluble problem, since it arises out of injustice and alienation. Interminable and senseless conflict, he adds, is caused by an internal machine, unacknowledged damaging alienation and the associated "spiral of shame and anger." If this theory is true, then there is "a possibility that the bad machine in ethnicity can be dismantled,"[36] by incorporating African egalitarian political values into a Western individualistic construct. Scholars in African ethnic studies often misunderstand the African social ideology when they view it as monolithic and lacking flexibility.[37] It is valid to argue that ethnicity can be an essential ingredient of both oppression and liberation. By itself, it does not induce either resistance or new projects. The truth is that civil society, family, and community provide unbreakable eternal codes around which a counter-offensive is mounted against the culture of ideological dominance. While the resistance politics from below can take ethnic form, at the same time it may include a wider and more inclusive civic and national consciousness.

This moral ethnicity is likely to present a genuine challenge to "political tribalism" that resorts to the divisive competition for state power by members of the political class, who unduly claim to speak for unified ethnic communities. In trying to understand Kikuyu definitions of a moral community in the origins of Mau Mau, John Lonsdale, for instance, argues that there was no uniform peasant consciousness in national identity in Kenya.[38] In Kenya, where ethnic groups are many, there has been some political production of a national ideology, nyayoism, love and unity, laws against "tribalism" or "political ethnicity." One interpretation is that the legitimization of Kenya's one-party form of government under Moi is based on efforts to overcome coups and chaos stemming from "ethnic alliances and sub-national factions."[39] The state has a deliberate proactive role in mediating the issues of pluralism through the constitutions and legal systems. In this role, the state and its agencies recognize the claims of and bestow legal standing on ethnic groups. In Kenya and Nigeria, ethnic group claims are not recognized legally, although they are central to constitutional debate and government practice, suggesting that ethnicity can be a part of a political discourse without harming the democratization process.

Few ethnonationalist movements in Africa have made intractable demands to form their own ethnic states. Many movements, such as the Sudan's People's Liberation Movement (SPLM) in the poverty-stricken south of the Sudan and the Oromo Liberation Front (OLF) in Ethiopia, have not sought secession as the solution to their ethnic issues. Despite many obstacles, The Sudan's "People's Liberation Movement" and the "Sudan's People's Liberation Army" do not perceive themselves as a disadvantaged racial or ethnic minority aspiring for federalism. Instead, they have the self-confidence to restructure national power to create a "new Sudan" in which race, culture, and religion would not determine participation in political and economic life. The southerners now hope for a "confederal arrangement."[40] The narrowly focused Inkatha Freedom (Zulu) Party (IFP) in post-apartheid South Africa has also clearly rejected independence in favor of some form of federal arrangement. Thus, there has been an adoption of a realistic goal to integrate different ideas to form a workable and peaceful new order in political life.[41]

Economic Order

Inspired by the command economy of socialism that called for economic and political discipline, the first generation African elites resorted to regimentation in all spheres of life in the wake of social unrest and political disorder. With the collapse of the Soviet economy and the continual "growth-tragedy" in macro-economy in Africa, the Marxian assumption lost its charm and as such liberal economy (mostly a variety of mixed economy) came into fashion. The general economic decay and consequent state contraction not only strengthened ethnic loyalties to civil society in sub-Saharan Africa but also sought new ways to economic development.

The "African" economic model accepts some basic premises of progressive liberalism such as the state's role to direct citizen organizations and associations that may cut across cleavage lines in conflict-ridden regions to build social trust. To an African, the state is the center surrounded by a relevant significant periphery and the active community, and as such, the state should help the pursuit of private affluence through the expansion of productivity, technology and access to raw materials inside and outside the nation. This is collective freedom in which both the economy of the villages and the industrial, though small, economy in the urban sector can contribute to the growth of a national economy. Several chief features in the model may be examined.

Moral lessons of social inequality arising out of the free market were questioned because African traditions place high value on care for the less fortunate members of society. In Kenya, for instance, the question of equity came to be subordinated to the quest for economic growth along overtly capitalist lines. Certain people, having political connections, raised loans to buy large farms, which had been excluded from general resettlement schemes, an unfair practice which novelist Ngugi wa Thiongo draws attention to in his much read novel, A Grain of Wheat. In the novel, the protagonists are surprised to discover that a member of parliament has bought the farm which belonged to the departing settler.[42] On balance, the majority of peasants in Kenya probably found themselves somewhat better off by the early 1980s, but there has been a debate as to whether the Kenyan path to development, departing from traditional norms, tended to lead to absolute impoverishment.[43]

One way to economic equity is to conform to the concept of development of social capital for human resources development. Various spokespersons and indigenous agencies believe that "social capital" would bring more people out of poverty. Neo-Weberian theorists construct social capital as the combination of ties and norms binding individuals within constituent elements of larger organizations, or linking them across different institutional realms, whereas others regard social capital as a moral resource such as trust, or a cultural mechanism used to reinforce the borders and fate of groups. It is unresolved whether social capital is the infrastructure or the content of social relations, or is it both? Matters become complicated further when social capital is classified as a public good that is under-produced by society. Michael Woolcock and Deepa Narayan examine the social capital issue under four distinct perspectives: the communitarian view (clubs, civic groups, and associations); the networks view (intercommunity ties that provides sense of identity and common purpose); the institutional view (the vitality of community work depends on political, legal, and institutional environment); and the synergy view (synergy between government and citizen action is based on complementarity and embeddedness). However, these two authorities are cautious to declare that the framework on analysis is not "to announce the arrival of a new paradigm."[44] What they suggest is that social capital should accompany institutional and technical development. An African claim is that social capital is to be produced by cooperation between the citizens and the government for the good of the people. Mwanga S. Kimnyi, an African historian, observes that ethnic groups may be organized on the "club model" for efficient social services. Ethnic attachments, he claims, can provide a significant substitute for Western contract law.[45]

Literary figures offered some suggestions. In 1966, Chinua Achebe's *A Man of the People*, made a scathing satirical attack on political and economic corruption leading to unequal accumulation of capital in some hands. In the same year, Ayi Kwei Armah's novel, *The Beautiful Ones Are Not Yet Born* bitterly made an exposition of the ruling classes in sub-Saharan Africa. Armah argued that "classical" understanding of social development contained two notions of culture—one in which culture represented the traditional, that which was pre-existing and contrary to development, and another in which culture stood for "a set of institutions" that emerges as a consequence and reflection of social development. The novelist suggested that an African had to reflect on both the social development and modernization theories.[46]

Various strategies have been tried to develop human capital. "The Undugu Society of Kenya" (Undugu means brotherhood) is committed through income-generating activities, community health, and shelter improvement, to help the poor in Nairobi and its environs. The experience of the society repudiates the thesis that civil society organizations directly engage the state on behalf of society to force political reform. Through several economic projects that enhance the political capacities of local communities, the Kenyan Society, like other organizations in East and Central Africa, helps to mobilize citizens and influence the direction of political change toward greater participatory economic democracy and managerial accountability. Nigerian and South African experiments show that organizations that have more direct mobilized constituencies with concrete goals succeeded more than organizations with abstract goals in democracy. In short, for sustainable development, civil society and private economic organizations become legitimate partners of, not replacements for, state institutions and market actors. They promote, as Robert Putnam and associates argue, "social capital" leading to reinforcement of African civic norms.[47]

Inter-ethnic Economic Cooperation

Although the design of public policies that promote interethnic economic cooperation remains poorly understood, a recent field research, despite its methodological shortcomings with small samples, suggests that the post-Julius Nyerere Tanzanian economic approach has allowed ethnically diverse communities in rural Tanzania to achieve considerable fund-raising for local public projects such as road construction and water wells. Under economic power-sharing in Tanzania, ethnic minorities have been assured some minimum representation in village and district governments and some influence over policy, including a veto power over certain policies concerning local economic planning. In the neighboring state of Zambia, this kind of regional activity is worth noticing. Zambia's smaller economic units like the "Women for Change," a donor supported NGO, are partly consciousness-raising and partly mutual helping. At present, this association is managed by urban educated women mainly to educate the women about national projects, management, and community values, although originally it was created from above, from the city out. Earlier it was poorly rooted in society because the group did not engage the state.[48]

Following a different strategy, the urban "home town" associations, which are community responses to modernization, also help the growth of social capital. These associations bind together individuals from across socioeconomic stations and in spaces far away from their ancestral communities. They serve for mobilization of resources, through levies on their members in order to promote development in their home towns. The elites are the patrons. They offer platforms for accumulating social capital that can be expended in the pursuit of political objectives. These home-town associations allow for some downward redistribution of wealth. Unwilling to be involved in these associations invites the labeling of the recalcitrant as morally community outcasts. Conflicts over conceptions of local citizenship are perhaps the most salient factor in ethnic tensions in rural society. It is worth observing that commercialization of agriculture is a struggle for resources. Members of communities whose rights are thus challenged typically resort to universalist definitions of citizenship, by placing the emphasis on settlement and ownership of property.[49]

All these endeavors, including civil activities, pose a related question. Are these anti-state programs which stand for fragmentation in economic planning? Some authorities suggest that the goal of most rural communities in Africa including Guinea-Bissau is not to "redistribute power" so much as to conserve legitimately based local control over community-level social and economic authority structures. Indeed, peasants have benefited from their investment in agrarian struggles but at the same time they merged their interests into a "common organic principle." In this sense, the rural civil society has kept the autonomy of the groups and social formations and also contributed to the national cohesion.[50] The great anthropologist Jean-Francois Bayart argues that production agencies and rural social agencies in Angola, Mozambique, Ethiopia, Madagascar, and Congo have not "chipped away" state authority despite the fact that the rural agents have gained benefits from their resistance and struggles.[51] Lineages, chiefdoms, secret societies, and local communities have constructed, altered, and reconstructed their own authority and leadership structures. In short, historically generated community-based social formations are central to our understanding the legacies of state weakness in sub-Saharan Africa. The problem as spelled out in modernization theories is that "the affairs of rural Africans," are submerged below the "gaze of government and even of African leaders."[52] The rural actions are hidden from the public view. Social capital development demands a progressive coverage that should include the rural sectors as well.

Although the state is the ultimate agency of self-conscious political action and economic planning, other civil institutions and affiliations, such as family, religious bands, regional groupings, and ethnic affiliations, provide other significant sites of identification and produce aggregate social effects through their actions and economic transactions. Several NGOs and governments now assume that a prime way to survive and accumulate is through retreat from state dependence to national interdependence, with an economic priority rather than political statements. Informal business enterprises, even illicit trading, and urban welfare associations, in lieu of ineffective trade unions mobilize social and economic development. The well-intentioned government efforts have created some problems. The involvement of the Kenyan state in regulating access to public land after independence increased rather than decreased and contributed to the deepening of the land question rather than its resolution. The state's practice of individualizing public land in the coastal district according to political considerations created more people without rights to land and generated new types of disputes over ownership. Resistance from below became an important mechanism for limiting such forms of land accumulation.[53] There is little societal base for contesting state prerogatives or even advocating institutional neutrality.

The African orientation is not irrationality and simple reproduction of old values. It is a means to introduce the modern complexity of profit–and participation–oriented institutions. Eventually, there is the development of dynamic and calculating personalities and the duality of "mass" and "high" cultures which become liberated from traditional narrow subsistence functions. Self-reliance, national unity, mass education and health are the developmental themes echoed by African creative and performing literature as well. The Ndebele artistic works in Zimbabwe reflect a spirited cooperative spirit. For instance, the play "Bulawayo's Elimnyama Theatre Cooperative" drew 300 audiences in the 1980s. Cain Mathema's play, "Silbhekise Ngaphi," reflects through its hero in the play, the equal social rights for all ethnic groups–the Shona, Ndebele, Manyika, and other groups. This native presentation is a kind of cultural emancipation that is thus seen as a precondition for socioeconomic development.[54] Two other books, *Land, Freedom & Fiction: History and Ideology in Kenya* and *Theatre and Cultural Struggle in South Africa* utilize a Gramscian notion of cultural hegemony in national reconstruction,[55] and African culture presumes that considering the gross imbalances between high and low earners in market fundamentalist America, most Africans would prefer slower growth as a price to pay for more economic equity.

Assessment

"The New African," with an adoption of some Western liberal ideas, seeks economic planning on the basis of limited capitalism and a mixed bag of socialism, but at the core of the system, there is a need "for social legislation affecting the economy,"[56] an economy that is beyond ethnic influence. In this context, migrations throughout Africa are helping interaction between groups to bring about economic integration. Streams of labor migrations to Zambia's "copperbelt" mining, for instance, emphasize group membership as more relevant than original ethnicity. Since the workers are individually tied to the mining enterprises, ethnicity is deliberately shown off. But the bulk of the subordinate classes consist of peasants, workers, and petty-commodity producers. The peasants are still deeply involved in the production of use value, and their involvement in commodity relations is limited. Here the differentiation of economic interests is rudimentary. The individual has not fully emerged as a legal subject. In some countries, such as Kenya and Ivory

Coast, large farmers are a powerful interest group. Of course, peasants have yet to get a deal from state and civil society.

Under the existing conditions, the state-controlled social services expanded in a haphazard manner, which tended to reinforce regional disparities; the income gap between the richest and the poorest have widened markedly. But the emphasis which was placed on the national interest has narrowed the scope for ethnically based competition in several states, including Kenya and Tanzania. Ethnic pluralism is not necessarily antithetical to the formation of inclusive political community and a generalized public economic sphere. Yet, it must be admitted that the exercise of authority by ethnic patrons, often according to traditional criteria, isolates small groups from wider arenas of association. Markets for capital, labor and commodities are still regionally or ethnically segmented and often localized,[57] and neither traditions nor modernizations have given any solution.

Religious Fundamentals in State-building

In the fourteenth century, Ibn Battuta noted the impact of the circulation of Shiite ideas in West Africa, indicating their potency in social and political reform. Currently, an assorted spiritual past has generated an urge for social and political reforms to make better conditions for state stability in sub-Saharan Africa. M. Louise Pirouet insightfully concludes that it is the African religious institutions and organizations, including Roman Catholic and Protestant churches in Africa, which have the capacity to help "modify undemocratic and repressive governments. One religious group in Kenya declared, "Our task is to provide the moral alternative of non-violent reformation through communication and dialogue."[58]

Historical experience suggests that religious grass-roots movements are significant driving forces in patterning the reformulation of state structure. Religious ideas generally govern relationships of people with a perceived spirit world. This principle can govern relations of one person to another, or of one person to a community, but also of people to the country they live in. An admission that religion is a source for development does not mean that policy makers can simply add religious institutions to the range of policy instrument at their disposal. Given this principle, it is certainly possible to identify specific sectors in which religion can play a positive role in social and political progress. However, there are difficulties in attempting to add religion to the list of tools that are basically used in economic development and political state formulation, but there are some sectors in which religion may play a role.[59] There is a corpus of beliefs and religious practices that are common in Africa and to a certain degree constitute an underlying worldview of public life.[60]

Historical literature, attuned to the developmental history of religious culture in relation to state, has taken on the paradoxical task of documenting the influential impact of cultures while, at the same time, demonstrating the powerful modernizing effects of the global flow of styles, fashions, discourses, and practices. Without directly engaging in the relative merit of either side, I argue that despite their rejection of the liberal label, many African intellectuals, religious philosophers, and traditional community leaders have never failed to incorporate Western liberal values into political and social ideas. As admitted by the distinguished anthropologist, E.E. Evans-Pritchard, there are sets of questions in society that include technology, morality, and religious beliefs, all of which govern our lives "with a mixture of skepticism and belief."[61] There is a belief in Africa that religious values and ethics may provide a good foundation for a political kingdom. Several spiritual dimensions may be examined to support my hypothesis that religions have played a meaningful role in state formulation, and are likely to do more, partly because there have been no ethnicity-related issues in religious discourse.

First, there has been a conventional argument that Africans are satisfied with the existing economic conditions and as such wealth creation has not been a priority. My argument is that wealth generation has been an important goal in African faiths. Vaguely defined "Protestant ethics" in the West has, it has been argued, led to free enterprise and overall social progress. The spiritual "ethics" supports the legitimacy of wealth and the moral value of saving or sustained investment. In the same spirit, the wealthy and politically powerful men and women in sub-Saharan Africa are glad of the "blessing of God and the ancestors and the poor are always challenged to ponder critically about human responsibility."[62] In the African mind-set, there is nothing wrong in accumulating life-sustaining wealth. Preaching the so-called "prosperity gospel" in Africa, certain religious networks, such as the Mourides of Senegal, called for creation of wealth to satisfy earthly need.[63] Here there was an avenue for state leaders to identify opportunities for policies aimed at wealth creation or enhancement. In recent times, this gospel has tuned into development of "social capital" in Africa. God, according the Kikuyu in Kenya, wants people to be prosperous but can work only through obedient human hands. A Kikuyu must justify his existence by hard work. "Wealth rewards virtue as poverty punishes disobedience." The economic message is clear: the Kikuyu theology concedes the power of God or the ancestors but still holds that man can master his fate by generating wealth.[64] The implicit assumption is that virtue and power, property and labor reinforce each other.

But there is a moral debate about the principle of social justice in Africa. To Plato, justice means "just" (right as opposed to wrong); to John Rawls, "justice" involves morally approved individual (mostly political in nature) liberty," and to Aristotle, it is ethical "fairness," treating (behavior) a people proportionately. Rawls's paradigm has some meaningful relevance to our present analysis. He argues that the fundamental liberties of the person, the social and economic policies, are aimed at maximization of the long-term expectations of the least advantaged, under conditions of their fair equality of opportunities.[65] In the same vein, Kenya's youthful and energetic Oginga Odinga argued that there was no alternative to the total mobilization and development of human resources for social capital.[66] Sub-Saharan current state elites should consider how people's full range of resources, including their spiritual or religious resources, can be used for their general well-being.

Second, religion has a solidarity aspect among people. A study of the Ewe ethnic group in Ghana reported that the Western Christian missionary idea, free of any ethnic element, had not diminished the African desire to form "collective forms of identity based on lineage or clan." For the Ewe, involvement with modernity went hand in hand with new enchantment, rather than disenchantment, of the cotemporary world.[67] Despite occasional open religious conflicts in West Africa, a pacific tradition in Islam, largely influenced by local traditions, gave ideological support for peaceful coexistence among various ethnic groups. There are numerous cases in Sierra Leone, Ghana and Liberia where one partner of a couple was either a Christian or a Muslim, thereby lowering social conflict. As opposed to the Western tradition of reliance on individual critical judgment, an African peasant would say, "I am because we are." A Vai proverb in Liberia declares, "What is mine goes; what is ours abides."[68] Many cultural and religious institutions expressed collective identities, such as clan, age-set, and religious brotherhood, to which rural folk would continue to grant allegiance. Whereas the African state elites try for "departicipation" of the rural majority, the African religious institutions ask for solidarity and brotherhood, at least in the name of God.[69]

Third, the African religious orientation recognizes the centrality of state. Several African religions, by virtue of their distinct combination of geoterritorial religiosity and multi-ethnic incorporatism have captured the social allegiance to the state. In this African vision, the social contract, (John Locke, *Two Treatises of Government*) have two sides—mandate and accountability. The African traditional religions demand that there must be accountability for misdeeds of state elites. Upset by the contemporary chaotic social order and pervasive political corruption, the indigenous religious systems as well as organized churches developed a "reformist" character to offer a clear spiritual direction to state managers. The Lutheran congregants in Tanzania demanded, in a legal/religious vein, an end to racially based control over the church. On a more serious scale, independent religious movements such as Kimbanguism in Zaire, the Lumpa Church of Alice Lenshina in Zambia, and the Zionist churches in South Africa, demanded social justice from the state. Assisted by her husband, Lenshina, a church leader, created a peasant movement and since 1960 has been denouncing *boma* (district) government, chiefs and local courts all failing to adhere to African norms in collective good. Religious leaders like Chana, Mwana, and Lenshina all introduced a counter-ideology of individualism, with a strong emphasis on the suffering individual and the downplaying of kinship obligations and morality.

In both Central and East Africa, several prophetic movements, watchtowers, and Christian independent churches attempted to eradicate witchcraft and establish new forms of community ethics that could be extended to affairs of state. Here religion became a mode of knowledge or an ideology for social change, and these ideas led the religious groups to confront the state, as in the case of Lenshina versus the UNIP government under Kenneth Kaunda. Most importantly, the very concept of syncretism, as demanded by Lenshina, introduced a theme—the importance of religion in state restructuring social reorganizations. Movements such as *Zar* cults in the Sudan remained "counter-hegemonic," expressing concern about a modernity that calls for individualism.[70] At the same time, Simon Kimbangu in Zaire/Congo (formerly Belgium Congo) argued that witchcraft must be controlled and thus, as a cult leader, he gained status and power in his position as a suppressor of witchcraft.[71] Autocratic traditional rulers were denounced as witches, thereby giving the impression that resistance to traditional misrule was a moral demand.

In Kenya, individual bishops and ministers within the Presbyterian and Anglican churches criticized the abuses associated with single-party rule and lended their voices to demands for the holding of a national conference. When this provoked a furious response from the autocratic Moi regime, the Catholic Church hierarchy rallied to the side of the Protestant churchmen. As a broad pattern, the mainstream Christian churches intervened in political matters once the government power structure seemed vulnerable to attack. When they did so, their contribution was weightier than that of the independent and Pentecostal churches that were often apolitical or complicit.[72]

Society and Morals

African church leaders advocated universal moral values for social equality as well as the state's stability. South Africa's liberation theology, The Kairtos Document of 1985, opposed apartheid in order to save souls. Of course, its militant tone was disliked by more orthodox clerics. The broader goal was to introduce the elements of a non-racial and non-ethnic society, as was the norm in most Western states. In fact, the founders of the ANC envisioned the emergence of a nation that would transcend the ethnic identities of its citizens. This goal appealed to black republicans as well as multiracial unionists. It should be emphasized that black republicans and non-European unity churches generally believed that citizenship should be rooted in African communal identities, values, and virtues ("an Azania state").[73]

To put teeth to the African demand for social reforms, after the 1960s, Christian church hierarchies were rapidly Africanized; and by 1993, the Roman Catholic Church had sixteen African cardinals. There was a growth of a peasant Christianity in the Ethiopian Church manner, with strong village congregations, sparsely trained evangelists, and little superstructure. The independent churches multiplied. About 1,300 churches were founded in Zaire alone between 1960 and the early 1980s, and all of them had similar structures.

Whereas organized Christianity and Islam spawned millennia sects, rejecting many evils of the post-colonial modernity,[74] the fight against Satan became basically a permanent inner struggle. The "personified Devil" was transposed in Ghana into the realm of the imaginary, which Christian African Pietists considered the source for the revelation of truth. The allegory and the lithograph defined bad and worldly attitudes and depicted them as satanic temptations. The "Devil" was then held responsible for all kinds of sexual, culinary, anti-social and egotistic desires that enticed people to forego the heavenly kingdom and finally face Satan in hell. All these depict an existence of a moral collective identity in favor of collectivity that is likely to enhance national unity.[75]

Even "black magic" spoke against selfishness and exploitation, so far tolerated by corrupt politicians as well state elites. An investigative anthropological study found that discussions of witchcraft flourished in popular media among the Igbo in Nigeria and provided new material for describing the experience of deprivation and evil in the urban world. In fact, witchcraft, when considered as a relatively empty category in the social lives of Igbo-speaking peoples, was broadly "about" selfishness, exclusiveness, and a pervasive evil in society. Rather than being antirational, or anti-modern, witchcraft continues today to offer a possible description for actions that are morally wrong. It speaks against "selfishness and exploitation under an alien system of government and economies."[76] Some beliefs remained as movements of resistance, part of a reaction against either organized Christianity or the vicissitudes of capitalist "modernity," creating new socio-economic structures. Many Africans began to fear the secularizing thrust of modernity and so desperately looked for allegiance to faiths and traditions.[77] The religious clash between the Kikuyu and British was wrapped in culture; this was "cultural resistance." On the basis of available cultural materials, many religious actors including smaller church leaders, tried to build a new identity defining the religious position in society, and by doing so, sought to transfer the overall social structure. This identity, coupled with resistance, remains today somewhat dominant, and yet becomes a legitimizing identity to rationalize their domination of the large sections of society.

The European missions' introduction of the modern conception of the individual person might have been highly relevant to both capitalism and Protestantism, but the issue gave rise to resistance both within and between people. Some creative processes such as "creolization" and "pidgination" took place in Africa. Devil and demons are the means by which to address the attractive and destructive aspects of the Ewe group's encounter with Western concepts. Their response is a relationship between enchantment and modernity.[78] In the same vein, Moses and his fellow witch-finders in Zambia, working among the Ngoni people, are attuned to the major trends in late twentieth-century Africa—to periodic popular withdrawals from the state, to the proliferation of complex economic networks in roadways, and the emergence of global popular cultures. The prevalent One-Party states in Africa alternately attempt to suppress or co-opt these charismatic religious leaders.[79]

In sum, African religious orientation has been for territorial nationalism rather than ethnic nationalism. On a wider scale, Africa's religious encounter with colonialism required separating Christianity from the West's political project in assimilation and uniting it with Africa's own religious and cultural priorities.

Environment and African Belief

Modernization's triumph in variously taming natural environments carries with it a deep distortion of consciousness, a deviation that threatens today many African values and gives rise to the "deep ecology" movement and nature religion. The African traditional societies' demand for a better environment relies on persuasion rather than force. For a noted Kenyan scholar and social activist, the preservation of water, trees and forests is no less significant than women's social freedom. Wangari Maathai of Kenya, a Nobel peace prize winner in 2004, established the "Green Belt Movement" to highlight the links between the green and feminist movements in Africa and to encourage planting tree seedlings—indigenous acacia, fig, cedar and baobab—and help reverse deforestation. Kenyan women have so far planted 30 million seedlings, and her movement has caught on in other African countries. A respecter of water, she laments, in an inspirational new book, that in her mother's childhood, the "Gura" river used to roar down from the Aberdare range, clear and glittering with trout but the situation has changed for the worse.[80] To the development-oriented Western environmentalists, land and waters are simply resources; but the African traditional cultures hold that they occupy a sacred space and that all their actions, therefore, need sanction from gods, often accompanied by the appropriate ritual.

African masses have paid more attention to nature than the modern African political rulers. African hunters have tended to protect parts of nature, as a manifestation of the supernatural, as has been the case of protection of the Mwari cult and its natural vegetation in the mountains of Zimbabwe. There, people care about the trees, because trees give evidence of the supernatural, because the lands may reveal God. Nature is potentially sacred, or rather, it turns into sacred matter when humans experience the supernatural in vision, or ritual. A Zulu village in South Africa has a direct relationship to the ancestors; the hills have a direct relationship with the "God of the Sky."[81] Africa has a different social texture, and understanding the social achievements of sub-Saharan states thus requires an approach integrating historical, political, and environ-related religious dimensions. To a Bantu, cattle is an investment, milk and meat provider, beast of burden, and fellow living entity living in the space as occupied by all members of a family.

In African consciousness, an ethic of the environment demands that the moral standing of the non-human entities of the cosmos is given equal value with the human species. This ethic in environment is as valid in a secular context as in a transcendental one. Africans call for ecological wisdom, grassroots democracy, and personal responsibility over lifestyles, community-based economies, evolving post-traditional values, respect for diversity, and a vision for the state that asks for the quality of life as well the preservation of sacred nature. These are not romantic assertions. Several cult organizations made tremendous contributions to the preservation of nature and environment which became a spiritual/ethical issue. In Malawi, people maintain "a ritually directed ecosystem" on various social occasions. In the Kwahu district of the eastern region of Ghana, an "inselberg" in the local landscape whose surroundings are thickly forested is very much revered by the local inhabitants, who regarded it as the "home" of one of the most powerful gods in the district. This peak and its surrounding forests remain unexploited because the people are faithfully committed to nature. Local "spiritual healers" have become a powerful force in the control and management of natural resources in the region. Here, shrine activities and ecological processes have become mirror images of each other.[82]

There are many cases of an expression of phiosophical ideas about ecology. Michel Serre (1990) calls for the development of a "philosophical ecology" invoking a new a contract with nature, limiting real and symbolic violence against environment. This is similar to the social contract that excludes war and violence from society. Heike Behrend (1995) has applied this concept to explain the work of an ecological movement in northern Uganda. He argues that the Holy Spirit Movement (HSM) there has developed a political concept known as "green consciousness." Led by holy medium, Alice Auma, a young woman, the Holy Spirit Movement from 1986 wished to overthrow the Uganda government to cleanse the world of evil and to build a new world in which humans and nature would be reconciled. To achieve these goals, Holy Spirit bush soldiers and 140,000 spirits including bees, snakes, rivers and rocks would bring a cosmic uprising to save man and nature. The significance of the movement is that it was intended to save nature. This was an example of the implementation of a new social contract in which the well-being of the community would be guaranteed.[83]

Thus, the African environmental (nature as well as natural systems) values are linked to the sub-continent's religious spirit that calls for devotional attachment to environment. In the West, glorification of the individual rights creates a sense of notional equality that emphasizes abuses and misuses of species and natural resources to such an extent that "deep ecology" is largely neglected. The ethics of "deep ecology" was formulated by the Norwegian philosopher Arne Naess who in the 1930s worked with the Vienna School of positivists. He demonstrated an intimate linkage between human and nonhuman. There can be no dichotomy of reality, or value between the human and nonhuman. In the same vein, African holistic medicine, healing, and nature religion are for environment preservation.[84] They are far from the radical Green politics of the West that has a political connotation. As Vandana Shiva, a distinguished ecology scholar and an influential activist in India, eloquently observes, "natives of Africa" and Amazonia had survived over centuries with their ecologically evolved, indigenous knowledge systems. Western experts have destroyed the systems in a few years. Her message is that exploitation of the life in nature may not help nature's life-supporting capacity.[85] In our present context, an ethical study of environment means an evaluation of normative claims, judgments, beliefs, and social and state obligation.

For many traditional environmentalists in Africa, human value resides in the natural object itself and is not conferred upon it from outside. The Ethiopian Oromo environmental ethic subscribes to this view. The Oromo are a traditionally pastoral people in South-West Ethiopia, comprising about 30 percent of the Ethiopian population. A report affirms that the Oromo people have developed a complex system of agriculture and intensive soil, water, vegetation and wildlife management that have survived the test of time and the vagaries of the environment. These traditional ethnic practices incorporate Oromo values and beliefs more than Western practices incorporate Western traditional values. Unlike anthropocentrists, the Oromo have deep emotional concerns for the future and health of both human beings and nonhuman creatures. This report reinforces the arguments of some others who claim that indigenous and modern knowledge are not mutually exclusive; in some instances, one may be superior to the other.[86]

Anthropologists have long appreciated the interaction of religion and management of the environment, especially in agricultural systems. Thus, Zionist churches in South Africa place exceptional importance on water baptism, believing that water is perhaps the most influential connection to the revered past. According to one regional belief, humanity emerges out of a marshy area near the bank of a river, and thus water also is a central component of the process by which people become healers. In Africa, water is a very essential element that welcomes the person to the community of the faithful that is connected and sustained by the past. Water is capable of relocating the faithful within the fabric of history ultimately rooted in the very birth of humanity, a time that people associate with the "proper morality."[87]

Is this African appeal "eco-romantic" that dislikes modernity? Does the African call for nature preservation testify to the continent's desire to regain the supposed lost paradise of the distant past? Do these traditionalists possess a rational level of awareness that can seek practical solutions to economic development? Some authorities claim that ecophilosophers, particularly deep ecologists and nature mystics, tempt us to look backward to a supposed "paradise" before human-kind was polluted with material culture and society.[88] My counter-argument is that African deep ecology has led to some direct action, though limited. Philosophically, Jurgen Habermas's argument helps to clarify my position on African environmental principles. Habermas argues that the hunting peoples did not distinguish the boundaries "of their societies" from the natural world.[89] Management of natural resources is internationally regarded as crucial to Africa's development, in which traditional religious networks (not organized religions like Islam or Christianity) continue to play a positive role. There is a conviction that relationships between people and the land they live on or cultivate are governed by identifiable spirits, whose favor may be earned by maintaining a healthy relationship with the land itself.[90] Farmers consider the hunter-gatherers of the hills to be of the land; intruders are visitors. The land in the Eastern Cape has been destroyed, resulting in ecological disaster. If democracy in South Africa has arrived, will it bring rain, as well? At the core of the new political history will be an exploration of the relationship between politics and suffering, about social health and a healthy environment.[91]

In sum, the sub-Saharan states need to have some useful ingredients, such as a strong commitment to the preservation of land and water, political processes promoting environmental protection, the decision to prioritize ecology, and above all a focus on peasant agriculture and improving the livelihood of the rural poor.

Conclusion

There are competing arguments between ethnic communities and states, nations and "peoples," and civil society and national government, and as such there is no point in fully criticizing the modern state system because the rule of equal treatment and social justice may be interpreted in the light of claims and counter claims. Rights and social justice have rival moral claims. This essay has argued that the requirements of logic and the long-term requirements of universal justice commend the idea of accepting local communities as right-and-duty-bearing units.[92]

The underlying assumptions in my analysis are several. First, the measure of success in the expansion of the people's ideology has been evident in the development of a public with clear opinions, that expects governments to govern, but holds them accountable for the quality of their governance. The African publics ask for a close examination of vital issues in the mindscape, the cultural feelings, the interests, and the judgments of the common citizenry.

So the ethnic perspective has been situated within the modernization paradigm which seeks to explain sub-Saharan underdevelopment in ahistorical terms of the sense of modernity. Modernization and Westernization were expected to bring the withering away of ethnicity,[93] as if ethnic intimacy itself is a problem. Even small clashes between groups have been interpreted through the master narrative. Community identity does not necessarily lead to conflict. The master narrative has acquired hegemony in a Gramscian sense, in that more and more people have come to believe it. Others would make a distinction between hegemony and dominance, the latter term meaning imposition from above but not acceptable from below.[94]

A major problem in sub-Saharan Africa is the prevalence of poverty, which has been seen as the main cause of institutional crisis rather than a result of institutional failure. Research using public choice theory provides alternative explanations for political instability. Africa's unitary centralized states do not compromise optimal units of collective choice. Unifying ethnic groups by state decree has resulted in institutions that are not suited to achieving cooperative agreements among various groups.

Second, an ethnic process by itself has no real meaning unless understood in its interactions with other processes in human relationships. When people identify themselves more closely with their ethnic group or faith than with the country, political parties can become the means of promoting narrow communal interests, or worse, fomenting ethnic grievances. Ethnicism and ethnic mentality are political culture rather than a theoretical masterpiece from one individual mind. It is a body of thought resting on a cumulative consensus, linking the past with the present and future. For instance, the attempt to reinstitute the kingdom of Buganda in modern Uganda as an "ideal ethnic identity" may at best be defined as "cultural." Kwame Appiah has correctly argued that this reorganization of an old institution, "however revered does not fit into the public" worldview. This Uganda "Mikado" is only a vague reference to a historic connection and has no ethnic linkage.[95]

As Partha Chatterjee, the noted sub-alternist historian, succinctly states, the nationalist cultural project in producing disciplined citizens for emerging nations should take notice of the "root in the inner spaces of the community, especially in the new restructured everyday wife of the family, and not simply in the public institutions of civil society." Publics have to be aware of moral corruption in the existing state formulation.[96] As some scholars propose, there is a need for a change in theoretical focus and terminology in both politics and economy. Instead of having phrases such as "imagined communities" and "imagined nations," phrases that betray a finality, social engineers and actual state-builders should emphasize the multiple and often fragments of ideology that underlie continuing shifting conceptions of any given nation. African national imaginary is a living imaginary that rejects universalism, a stance upheld by the sub-alternists.[97]

Third, social movements supported by ethnic groups and civil society may provide avenues for conflict resolution in several countries such as the Democratic Republic of Congo (formerly Zaire), Rwanda, Burundi, Sierra Leone, Liberia, Nigeria, and Somalia. What is not stressed in the existing literature is that ethnic violence is not primordial in most cases in sub-Saharan Africa. The Angolan civil war had its own internal dynamic. Although originally it was interpreted as a mixture of ideological and ethnic differences, recent researchers demonstrate that the line of division is blurred. The ascetic strain in the MPLA government gave way to elite corruption. The privatization provided the perfect cover for MPLA politicians to enrich themselves. As the MPLA and UNITA used increasingly refined weaponry to continue their feud, they stopped to view ethnicity as a weapon. Extra-judicial killings of ordinary citizens remained fashionable in the corrupt atmosphere in Angola. The highly factional and regionalized nature of Chadian politics means that a consensus is highly unlikely. The endemic weakness of the central government of Chad helps the rebel movements to receive the monetary support of the Libyan and Sudanese regimes. Many of these vicious civil conflicts, fought in a Post-Cold War environment, did not turn on differences of ideology, religion and ethnicity, but on the struggle for material resources, especially mineral wealth (e.g., diamonds in Congo-Brazzaville and Sierra Leone). Unfortunately the international community, ignoring a common humanity, fails to over-ride traditional respect for "state sovereignty."[98]

In conclusion, most African studies have ignored the true role of culture in the state reconstruction. Originally, "culture" deriving from the Latin *cultura/colo*, meant to care for, refine, grow, or raise up, especially in an agricultural sense, a setting not different from the African scene. When applied to public questions, culture is commonly understood to have an organic historical as opposed to a philosophic or creedal connotation. "Cultural conditions are the soil and fertilizer in which political systems take root and grow and out of which they define themselves with reference to particulars"—this land and this people.[99]

Notes

1   Michael D. Levin, ed., *Ethnicity and Aboriginality: Case Studies in Ethnonatioanlism* (Toronto: University of Toronto Press, 1993).

2   Joel S. Migdal, *Strong Societies and Weak States: State-Society Relations and State Capabilities in the Third World* (Princeton: Princeton University Press, 1988), 256-58.

3   Immanuel Wallerstein, *The Capitalist World-Economy* (Cambridge: Cambridge University Press, 1979).

4   Kelley M. Askew, *Performing the Nation: Swahili Music and Cultural Politics in Tanzania* (Chicago: University of Chicago Press, 2002), 272-83.

5   George Steinmetz cited in Askew, *Performing the Nation*, 11.

6   Robert Putnam, *Making Democracy Work* (Princeton: Princeton University Press, 1993), 90.

7   Stephen Ellis, *The Mask of Anarchy: The Destruction of Liberia and the Religious Dimension of an African Civil War* (New York: New York University Press, 199), 291.

8   Ulf Hannerz cited in John Hargreaves, *Decolonization in Africa* (London: Longman, 1988), 67.

9   Ronald Beiner, "Community versus Citizenship," *Critical Review* 14 (4) (2000), 463.

10   *Recent Studies on Ethnicity in South Africa: Ethnicity in Focus*, 89.

11   Carl G. Rosberg, "Why Africa's Weak States Persist: The Empirical and Juridical in Statehood, "*World Politics*, 27 (October 1982), 2-3.

12   Jomo Kenyatta cited in Frank Fueedi, *The Mau Mau War in Perspective* (London: James Currey, 1989), 89.

13   Benedict Anderson, *Imagined Communities: Reflections on the Origins and Spread of Nationalism* (London: Verso, 1983), 114-15; Clifton Crais, *The Politics of Evil: Magic, State Power, and the Political Imagination in South Africa* (Cambridge: Cambridge University Press, 2002), 124-25.

14   C.R.D. Halisi, *Black Political Thought in the Making of South African Democracy* (Bloomington: Indiana University, 1999), 58.

15   Ernest Gellner, *Nations and Nationalism* (Ithaca, N.Y.: Cornell University Press, 1983); Eric J. Hobsbawm, *Nations and Nationalism since 1780* (Cambridge; Cambridge University Press, 1990).

16   Mahmood Mamdani, *Citizen and Subject: Contemporary Africa and the Legacy of Late Colonialism* (Princeton: Princeton University Press, 1996).

17 Olufemi Vaughan, ed., *Tradition and Politics: Indigenous Political Structures in Africa* (Trenton, N.J.: Africa World Press, 2005), 7, 27, 121.

18 R.A. Adeleye, *Power and Diplomacy in Northern Nigeria, 1804–1906* (New York: Humanities Press, 1971), 52–53.

19 Peter Morton-Willimas, cited in Jeffrey Herst, *States and Power in Africa: Comparative Lessons in Authority and Control* (Princeton: Princeton University Press, 2000), 54.

20 Jeffrey Herbst, "The Dilemmas of Land Policy in Zimbabwe," in Simon Baynham, ed., *Zimbabwe in Transition* (Stockholm: Almqvist International, 1992), 90.

21 Steven Feierman, "Colonizers, Scholars, and the Creation of Invisible Histories," in Victoria E. Bonnell and Lynn Hunt, *Beyond the Cultural Turn* (Berkeley, Calif.: University of California Press, 1999), 183.

22 Peter P. Ekeh, "Colonialism and the Development of Citizenship in Africa: A Study in Ideologies of Legitimation," in Onigu Ottie, ed., *Themes in African Social and Political Thought* (Enugu, Nigeria: Fourth Dimension Publishing Company, 1978), 28–29.

23 Jacqueline M. Klopp, "Can Moral Ethnicity Triumph Political Tribalism? The Struggle for Land and Nation in Kenya," *African Studies* 61 (2) (December 2002), 286.

24 Kymlicka cited in Yusef Waghid, "Communitarian Deliberative Democracy and Its Implications for Political Discourse in South Africa," *Politikon: South African Journal of Political Studies* 29 (2) (November 2002), 184.

25 Michael Mann cited in Migdal, *Strong States*, 23.

26 Michael D. Levin (ed.), *Ethnicity and Aboriginality: Case Studies in Ethno-nationalism* (Toronto: University of Toronto Press, 1993), 177.

27 Arend Lijphart, *Democracies: Patterns of Majoritan and Consensus Government in 21 Countries* (New Haven: Yale University Press, 1984).

28 Department of Provincial and Local Government, "A Draft Discussion Document towards a White Paper on Traditional Leadership and Institutions" (April 11, 2000); Clifton Crais, *The Politics of Evil: Magic, State Power, and the Political Imagination in South Africa* (Cambridge: Cambridge University Press, 2002), 31.

29 Jonathan Moyo cited in Terence Ranger and Olufemi Vaughan, *Legtimacy and the State in Twentieth Century* (Oxford: The Macmillan Press, 1993), 260.

30 Solomon Gashaw, "Nationalism and Ethnic Conflict in Ethiopia," in Crawford Young, ed., *The Rising Tide of Cultural Pluralism: The Nation-State at Bay* (Madison: The University of Wisconsin Press, 1993), 141–42.

31 Herbert S. Lewis, "Ethnicity in Ethiopia: The View from Below," in Crawford Young, ed., *The Rising Tide of Cultural Pluralism*, 160.

32 Bonnell, *Beyond the Cultural Turn*, 127.

33 Kwame Anthony Appiah and Henry Louis Gates, eds., *Africana 2* (New York: Oxford University Press, 2005), 568–69.

34 Marina Ottaway and Thomas Carothers, eds., *Funding Virtue: Civil Society Aid and Democracy Promotion* (Washington, D.C.: Carnegie Endowment for International Peace 1998), 79.

35 Anthony D. Smith, *Ethnic Origins of Nations* (Oxford: Blackwell, 1987).

36 Craig Calhoun, ed., *Social Theory and the Politics of* Identity (Oxford: Blackwell, 1994), 300.

37   Linda M. Heywood, "Towards an Understanding of Modern Political Ideology in Africa: The Case of the Ovimbundu of Angola," *The Journal of Modern African Studies*, 36 (1) (1998), 145.

38   John Lonsdale, "Kikuyu Political Thought and the Ideologies of May Mau," Paper for the Institute of Commonwealth Studies Seminar, University of London, January 16, 1986.

39   Judith M. Abwunza, "Ethnonationalism and Nationalism Strategies: The Case of the Avalogoli in Western Kenya," in Michael D. Levin, *Ethnicity and Aborginality: Case Studies in Ethnonationalism* (Toronto: University of Toronto Press,1993), 127.

40   Francis Deng Mading, "Negotiating a Hidden Agenda: Sudan's Conflict of Identities," in I. William Zartman, ed., *Elusive Peace: Negotiating an End to Civil Wars* (Washington, D.C.: The Brookings Institution, 1995), 95.

41   Kidane Mengisteab and Cyril Daddieh, "Why State Building Is Still Relevant in Africa and How It Relates to Democratization," in Kidane Mengisteab and Cyril Daddieh, eds., *State Building and Democratization in Africa: Faith, Hope, and Realities* (Westport, Conn.: Praeger, 1999), 9.

42   Ngũgĩ wa Thiong'o, *A Grain of Wheat* (London: Heineman Educational Books, revised edition, 1988), 169.

43   Paul Nugent, *Africa Since Independence: A Comparative History* (New York: Palgrave 2004), 161.

44   Michael Woolcock and Deepa Narayan, "Social Capital: Implications for Development Theory, Research, and Policy," in Elinor Ostrom and T.K. Ahn, eds., *Foundations of Social Capital* (Northampton, Mass.: An Elgar Reference Collection, 2003), 347–50.

45   Mwanga S. Kimenyi, "Harmonizing Ethnic Claims in Africa: A Proposal for Ethnic-Based Federalism," *CATO Journal* (02733072) (Spring/Summer 1998), 14.

46   Chinua Achebe, *Girls at War and Other Stories* (London: Heinemann, 1972); Thiong'o, *Grain of Wheat*.

47   Marina Ottaway, "Social Movements, Professionalization of Reform, and Democracy in Africa," Marina Ottaway and Thomas Carothers, eds., *Funding Virtue: Civil Society Aid and Democracy Promotion* (Washington, D.C.: Carnegie Endowment for International Peace, 2000), 82; Stephen N. Ndegwa, *The Two Faces of Civil Society: NGOs and Politics in Africa* (Hartford: Kumarian Press, 1996), 6 and 58; Christopher Landsberg, "Voicing the Voiceless: Foreign Political Aid to Civil Society" in Marina Ottaway, "Africa's 'New Leaders': African Solution or African Problem," *Current History* (1998).

48   Ngwabi Bhebe and Terence Ranger, eds., *Society in Zimbabwe's Liberation War* (Oxford: James Currey, 1996), 90.

49   Dickson Eyoh, "Community, Citizenship, and the Politics of Ethnicity in Post-Colonial Africa," in Paul Tiyambe Zeleza and Ezekiel Kalpeni, eds., *Sacred Spaces and Public Quarrels: African Cultural and Economic Landscapes* (Trenton, N.J.: Africa World Press, Inc., 1999), 287–89.

50   Joshua B. Forrest, *Lineages of State Fragility: Rural Civil Society in Guinea-Bissau* (Oxford: James Currey, 2003), 246.

51   Jean-Francois Bayart, "Civil Society in Africa," in Patrick Chabal, ed., *Political Domination in Africa* (Cambridge: Cambridge University Press, 1986), 251–52.

52   William Beinart and Colin Bundy, *Hidden Struggles in Rural South Africa* (London: James Currey, 1987), 1.

53 Karuti Kanyinga, *Redistribution from Above: The Politics of Land Rights and Squatting in Coastal Kenya* (Research Report No 115) (Uppsala: Nordic Africa Institute, 2000), 121.

54 Luke Mhlaba, "Local Cultures and Development in Zimbabwe: The Case of Matabeleland," in Preben Kaarsholm, ed., *Cultural Struggle & Development in Southern Africa*, London: James Currey, 1991), 213-14.

55 T. P. Gorman, "The Development of Language Policy in Kenya with Particular Reference to the Educational System," in W.H. Whiteley, ed., *Language in Kenya* (Nairobi: Oxford University Press, 1974), 89.

56 Otite, *Themes in African Social Thought*, 291.

57 Peter M. Lewis, "Political Transition and the Dilemma of Civil Society in Africa," *The Journal of International Affairs* 46 (1) (1992), 41.

58 *Nairobi Law Monthly* 25 (September 1990), 36.

59 Stephen Ellis and Gerrie ter Haar, "Religion and Development in Africa," in Gerie Ter Harr, *Half Way to Paradise: African Christians in Europe* (Cardiff, U.K.: Cardiff Academic Press, 1998).

60 Ivor Kopytoff, cited in Brian Morris, *Religion and Anthropology: A Critical Introduction* (Cambridge: Cambridge University Press, 2006), 149.

61 E.E. Evans-Pritchard, "The Zande State," *The Journal of Royal Anthropological Institute* 93 (1) (1963), 202.

62 John Lonsdale, "The Moral Economy of Mau Mau: The Problem," in Bruce Berman and John Lonsdale, *Unhappy Valley: Conflict in Kenya and Africa* (London: James Currey, 1992), 336-37.

63 Ellis, "Religion and Development in Africa," 67.

64 Lonsdale, "The Moral Economy, " 343.

65 John Rawls cited in Maurice Mullard and Paul Spicker, *Social Policy in a Changing Society* (London: Routledge, 1998), 220-22.

66 Ali A. Mazrui, "Ideology and African Political Culture," in Thedros Kiros, ed., *Explorations*, 102.

67 Bright Meyer, *Translating the Devil: Religion and Modernity Among the Ewe in Ghana* (Trenton, N.J.: Africa World Press, 1999), xxi-xxii.

68 Cited in George B.N. Ayittey, *Indigenous African Institutions* (New York: Transnational Publishers, 1991), 16.

69 Michael Bratton, "Civil Society and Political Transition in Africa," *IDR Report* 11 (6) (1994), 3-8.

70 Brian Morris, *Religion and Anthropology: A Critical Introduction* (New York: Cambridge University Press, 2006), 315.

71 Linda M. Heywood, "Toward an Understanding of Modern Political Ideology in Africa...," *Journal of Modern African Studies*, 36 (1) (1998), 145.

72 Nugent, *Africa Since Independence*, 377.

73 Halisi, *Black Political Thought*, 59.

74 John Iliffe, *Africans: The History of a Continent* (Cambridge: Cambridge University Press, 1995), 265.

75 Meyer, *Translating the Devil*, 45.

76 Jean Comaroff and John Comaroff, eds., *Modernity and Its Malcontents* (Chicago: The University of Chicago Press, 1993), 156.

77 John Iliffe, *A Modern History of Tanganyika* (Cambridge: Cambridge University Press, 1979), 90.

78 Meyer, *Translating the Devil*, 213–215.

79 Comaroff and Comaroff, eds., *Modernity and Its Malcontents*, 188.

80 Review of book, *Unbowed: A Memoir* (London: Heineman) in *The Economist* (23 September 2006), 94.

81 H. Byron Earhart, ed., *Religious Traditions of the World* (San Francisco: Harper, 1993), 53.

82 Charles Anyinam, "Ecomedicine, Sacred Spaces, and Ecosystem Preservation and Conservation in Africa," in Paul Tiyambe, et al, *Sacred Spaces*, 128–130; J.M. Schoffelers, ed., *Guardians of the Land: Essays on Central African Territorial Cults* (Gwelo: Mambo Press, 1978).

83 Heike Behrend, "The Holy Spirit Movement and the Forces of Nature in the North of Uganda, 1985–1987," in Holger Bernt Hansen and Michael Twaddle, eds., *Religion and Politics in East Africa* (London: James Currey, 1995), 59–62.

84 B. Devall and G. Sessions, eds., *Deep Ecology: Living as if Nature Mattered* (Salt Lake City, Utah: Peregrine Smith Books, 1985).

85 Vandana Shiva, "Staying Alive: Women, Ecology, and Development," in Nora Haenn and Richard R. Wilk (eds.), *The Environment in Anthropology: A Reader in Ecology, Culture, and Sustainable Living* (New York: New York University Press, 2006), 189.

86 Workineh Kelbessa, "Indigenous and Modern Environmental Ethics: A Study of the Indigenous Oromo Environmental Ethic and Oromo Environmental Ethics in the Light of Modern Issues of Environment and Development," Ph.D. Dissertation, University of Wales (Fall 2001) <http:lamar.colostate.edu/~rolston/GRAD-INT.HTM> (Accessed 8/28/2006).

87 Michael Taussing, "The Sun Gives without Receiving: An Old Story," Comparative Studies in Society and History, 37 (2) (April 1995): 368–98; Clifton Crais, *The Politics of Evil* (Cambridge: Cambridge University Press, 2002), 133.

88 Ken Wilber, *A Brief History of Everything* (Boston: Shambala, 1996), 166 (31). For a sound analytical discussion on Wilber's thesis see "A Critique of Ken Wilber's Account of Deep Ecology & Nature Religions," <http://trumpeter.athabascau.ca/content/v13.2 /dizerega.html> (Accessed 9/29/2006).

89 "Critique of Ken Wilber's Account of Deep Ecology & Nature Religions," <home.clara.net /heureka/art/snyder.htm> Accessed September 29, 2006.

90 Ellis, "Religion and Development in Africa."

91 Clifton Crais, *The Politics of Evil: Magic, State Power, and the Political Imagination in South Africa* (Cambridge: Cambridge University Press, 2002), 23.

92 Vernon Van Dyke, "The Individual, the State, and Ethnic Communities in Political Theory," *World Politics* 29 (April 1977): 53–54.

93 Eghosa E. Osaghae, "Redeeming the Utility of the Ethnic Perspective in African Studies: Towards a New Agenda," *The Journal of Ethnic Studies* 18 (2) (1990), 43–45.

94 Ashutosh Varshney, "Postmodernism, Civic Engagement, and Ethnic Conflict," *Comparative Politics* 978 (1) (October 1997), 18.

95   Mazrui, "Ideology and African Political Culture," 102; Kwame Anthony Appiah, "Ethnic Identity as a Political Resource," in Kiros, Explorations in African Political Thought, 51–52.

96   Parha Chatterjee cited in Dipesh Chakravarty, Provincilizing Europe: Postcolonial Thought and Historical Difference (Princeton: Princeton University Press, 2000), 67.

97   M. Askew, Performing the Nation: Swahili Music and Cultural Politics in Tanzania (Chicago: University of Chicago Press, 2002), 11.

98   Nugent, Africa Since Independence, 449–50.

99   Bradley C.S. Watson, "Creed & Culture in the American Founding," Intercollegiate Review 41 (2) (Fall 2006), 35.

Bibliography

Adam, Herbert. "Ethnic Versus Civic Nationalism: South Africa's Non-Racialism in Comparative Perspective." *SA Sociological Review* 7 (1) (1994).

Aguirre, B. E., Rogelio Saenz, and Sean-Shong Hwang. "Discrimination and the Assimilation and Ethnic Competition Perspectives." *Social Science Quarterly* 70 (1989).

Ake, Claude. "Presidential Address to the Nigerian Political Science Association." *West Africa* (May 25, 1981).

Alexander, Neville. "An Approach to the National Question in South Africa." *Azania Worker,* 2 (2) (1985).

Anderson, Benedict. *Imagined Communities: Reflections on the Origin and Spread of Nationalism,* Second Edition. London: Verso, 1991.

Ayittey, George. *Africa in Chaos.* New York: St. Martin's Press, 1999.

Bailey, Thomas and Roger Waldinger. "Primary, Secondary, and Enclave Labor Markets: A Training System Approach." *American Sociological Review* 56 (1991).

Barkan, Steve. "Legal Control of the Civil Rights Movement." *American Sociological Review* 49 (1984).

Bates, Roberts H. *Ethnicity in Contemporary Africa: East African Studies XIV.* Syracuse: Syracuse University Press, Maxwell School of Citizen and Public Affairs, 1973.

———. *Markets and States in Tropical Africa.* Berkeley: University of California Press, 1981.

Bayart, Jean-Francois. *The State in Africa: The Politics of the Bell.* London: Longman, 1993.

Beck, E. M. "Guess Who's Coming to Town: White Supremacy, Ethnic Competition, and Social Change." *Sociological Focus* 33 (2000).

Belanger, Sarah and Maurice Pinard. "Ethnic Movements and the Competition Model: Some Missing Links." *American Sociological Review* 56 (1991).

Bobo, Lawrence and Vincent L. Hutchings. "Perceptions of Racial Competition in a Multiracial Setting." *American Sociological Review* 61 (1996).

Bollen, Kenneth A. *Cross National Indicators of Liberal Democracy, 1950 to 1990: Codebook.* Chapel Hill: University of North Carolina Press, 1998.

Bonachi, Edna. "A Theory of Ethnic Antagonism: Split Labor Market." *American Sociological Review* 37 (1972).

Bowen, John R. "The Myth of Global Ethnic Conflict." *The Journal of Democracy* 7 (1996).

Butler, Anthony. *South Africa's Political Futures: The Positive and Negative Implications of One-party Dominance.* Cape Town: University of Cape Town Press, 2001.

Chabal, Patrick. *Power in Africa: An Essay in Political Interpretation.* New York: St. Martin's Press, 1991.

Chatterjee, Partha. *The Nation and Its Fragments: Colonial and Post-Colonial Histories.* Princeton, NJ: Princeton University Press, 1993.

Clapman, Christopher."The Horn of Africa: A Conflict Zone." In Oliver Furley, *Conflicts in Africa.* London: Tauris Academic Studies, 1995.

Cooper, Frederick. *Africa Since 1940: The Past of the Present.* Cambridge: Cambridge University Press, 2003.

Copson, Raymond W. *Africa's Wars and Prospects for Peace.* New York: M.E. Sharpe, 1994.

Correy, John. "A Formula for Genocide." *The American Spectator.* (September), 1998.

Crawford, Beverly, et al., eds., *The Myth of 'Ethnic Conflict': Politics, Economics, and 'Cultural' Violence.* Berkeley: University of California Press, 1998.

Crawford, Brough Macpherson, *The Real World of Democracy.* Montreal: CBC Enterprises, 1983.

Crocker, Chester, et al., eds. *Managing Global Chaos: Source of and Responses to International Conflict.* (Washington, DC: United States Institute of Peace Press, 1996).

Daniel, John and Southall, Szeftel, *Voting for Democracy: Watershed Elections in Contemporary Anglophone Africa.* Burlington, VT: Ashgate Publishers, 1999.

Davidson, Basil, et al. "The Crisis of the Nation-State in Africa." *Review of African Political Economy* (Winter 1990).

Deng, Francis M. "Negotiating a Hidden Agenda: Sudan's Conflict of Identities." In I. William Zartman, eds., *Elusive Peace: Negotiating an End to Civil Wars.* Washington, DC: The Brookings Institution,1995.

Diamond, Larry. *Class, Ethnicity and Democracy in Nigeria: The Failure of the First Republic.* Syracuse: Syracuse University Press, 1988.

——. *Developing Democracy: Toward Consolidation.* Cambridge: Cambridge University Press, 1999.

Dione, Douglas. "Competition and Ethnic Conflict: Artifactual? *Journal of Conflict Resolution* 41, 5 (1997).

Donald, Horrowitz, L. *Ethnic Groups in Conflict.* Berkley: University of California Press, 1985.

Dunaway, Wilma A. "Ethnic Conflict in the Modern World-System: The Dialectics of Counter-Hegemonic Resistance in an Age of Transition." *Journal of World Systems Research* 9 (2003).

Ebere Onwudiwe. "A Reason for Optimism." *Nigerian Guardian.* Sunday (May 4, 2003).

Edozie, Kiki R. *People, Power, and Democracy:The Popular Movement Against Military Despotism in Nigeria, 1989–1999.* New York: Africa World Press, 2002.

Elazar, D. *Exploring Federalism.* Tuscaloosa: University of Alabama Press, 1987.

Fage, J.D. *A History of Africa.* London: Routledge, 2002.

Falola Toyin. *Nationalism and African Intellectuals.* Rochester, NY: University of Rochester Press, 2001.

Francisco, Ronald A. "The Relationship between Coercion and Protest." *Journal of Conflict Resolution* 39 (1995).

Frye M., Timothy. "Ethnicity, Sovereignty and Transitions From Non-Democratic Rule." *Journal of International Affairs* 45, 2 (Winter 1992).

Furtado, Charles. "Nationalism and Foreign Policy in Ukraine." *Political Science Quarterly* 109, 1 (1994).

Gagnon, V. "Ethnic Nationalism and International Conflict." In Lynn, S. and Miller, S., eds., *Global Dangers: Changing Dimensions of International Security.* Cambridge, MA: MIT Press, 1995.

Gershoni, Yekutiel. War Without an End to a War: The Prolonged War in Liberia and Sierra Leone. *African Studies Review* 40 (1997).

Glcukman, Max. "Tribalism in Modern British Central Africa," *Cahiers d'Etudes Africaines* 1 (1960).

Gurr, Ted Robert. "Minorities, Nationalists, and Ethnopolitical Conflict." In Chester Crocker et al. (eds.). *Managing Global Chaos: Sources of and Responses to International Conflict.* Washington, DC: United States Peace Institute Press, 1996.

———. *Minorities at Risk: A Global View of Ethnopolitical Conflict.* Washington, DC: United States Institute of Peace Press, 1993.

———. "Peoples Against States: Ethnopolitical Conflicts and the Changing World System." *International Studies Quarterly* 38 (1994).

———, and Barbara Harff. *Ethnic Conflict in World Politics.* Boulder, CO: Westview Press, 1994.

Gutkind, Peter. "Preface: The Passing of the Tribal Man in Africa." *Journal of Asian and African Studies* 5, 1 (1970).

Gyimah-Boadi. "Civil Society in Africa." In *Consolidating the Third Wave Democracies.* Edited by Larry Diamond, Marc Plattner, Yun-han Chu, and Hung-Mao Tien. Baltimore: Johns Hopkins Press, 1997.

Hamilton, Alexander, and Thomas Madison. *The Federalist Papers.* Washington, DC: 1787.

Henderson, Errol "A. Culture or Continuity: Ethnic Conflicts, Similarities of States and the Onset of War." *Journal of Conflict Resolution* 41 (1997).

Herbst, Jeffrey. *States and Power in Africa: Comparative Lessons in Authority and Control.* Princeton, NJ: Princeton University Press, 2000.

Heribert Adam, "Ethnic Versus Civic Nationalism: South Africa's Non-Racialism in Comparative Perspectove." *SA Sociological Review* 1 (1994).

Holsti, K.J. "National Role Conceptions in the Study of Foreign Policy." *International Studies Quarterly*, 14 (3) (September 1970).

Horowitz, Donald L. *A Democratic South Africa? Constitutional Engineering in a Divided Society.* Berkely: University of California Press, 1991.

———. "Comparing Democratic Systems." In *The Global Resurgence of Democracy.* Edited by Diamond and Plattner. Baltimore: Johns Hopkins University Press, 1996.

———. *Ethnic Groups in Conflict.* Berkeley: University of California Press, 1985.

Human Rights Watch. "Preparing for Elections: Tightening Control in the Name of Unity." New York: *Human Rights Watch Report.* 2003.

Huntington, Samuel P. "The Clash of Civilizations." *Foreign Affairs* 72 (3),1993.

Hwang, Sean-Shong and Steve H. Murdock. "Ethnic Enclosure or Ethnic Competition: Ethnic Identification among Hispanics in Texas." *The Sociological Quarterly*, 32 (1991).

Jasso, Guillermina. "Analyzing Conflict Severity: Predictions of Distributive Justice Theory." *Social Justice Research*, 6 (1993).

Jenkins, J. Craig, and Charles Perrow. "Insurgency of the Powerless." *American Sociological Review*, 42 (1977).

———, and William Form. "Social Movements and Social Change." In *The Handbook of Political Sociology*, edited by Thomas Janoski, Robert Alford, Alexander Hicks, and Mildred A. Schwartz, Cambridge: Cambridge University Press.

Johnson, H. Douglas. *The Root Causes of Sudan's Civil Wars.* Bloomington: Indiana University Press, 2003.

Johnson, Janet B, et al. *Political Science Research Methods.* Washington, DC: *Congressional Quarterly.* Government Printing Office, 1991.

Jönsson, Christer and Ulf Westerlund. "Role Theory in Foreign Policy Analysis," In *Cognitive*

Dynamics and International Politics, edited by Christer Jönsson, New York: St. Martin's Press, 1982.

Joseph, Richard. *Democracy and Prebendal Politics in Nigeria.* Cambridge: Cambridge University Press, 1987.

Kaplan, Robert D. *Surrender or Starve: The Wars behind the Famine.* Boulder, CO: Westview Press, 1988.

Kohn, Hans. *The Idea of Nationalism: A Study in the Origins and Background.* New York: Macmillan, 2005.

Komolafe, Ajayi, Ahuima-Young, Adeyemi, "Strike: First Phase to Last 4 Days." *Vanguard* (October 9, 2004.)

Kunz, Frank A. "Liberalization in Africa :Some Preliminary Reflections." *African Affairs* 90 (1991).

Lawyers Committee for Human Rights. *Liberia: A Promise Betrayed* (A Report on Human Rights). New York: LCHR Publications, 1986.

Le Vine, Victor T. "Conceptualizing 'Ethnicity' and 'Ethnic': A Controversy Revisited." *Studies in Comparative International Development* 32 (2) (1997).

Mafeje, Archie, "The Ideology of Tribalism," *Journal of Modern African Studies* 9 (2) (1971).

Mamdani, Mamhood, *Citizen and Subject: Contemporary Africa and the Legacy of Late Colonialism.* Princeton, NJ: Princeton University Press, 1997.

Minorities at Risk Project (MAR). *Minorities at Risk Dataset, version MARv899* (College Park, MD: Center for International Development and Conflict Management, University of Maryland, 1999).

Marcus, Harold G. *History of Ethiopia.* Berkeley: University of California Press, 1994.

Mare, G. *Ethnicity and Politics in South Africa.* London: Zed Books, 1999.

Mason, Philip. *Race Relations.* London: Oxford University Press, 1970.

Maynes, J. "Invitation to War: Conflict in the Balkans." *Foreign Affairs* 73, 1993.

Mazrui, Ali A. *Cultural Engineering in East Africa.* Evanston, IL: North Western University, 1972.

McAdam, Doug. *Political Process and the Development of Black Insurgency, 1930–70.* Chicago, IL: University of Chicago Press, 1982.

McCarthy, John and Mayer N. Zald. "Resource Mobilization and Social Movements: A Partial Theory." *American Journal of Sociology* 82 (1977).

Melvin, Neil *Russians Beyond Russia: The Politics of National Identity,* London: Royal Institute of International Affairs, 1995.

Merton, Robert K. *Social Theory and Social Structure.* Glencoe, IL: Free Press, 1957.

Meyer, David S. and Suzanne Staggenborg. "Movements, Counter Movements, and the Structure of Political Opportunity." *American Journal of Sociology* 101 (1996).

Migdal, Joel S. *Strong Societies and Weak States: State-Society Relations and the State Capabilities in the Third World.* Princeton, NJ: Princeton University Press, 1988.

Molteno. Robert. "Cleavages and Conflict in Zambian Politics: A Study in Sectionalism." In William Tordoff , ed. *Politics in Zambia.* Berkeley: University of California Press, 1974.

Moore Jr., Barrington. *Injustice: the Social Bases of Obedience and Revolt,* New York: M.E. Sharpe, 1978.

Moroney, Jennifer, et al., eds. *Ukrainian Foreign and Security Policy: Theoretical and Comparative Perspectives.* Westport: CT: Praeger, 2002.

Nnoli, Okwudiba. *Ethnicity and Democracy in Africa: Intervening Variables.* Lagos: Malthouse Press Ltd., 1994.

Norvall, Arletta. "Rethinking Ethnicity: Identification, Hybridity and Democracy." In Paros Yeros, ed., *Ethnicity and Nationalism in Africa: Constructivist Reflections and Contemporary Politics.* New York: St. Martins Press, 1999.

Oberschall, Anthony. *Social Conflict and Social Movements.* Englewood Cliffs, NJ: Prentice-Hall, 1973.

Olivier, Johan L. "Causes of Ethnic Collectivity and Action in the Pretoria-Witwatersrand-Transvaal Triangle." *South African Sociological Review,* 1990.

Olonisakin, Funmi. "African Homemade Peacekeeping Initiatives." *Armed Forces and Society* 23 (1997).

Olzak, Susan. *The Dynamics of Ethnic Competition and Conflict.* Stanford, CA: Stanford University Press, 1992.

——, and Tsutsui, T. "Status in the World System and Ethnic Mobilization." *Journal of Conflict Resolution* 42 (6) (1998).

Outram, Quentin. "Liberia: Roots and Fruits of the Emergency." *Third World Quarterly* 20 (1999).

Packard, Gabriel. "Nigeria: 29 Opposition Parties Back One Man Run Against Obasanjo." *IPS/GIN* (December 11, 2004).

Patterson, Orlando. "The Nature, Causes, and Implications of Ethnic Identification." In C. Fried, ed., *Minorities: Community and Identity.* Berlin, Germany: Springer-Verlag, 1983.

Paxton, Pamela. "Social Capital and Democracy: An Interdependent Relationship." *American Sociological Review* 67 (2002).

Peoples, Clayton D. "How Discriminatory Policies Impact Interethnic Violence: A Cross-National, Group-Level Analysis." *International Journal of Sociology* 34 (2004).

Philippe Le Prestre, ed. *Role Quests in the Post-Cold War Era.* Montreal: McGill and Queen's University Press, 1997.

Pinkney, Robert. *Democracy in the Third World.* Boulder, CO: Lynne Rienner, 2003.

Portes, Alejandro, and Alex Stepick. "Unwelcome Immigrants: The Labor Market Experiences of 1980 [Mariel] Cuban and Haitian Refugees in South Florida." *American Sociological Review* 50 (1985).

Prizel, Ilya. *National Identity and Foreign Policy: Nationalism and Leadership in Poland, Russia and Ukraine,* Cambridge: Cambridge University Press, 1998.

Putnam, Robert D. *Making Democracy Work: Civic Transition in Modern Italy.* Princeton, NJ: Princeton University Press, 1992.

Rabie, Mohamed. *Conflict Resolution and Ethnicity.* Westport, CT: Praeger Publishers, 1994.

Rasler, Karen. "Concession, Repression, and Political Protest in the Iranian Revolution." *American Sociological Review* 61 (1996).

Reporter. "Togo: Buy Me; I'm the Best." *New African* (June 2003).

Robertson, Ian. *Sociology.* New York: Worth Publishers, Inc, 1987.

Sadowski, Yahya. S. "Ethnic Conflict." *Foreign Policy* (February, 1998).

Sahadevan, P. "Ethnic Conflict in South Asia." *Working Papers* (June 1999). Joan B. Kroc Institute for International Peace Studies. <ww.ciaonet.org.wps.sap01>

Salih, Mohamed, M.A. *Majoritarian Tyranny in a World of Minorities.* The Hague: Institute of Social Studies, 2002.

Sandbrook, Richard. "Patron, Clients, and Factions: New Dimension of Conflict Analysis in Africa." *Journal of Political Science* 5 (1972).

Scarritt, James R. "Communal Conflict and Contention for Power in Africa South of the

Sahara." In Ted Robert Gurr. *Minorities at Risk: A Global View of Ethnopolitical Conflicts.* Washington, DC: United States Institute of Peace Press, 1993.

Schermerhorn, R. A. *Comparative Ethnic Relations.* New York: Random House, Inc., 1970.

Schmitter, Philip. "More Liberal, Pre-liberal or Post-liberal." In Larry Diamond and Marc Plattner, ed., *The Global Resurgence of Democracy* (Baltimore: John Hopkins University Press, 1996).

Sesay, Max A. "Civil War and Collective Intervention in Liberia." *Review of African Political Economy* 67, 1996.

Shaw, Timothy M. "Ethnicity as the Resilient Paradigm for Africa: From the 1960s to the 1980s." *Development and Change*, 17 (1986).

Singer, J. D. "Accounting for International War: The State of Discipline." *Journal of Peace* 98 (1996).

Southhall, P. "The State of Democracy in South Africa," *Commonwealth and Comparative Politics* 38 (3) (November 2000).

Sumner, William G. *Folkways.* New York: Ginn, 1906.

Szporluk, Roman, ed. *National Identity and Ethnicity in Russia and the New States of Eurasia.* Armonk, NY: M.E. Sharpe, 1994.

Tamarkin, Mordechai. "Culture and Politics in Africa: Legitimizing Ethnicity, Rehabilitating the Post-Colonial State." *Nationalism & Ethnic Politics* 2 (3) (Autumn 1996).

Tilly, Charles. *From Mobilization to Revolution.* Reading, MA: Addison-Wesley, 1978.

Vanguard (Lagos), "Strike: First Phase to Last 4 Days" (October 9, 2004).

Vanguard (Lagos), "Why I Held Talks with Dokubo-Obasanjo" (October 1, 2004).

Walker, Stephen, ed. *Role Theory and Foreign Policy Analysis.* Durham: Duke University Press, 1987.

Wallerstein, Immanuel. *The Modern World System: Capitalist Agriculture and the Origins of the European World Economy in the Sixteenth Century.* New York: Academic Press, 1994.

White, Stephen, et al. "A European or a Slavic Choice? Foreign Policy and Public Attitudes in Post-Soviet Europe," *Europe-Asia Studies* 54 (2) (March 2002).

Wilkes, Rima and Dina G. Okamoto. "Ethnic Competition and Mobilization by Minorities   at Risk." *Nationalism and Ethnic Politics* 8 (2002).

Winter, Joseph. "Analysis: Nigeria's One-Party Creep." *BBC News UK edition*, Monday, 21 April, 2003, <newsbbc.co.uk/>.

World Bank. *Special Report on Sierra Leone.* Washington, DC: World Bank Publications, 1998.

Yeros, Paris, ed. *Ethnicity and Nationalism in Africa: Constructivist Reflections and Contemporary Politics*, New York: St. Martin's Press, 1999.

Zack-Williams, Alfred. Sierra Leone: The Political Economy of Civil War, 1991–98. *Third World Quarterly* 20 (1999).

Zartman, I. William. *Collapsed States: Disintegration and Restoration of Legitimate Authority.* Boulder, CO: Lynne Rienner Publishers, 1995.

——. *Governance as Conflict Management: Politics and Violence in West Africa.* Washington, DC: Brookings Institution Press, 1997.

Zolberg, Aristide R. "The Specter of Anarchy: African States Verging on Dissolution." *Dissent,*1992.

Contributors

Abdul Karim Bangura holds Ph.Ds in Political Science, Development Economics, Linguistics, and Computer Science, and is the author of 40 books and over 300 scholarly articles. He is currently a researcher-in-residence at the Center for Global Peace and a professor of International Relations in the School of International Service at American University in Washington, DC. He is the coordinator of the B.A. in International Studies—International Peace and Conflict Resolution (IPCR) focus, the coordinator of the Islamic Lecture Series, the coordinator of the National Conference on Undergraduate Research (NCUR), and the faculty advisor of the American University Undergraduate Research Association (AUURA), the International Peace and Conflict Resolution Association (IPCRA), the Student Organization for African Studies (SOFAS) and the Muslim Student Association (MSA) at American University, the United Nations Ambassador of the Association of Third World Studies (ATWS), and the director of The African Institution in Washington, D.C. From 1993 to 2000, Bangura taught Political Science and International Studies, served as Special Assistant to the President and Provost, founded and directed The Center for Success at Bowie State University of the University of Maryland System. He also has taught at Georgetown University, Howard University and Sojourner-Douglass College. He is Editor-In-Chief of both the *Journal of Research Methodology and African Studies* (JRMAS) and the *African Journal of Languages and Linguistics* (AJLL). He is a former President of the Association of Third World Studies (ATWS). Bangura's books include *United States Congress vs Apartheid* (in press), *Introduction to Islam: A Sociological Perspective* (in press), *Islamic Peace Paradigms* (in press), *Fettered–tions* (in press) *Surah Al-Fatihah: A Linguistic Exploration of Its Meanings* (2004), *Sweden vs. Apartheid: Putting Morality Ahead of Profit* (2004), *Islamic Sources of Peace* (2004), *The World of Islam: Country-by-Country Profiles* (2004), *The Holy Qur'an and Contemporary Issues* (2003), *Washington, D.C. State of Affairs* (2003), *Law and Politics at the Grassroots: A Case Study of Prince George's County* (2003).

Rita Kiki Edozie (Ph.D. Political Science, The New School University, NY, 1999) is an Assistant Professor at James Madison College, Michigan State

University, East Lansing. There, she specializes in Comparative Politics and International/African Affairs. Dr. Edozie has held appointments as the Deputy Director of the Institute of African Studies at Columbia University's School of International and Public Affairs (SIPA), and was a visiting assistant professor with the department of political science and international relations at the University of Delaware. Professor Edozie's current research interests include comparative democratization and developing world economic development. She is the author of *People Power and Democracy: The Popular Movement Against Military Despotism in Nigeria, 1989–1999* (Africa World Press, 2002); and has recently published an article in *African and Asian Studies*, entitled, "Promoting African Owned and Operated Development: Reflections on the New Partnership for African Development (NEPAD)", as well as in *Journal of Third World Studies* entitled, "Third World Democracies: South-South Learning from Each Other" (forthcoming). Dr. Edozie has contributed book chapters to several edited volumes, and is presently working on two book projects: a co-edited African politics volume with Dr. Peyi Soyinka-Airewele entitled, *Reframing African Politics: Politics, Culture and Society in a Global Era*, and scholarly text on democracy in Africa, entitled, *Reconstructing Africa's Third Wave: A Comparative Aanalysis of Democracy.*

Michael Grossman is an Assistant Professor of Political Science and the director of International Studies at Mount Union College in Alliance, Ohio. He received his PhD from the University of South Carolina. He has published and presented on a variety of topics including: post-Soviet foreign and domestic politics, US foreign policy, and International Relations.

David Emmanuels Kiwuwa is a final-year Doctoral candidate of Political Science and department teacher at the University of Nottingham. His thesis deals with Democratic Transition and Ethnicity in Rwanda. He has recently been to Rwanda for an extended research visit with The Unity and Reconciliation Commission, International Criminal Tribunal for Rwanda and the Centre for Conflict Management at the National University of Rwanda. His article, "Democratisation? The 2003 Rwanda Elections" is under active consideration for publication with the *Journal of Ethnopolitics*.

Paul J. Magnarella is Director of Peace and Justice Studies at Warren Wilson College, Asheville, N.C., USA. He holds the J.D. with honors, University of Florida College of Law, and the Ph.D., Harvard University. He serves on the editorial boards of several journals, including the *Journal of Social Justice* and the *Journal of Third World Studies*. He has served as Expert-on-Mission to the UN Criminal Tribunal for the Former Yugoslavia and serves as legal counsel to the American Anthropological Association's Human Rights Committee and to the Association of Third World Studies (ATWS). He also served as pro-bono attorney for former Black Panther, Pete O'Neal, who is now exiled in Tanzania. Paul is a past president of ATWS and a recipient of the Association's Presidential Award. He has authored over 100 academic articles and six books. His last book *Justice in Africa: Rwanda's Genocide, Its National Courts, and the UN Criminal Tribunal* (2000) received the ATWS's Book of the Year Award and was nominated for the Raphael Lemkin Book Award.

Clayton D. Peoples is Assistant Professor of Sociology at the University of Nevada, Reno. He received his Ph.D. from Ohio State University in 2005. His interests in ethnicity span ethnic inequality, ethnic-based policy, and ethnic conflict. He has published articles dealing with ethnicity in the *International Journal of Sociology* and the *Journal of Political and Military Sociology*, and has won an award from the American Sociological Association's section on Peace, War, and Social Conflict for his work on global ethnic conflict.

Santosh C. Saha is Professor of History at Mount Union College in Ohio. He had previously taught Asian and African history in colleges and universities in India, Ethiopia, Zambia, Liberia, and the United States. Dr. Saha was Editor-in-Chief of the *Cuttington Research Journal* in Liberia. Currently he is on the editorial board of the *Indian Journal of Asian Affairs* and also edits *Mount Union Academic Journal.*

He is the author of twelve books including *Dictionary of Human Rights Advocacy Organizations in Africa* (Westport, Conn.: Greenwood Press, 1999), *Culture in Liberia: An Afrocentric View of the Cultural Interaction between the Indigenous Liberians and the Americo-Liberians* (Lewiston, N.Y.: Edwin Mellen Press, 1998), and *Indo-U.S. Relations, 1947–1989: A Guide to Information Sources* (New York: Peter Lang, 1990). His civil-conflict related books are *Religious Fundamentalism in Developing Countries*, ed. with Thomas Carr (Greenwood, 2001); *Islamic, Hindu, and Christian Fundamentalism Compared–Public Policy in Global Perspectives*, ed. with Thomas Carr (Mellen, 2003); *Religious Fundamentalism in the Contemporary World* ed. (Rowman & Littlefield /Lexington Books, 2003). His articles have appeared in many journals including *International Journal of African Historical Studies*; *Journal of Negro History*; *Journal of Asian History*; *Pakistan Historical Journal*; *Indian Journal of Asian Affairs*; *Scandinavian Journal of Development Alternatives*, and *Canadian Journal of African Studies*.

In March 2006, Dr. Saha participated in the "Round Table Conference on Diversity," organized by Oxford Education Round Table at Oxford University, UK. Professor Saha's latest article, "The Logic of Ethnicity in Africa: Erosion of the Ethnic Identity in State-building," has been published by the Oxford University Journal *Forum on Public Policy* (October 2006).

Edward Lama Wonkeryor is currently a Dean's appointment and Lecturer/Assistant Professor in the African American Studies Department at Temple University in Philadelphia, Pennsylvania, U.S.A. Dr. Wonkeryor has authored three books, including *Liberia Military Dictatorship: A Fiasco Revolution; The Effects of United States' Political Communication and the Liberian Experience 1960-1990;* and *On Afrocentricity, Intercultural Communication and Racism.* His co-authorships are for these titles: *American Democracy in Africa in the 21ˢᵗ Century?*; and *New Jersey's Underground Railroad Heritage. "Steal Away, Steal Away..." A Guide to the Underground Railroad in New Jersey.* He also worked in Liberia in both the public and private sectors in the 1980s. Dr. Wonkeryor has presented papers at national and international conferences; he has written book chapters and scholarly articles which have been published in journals and newspapers. Dr. Wonkeryor has a forthcoming title: *Globalization and Its Implications for Africa* (2006).

Index